UPON A
WHITE HORSE

UPON A
WHITE HORSE

Journeys in Ancient Britain and Ireland

PETER ROSS

HEADLINE

First published in 2025 by Headline Publishing Group Limited

1

Cataloguing in Publication Data is available from the British Library.

Hardback ISBN 978 1 0354 1406 2

Designed and typeset by EM&EN
Printed and bound in Great Britain by Clays Ltd, Elcograf S.p.A.

Headline's policy is to use papers that are natural, renewable and recyclable
products and made from wood grown in well-managed forests and other
controlled sources. The logging and manufacturing processes are expected
to conform to the environmental regulations of the country of origin.

Headline Publishing Group Limited
An Hachette UK Company
Carmelite House
50 Victoria Embankment
London EC4Y 0DZ

The authorized representative in the EEA is Hachette Ireland,
8 Castlecourt Centre, Dublin 15, D15 YF6A, Ireland (email: info@hbgi.ie)

www.headline.co.uk
www.hachette.co.uk

For Eric and Susan

I have sought to evoke . . . an entity, the land of Britain,
in which past and present, nature, man and art
appear all in one piece.

– *Jacquetta Hawkes*

White chalk hills are all I've known
White chalk hills will rot my bones

– *PJ Harvey*

Between my finger and my thumb
The squat pen rests.
I'll dig with it.

– *Seamus Heaney*

Contents

Author's Note

Every book I write needs a guiding spirit or two; people whose work seems to offer a path, footprints, a lantern. During the writing of *Upon A White Horse*, that archaeological poet Seamus Heaney and the poetic archaeologist Jacquetta Hawkes have been dependable companions along the way. As have my late grandparents, who passed on their fascination with the ancient past and first led me down into an excavation trench. I have no trowel to follow you, Eric and Susan, but lay out these words as small finds – with love, and regret that you will never read them.

SHRINE

A MAN WALKED up the glen. The year was growing old. The hills sounded with the roar of the stag and the answering shush of the burn.

As he turned off the track and approached the shrine, he left no prints on the tussocky, bog-sprung ground. But he had come this way many times, always for the same purpose, and the land had left its mark on him, as it had on those who had come before: the past keepers of the stones.

The ritual takes place twice a year, as spring grown strong becomes summer, and as autumn weakens to winter. Getting to and from the shrine is not easy. The walk is several miles, some of it steep, and you have to go through the burn, which can be high and fast; dangerous in spate. But the journey feels like an offering. Weary limbs and hard breath are the price of being in the company of the Wee People.

It is a price worth paying. This part of Scotland – I have promised not to say where – is a little world to itself. A place of stone and story. The landscape seems tale-worn, shaped by legend as much as the slow grind of ice and wind: a warrior's head on a crag; a dead man's face in the mossy bark of a tree. The hills hunch over the glen, like an eagle mantling its prey, so that in some places the sun is not seen for months. It is not an easy place to live. Long winters. Loneliness. Storms that stoop and kill. So the folk take trouble to seek blessings where they can.

He wasn't alone, the keeper. There were a dozen or so following, strung along the way. Blackface sheep stood in withered bracken and watched us pass. Everyone went at their own pace, some preferring to walk alone, others falling into groups of two or three, telling stories of how the Wee People came to be in the glen.

One version goes that a long time past, before there was writing to record this tale and it was a thing told in shadow and firelight, a man and a woman came down from the hills on a night of wind and snow. She was pregnant, greatly so, and in want of food and warmth. The local culture was then, as now, to offer welcome to those in need, but the people must have gulped a bit at the size of their guests. They were giants, the wife twice as big as her mate, and bigger still with child; it would require the sacrifice of much meat and milk to satisfy their hunger. Still, the couple were fed and, more than that, a house was made, large enough to shelter them – and there the woman gave birth to a daughter.

The family lived in the glen for many years, and for as long as they stayed it was a gentle place: good crops, healthy cattle, sun and rain in the right proportion. The people understood this fertility as hospitality repaid, so that when the day came for the giants to return to their own land – three figures walk-ing into the hills from which two had come down – it was felt necessary to somehow keep their presence alive. A small house was built, and into it were placed three water-stones taken from the burn. The largest was the wife, the smallest the daughter, and the mid-sized stone was the husband. At the start of every summer the Wee People were brought from this shrine, washed in the flowing water, and set out on the land. At the start of winter they were put back into darkness, shielded from wind and rain, and the door shut. As long as this ritual was observed, the glen and its people would be blessed. And if it was not? Well, no one cared – or cares – to think about that.

'I feel it as a duty and a great responsibility,' the keeper told me. 'It has to be done. If you don't, that might be disaster for the glen. And also, nowadays, in our times of climate change, it's ever more important to worship these nature idols. Who knows what power is in these stones?'

The mother stone, in particular, is associated with a creation myth. She is said, in other stories, to represent a goddess who formed the hills and glens and lochs and islands; she set whirlpools spinning and made waterfalls run white. It is fitting that she should be embodied by a rock, she who shaped the rocks. She is where theology and geology meet.

If one believed in such things, one might worry that, lately, she has been showing her displeasure. This year there was drought in the glen for the first time in living memory. Then it rained so hard that a road was washed away. We could see, as we walked, where there had been landslides close to the path. Great chunks of the hill had slipped, exposing darker earth beneath.

We arrived at the shrine: a sturdy little building, about waist height, of stacked flat stones. Above the lintel, an oak roof had been topped with a thick layer of grassy turf and a few pieces of quartz. The doorway was open; it was dark within. The Wee People sat outside the entrance. The keeper looked them over without touching.

Out in front, facing down the glen, tilted by a molehill, was the largest of the three stones. This was the woman, the giantess. She was not quite two feet tall, with a round body, slender neck and mushroom-cap head. Behind her was the giant; he was squat and rather pot-like. To her right was a third stone, the smallest, the daughter, who seemed to have inherited characteristics of both. None were sculpted by hand, but rather by the action of the water in which, long ago, they were found. There was something fungal about them, too, and nothing amusing. They were to be taken seriously. They insisted upon it.

The rest of our party was arriving. One or two had dressed for the occasion: a long-haired man in a kilt picked up a sheep skull and placed it on top of the shrine; a woman in a green cloak set down her staff crowned with oak leaves and sat leaning against the back of the building, seemingly in prayer. Most, including the keeper, were ordinary-looking people in ordinary winter gear – woolly hats, thick jackets, waterproof trousers. The sky was blue, but there was no heat in the sun. Not walking, you felt the wind. 'It's so cold,' someone observed, 'that my bum cheeks are twitching.' A few nodded at this deep truth.

We sat in a circle, nothing formal, just the way people do. A tub of scones went round, and a hipflask with an Extinction Rebellion logo – and soon it was time to put away the stones.

The keeper lifted the first, the mother, cradling her weight and settling her at the back of the shrine. The man in the kilt took the second, the father, placing him beside his wife in the dark. A young woman picked up the third stone, the daughter, and the family was complete. Another woman began a sing-song chant, 'Welcome to the house of the stone people. Welcome to the house of the stone people,' which others took up. Pilgrims – I think we can use that word – began to leave offerings of food in the shrine, to see the Wee People through winter: oats grown for this ceremony; butter made for it; fat from a deer; an apple or two.

Now all that remained was to close the entrance. The keeper packed stones from ground to lintel, tight enough to stay in place through winter, and then the rest of us pushed grass and moss into the gaps, making the shrine wind-tight and snug.

A walker happened by and stopped to see what was going on; he was, it emerged, a singer in a Gaelic choir. Would he give us a tune?

Aye, he would, and did:

SHRINE

O, mar a bha nuair a bha sinn òg,
A' mireag air an àirigh le mànran is ceòl . . .

The mood, during the putting-away, had been focused and purposeful. Now, the work done, the songs sung, people began to drift off, taking the long path home. Autumn had laid out one last spread. The hills were marmalade orange, the loch a silver knife.

Walking back, I asked people why they had come. One older woman explained that she had been raised in a strict Christian family, all rules and dogma, and so takes pleasure in an act of devotion open to happenstance; one that changes depending on who takes part. She'd had her fill of thou shalt nots.

Among the others, the reasons were various:

'It's about honouring the ancestors, carrying on a tradition.'

'We get so much from the land. We should give something back.'

'You feel in your heart it's the right thing to do.'

For myself, it was a privilege to see this done, and to make my own offering: these inadequate words. The ritual is made of stone and flesh and earth and water and air. I may write it down and put it in a book, but paper and ink can never define it; a photograph cannot capture it; pages will never contain it.

It is older and better than books – a small, quiet thing in a large and noisy world.

RING

IT WAS HALF PAST FIVE in the morning, three days before Christmas, and King Arthur was on the bus to Stonehenge.

King Arthur is a druid. He's also a biker – his ringtone is 'Born To Be Wild' – but his bike, the Iron Steed, was off the road with a dodgy clutch. Also, although he's one of the pagan priests who leads the ceremonies within the ancient circle, he doesn't believe in paying the charges at English Heritage's car park. So I had met him at the bus stop in Salisbury, just across from Nando's, and now we were on our way to the stones.

It was dark outside the bus windows. It would be cold for the sunrise, though Arthur, a Stonehenge veteran in his late sixties, had known it colder. There have been occasions when he's had to crack ice out of his beard. Dressed formally but with an eye on the weather, he was wearing a fur cloak over a white robe on the front of which was embroidered a red dragon. His long white hair was held in place by a gleaming circlet: a silver dragon's wings spreading wide upon his forehead and its tail dangling between his eyebrows. If this was a regular journey, he might have got a few looks, but on a special service to a sacred ritual the presence of a druid is to be expected. Even the route number (333) and the fare, £13 return, seemed imbued with mystical significance.

'Stonehenge is like a great cathedral for us,' Arthur said, adjusting his sword, Excalibur, so that it slotted between our seats. 'And today is about hope and renewal.'

The winter solstice, the shortest day, is one of four occasions in the year when the public can wander freely – and for free – within the circle. The others are the summer solstice and the spring and autumn equinoxes: astronomical markers important to those for whom the change of seasons is part of their spirituality. The feeling of rare access to a magical place creates a festive air. But it is a party with rules: no drugs, no booze (not even druid fluid, as cider is sometimes known) and absolutely no climbing on the stones.

Arthur Uther Pendragon is his real name, by the way. He changed it, in 1986, from John Rothwell. The 'King' bit is an honorific with no legal standing, but he's sincere about it, and it's fun to say. I had enjoyed calling him up – 'Hello? Is that King Arthur?' – when planning this midwinter trip.

But the bus didn't work out. Too much traffic. Horrible tailbacks. What should have been a forty-minute journey had stretched to almost two hours. In the end, the driver opened the doors. We'd have to walk the rest of the way if we were to be there for dawn. Two young American women, unsure where to go, asked King Arthur. 'Follow me!' he said cheerily, striding off into the dark. 'If a druid doesn't know the way, nobody does!'

There was light to the east, a watery smear of silver-blue. But it was still too early to make out the stones, which were somewhere ahead, or the faces of the people making their way by path and field. The outlines were interesting, though. One tall figure appeared to have antlers. Another was fir-shaped and covered with rags, like a wishing tree with legs; from deep within this tattered mass came a concertina's carnival wheeze. Black mounds in the land to our left were Bronze Age barrows – inside one of which, in 1723, the antiquary William Stukeley found the cremated remains of what he took to be a teenage girl and the amber beads of her necklace. We were the living, thousands of us, passing through the territory of the dead.

Before Stonehenge was Stonehenge, before the famous stones had been brought from great distances, then shaped and lifted into place, it was a cemetery – for several hundred years from around 3000 BC, ashes were buried in pits and within the circular ditch and bank that enclosed the site.

Once Stonehenge was Stonehenge, long after the stones were raised and those who had raised them were dead, the landscape had become so significant, so sacralised by the presence of the monument, that people chose to be buried close by, within its spiritual blast radius – irradiated by its crackling lithic energy. There are so many barrows in the fields around Stonehenge that, seen from above, they appear like the patter of rain in a puddle, their rippling circles a kind of sepulchral fallout.

It is tempting to regard such a landscape as a spectacle of death and remembrance. To be buried here, whether with stone axes or bronze daggers or shroud-pins of bone, was surely to enter prayerful earth, ground made rich and holy by the mulch of generations past.

'There wasn't one Stonehenge,' is how the English Heritage historian Jennifer Wexler had put it when we spoke the day before the solstice. 'It's multiple monuments in a sacred landscape. It's a place that people returned to, and put their own meaning on, over a long period of time.'

The stone circle was built around 2500 BC; about the same time as the Great Pyramid of Giza. One theory, advanced by the archaeologist Mike Parker Pearson, who excavated between 2004 and 2009, is that it was a monument to the ancestors, more than a hundred of whom were buried there. If that was indeed its intended function, then we might regard Stonehenge as the prehistoric equivalent of Westminster Abbey, a grand architectural statement marking in stone the place of hallowed bones.

Evidence from nearby Durrington Walls, a large settlement thought to have been where the builders of Stonehenge had their base, suggests that it was a place of mass seasonal assemblies, to which people would travel a long way, driving cattle

and pigs for feasting, to work on the stones and participate in solstice rituals. The most important moment, it has been argued, was midwinter's day, when the sun would set between the uprights of the Great Trilithon – which, until it fell, was the largest of the doorway-like arrangements of three stones.

Though there is little to see on the surface at Durrington Walls, this land is haunted by chemical ghosts. Analysis of one house uncovered during Parker Pearson's excavation showed high levels of phosphorus where a wooden box-bed had once stood – the result, it is conjectured, of infants wetting the bed. In the same dwelling, by the hearth, the chalk-plaster floor bore the impression of a pair of knees, worn into the surface by someone who must have spent a long time preparing meals there. One can imagine, at the time when the stones were being raised, this other labour: the child on the hip and at the breast;

the sore back, the smoke and heat; the tingling legs and feet as a woman rose from the fire with pots of food.

This history of communality, Stonehenge as a pilgrimage site, is what makes the contemporary gatherings feel authentic. Whatever individual reasons people have for being here, from deep personal faith to a tick on a bucket list, the presence of so many is an enactment of tradition. Footsteps and voices make little or no trace in the archaeological record, but Stonehenge has, for many centuries, been rich in them – and we leave our own as an intangible tribute to the spirit of this place.

There is, too, something about ancient places that seems to fill some hollow in our souls. We are coming to an end of things, or that is how it feels, and so I find myself drawn, in retreat and in search of consolation, to the beginning. 'It is plain,' the archaeologist and writer Jacquetta Hawkes observed in 1951, 'that we have now reached a stage in our development, in our decay perhaps, at which a knowledge of our origins, an ability to re-identify ourselves with them, has come to satisfy an emotional and intellectual need.'

The horizon was by now getting light – there was no getting away from that. King Arthur, walking fast and a bit out of puff, took a call from Rollo Maughfling, the Archdruid of Stonehenge, who had arrived in the circle and was about to start the ceremony.

'If you hold fire for five, ten minutes,' Arthur reassured him, 'I'll be there.'

Druids, one finds, tend not to be sticklers for punctuality. But the solstice sunrise would not wait and I was beginning to worry we might miss the show. Then, just ahead, unmistakable in silhouette – the stones.

We no sooner saw them, it seemed, than we were inside, stepping between two fallen sarsens, the large and very hard sandstones which, around four thousand five hundred years ago, were brought here from their place of origin, fifteen miles to the north. The circle was packed tight with people. There was drumming, soft and low, a collective heartbeat. A man in a leather mask blew an animal horn. There was a smell – not unpleasant – of patchouli and armpits and pot.

It should have been impossible to get to the centre, but Arthur, in his white robes, passed through the throng like a swan crossing a pond and took up position next to the Archdruid.

How to describe Rollo Maughfling? A gentlemanly figure in a Panama hat, his long white hair brushed the shoulders of his faded red cloak; a long green and orange scarf was wound round his neck. I have always felt, whenever I have seen him in action, that he ought to be umpiring a cricket match on a village green or piloting the Tardis through time and space. He has an avuncular plummy charm, but there's something a bit cosmic about him too.

His voice, full of mild authority, carried from the middle of the circle to the outer ring: 'Can I please ask the people at the back to get off the stones? Otherwise we'll get in trouble for it. If you wouldn't mind, please.'

The crowd, taking up his cause, were less polite. 'Off the stones!' they chanted.

Off the stones!

Off the stones!

Off the stones!

People power prevailed. Those who had been standing on fallen sarsens, hoping to watch the ceremony from that vantage point, climbed down.

'Thank you very much,' said Rollo. 'That's very kind of you. Lovely.'

Now the ritual could begin.

*

Stonehenge is the 'Stairway to Heaven' or 'Hey Jude' of mega-lithic sites – an epic masterwork, the greatness of which has become occluded by overfamiliarity.

It is part of our shared visual language, a signifier of both 'ancientness' and, less straightforwardly, 'England'. Seven hundred years separate the earliest depiction, a manuscript illustration showing Merlin creating Stonehenge, from one of the more notable contemporary representations: the artist Jeremy Deller's *Sacrilege*, a life-size inflatable version made in 2012 for an art festival in Glasgow. It has since toured the world, a monumental bouncy castle on which children leap and play.

Inside a portable loo near the site, I noticed, someone had drawn a trilithon – three strokes of a marker pen, like the symbol for *pi* – and scrawled FREE OUR STONES beneath. This seemed a long way from Turner's sublime watercolour of the circle during a lightning storm, but it was all part of the same compulsion to somehow capture the essence of the thing; to get it down on paper, or vellum, or on a toilet wall. Yet each portrayal seems to further obscure rather than illuminate. The images pile up and get in the way. Stonehenge, thanks to restricted access, can be hard to see. But it is also hard to *see*.

Even standing within it, I could hardly believe I was there. There was an unreality to the occasion, a feeling of being on a film set or in a dream.

The antiquary William Stukeley, whose relationship with this place was one of obsession and adoration, wrote about the monument in his 1740 work, *Stonehenge: A Temple Restor'd to the British Druids*. I had seen a copy in Salisbury Museum, open behind glass. The right-hand page was given over to an engraving of an ancient druid, staff in hand, standing beside a trilithon – a term Stukeley invented – through which one could see into the centre of the circle where some sort of ritual seemed to be taking place. On the facing page I read these words:

When you enter the building, whether on foot or horse-back and cast your eyes around, upon the yawning ruins, you are struck into an ecstatic reverie, which none can describe, and they only can be sensible of, that feel it.

An ecstatic reverie is about right. Stonehenge can make one feel adrift, and so, as the ceremony got underway, I tried to get my bearings.

The sea of people made it impossible to distinguish any-thing below head height, but the larger stones, towering above, acted as landmarks. To my left was the most complete part of the outer circle, four sarsens joined together by three lintels. Immediately ahead was a trilithon on which, if I had pushed closed enough, I would have been able to make out the carved graffiti – WREN – said to have been incised by Christopher Wren, the architect of St Paul's Cathedral, who grew up nearby. Stonehenge, with a diameter of about a hundred feet, would fit snugly within the inner dome of St Paul's.

To my right was the largest stone of all, the surviving upright of the Great Trilithon, the lintel and other upright having fallen at some unknown point before 1574; a watercol-our of that year shows it as already collapsed. The surviving stone is very big indeed – twenty-two feet above ground, with a further nearly seven feet of foundation. It is distinctive not only because of its size, but because it has a prominent bump on top. This is a tenon, a stone peg that would have fitted into a mortise hole on the underside of the lintel. Stonehenge, because of this unique construction method, has been likened to Lego, but it's more like carpentry; tongue and groove joints, four thousand five hundred years old, still hold together the lintels of the sarsen circle. When the circle was complete, if it ever was complete, which is debated, the outer ring would have comprised thirty uprights capped with thirty lintels. 'It's the most sophisticated engineered monument we have from this period of time in the whole of Europe,' is how Jennifer Wexler had summed it up.

It is often said that visitors, seeing Stonehenge for the first time, are underwhelmed; it seems smaller than they had expected. But that is perhaps the result of being kept at a distance. Inside the circle, as I looked around, the impression was of being in the palm of some stony giant. It held us as cupped hands hold water.

The time was now 8 a.m. A cloudy morning with a spit of rain. There would be no dramatic sunrise. You couldn't even be sure when it was happening. But that didn't matter. Everyone was up for it, whatever the weather. There were prayers and chanting and singing. There was, somewhere around, the inevitable didgeridoo.

You might expect a druidic ritual at midwinter to be a bit like Midnight Mass at Christmas – to feel quite formal and follow a structured liturgy. There was something of that, for sure, but it also had an improvised quality, a jazz club vibe. You never knew quite who was going to step into the centre or what they were going to do.

There was an older lady in a red beret who instructed the crowd: 'Let us tune into the sacred sound of the universe – the Om. As you make this sound, imagine that all the molecules of your body are vibrating like ping-pong balls.'

Then another woman – wearing a crown of twigs, berries and fairy lights – sang a song celebrating the rebirth of the sun. It was a catchy tune and everyone joined in.

There were tributes to the recent dead, who had 'passed into the summerlands', as the pagans say. One of them had been a member of The Troggs – and King Arthur, to honour his memory, roared out '*Wiiiiild Thing!*' to laughter and applause.

Finally, it was time for the closing ritual. Rollo Maughfling lifted his palms to the sky and prayed for peace in the four quarters of the globe. The crowd turned, hands up, to face each direction as the druid named them – east, south, west and north – until he came at last to 'the most important of all: may there be peace throughout the whole world!'

There may be years at Stonehenge when this call for an end to war feels hopeful, even possible; 2023 was not one of them. It didn't seem very likely that the raised voices of a few thousand hippies in a cold field in England could end the bombing and staunch the blood. But we shouted for peace anyway – and why not?

'Thank you, ladies and gentlemen,' said Rollo. 'Three cheers for Stonehenge and the winter solstice! Hip hip! Hooray!'

*

The druids are reliably picturesque. They have come to be regarded as part of the scenery at Stonehenge. Yet it was not always so. Their cultural association with the monument goes back to the antiquary John Aubrey who, in the mid-1660s, concluded that it was 'a Temple of the Druids' built by ancient British people, not – as had been suggested – by the Romans, Vikings or Phoenicians. The druid theory was taken up by other writers and thinkers, notably William Stukeley, and proved so influential, so hard to shake, that as late as the 1950s the words 'Druidic' could still be found on some Ordnance Survey maps to describe stone circles and other remains.

In *A Child's History of England*, Charles Dickens wrote that the druids practised their 'strange and terrible religion' at open-air temples, that this religion included human sacrifice, and that Stonehenge was the 'most extraordinary' of these surviving temples. 'It is pleasant to think that there are no Druids, *now*,' he continued, relieved, 'who go on in that way.'

There may have been no druids who went on in quite that way, but there were certainly druids – and in Dickensian London, too. Towards the end of 1781, in the King's Arms tavern in Soho, the Ancient Order of Druids had its founding meeting. In 1853, the year in which Dickens published his *Child's History*, the Noble Order of Female Druids formed in Lancashire. But it wasn't until 1905 that such revivalist groups began to congregate at Stonehenge. 'The Dukes of Marlborough and Leeds were both present, as was the Earl of Warwick,' Ronald Hutton has written of that first gathering in his history of the druids, *Blood and Mistletoe*. 'Members who did not possess their own false beards were equipped by a famous costume hire firm.'

The Victorian and Edwardian iteration of druidry was, in character, akin to something like Freemasonry: social clubs with a side order of mysticism. But on what historical reality was this revival based? The most important primary source is Julius Caesar, who wrote in his memoir of the conquest of Gaul that the 'Druides' were religious leaders in tribal society, as well as judges in criminal matters and secular disputes. 'The Druidic doctrine,' he added, 'is believed to have been found existing in Britain and thence imported into Gaul; even today those who want to make a profound study of it generally go to Britain for the purpose.'

Part of that doctrine, Caesar wrote, was the belief that those suffering from serious illness, or who hoped to survive in battle, could save themselves by offering to their gods the lives of others:

> Some tribes have colossal images made of wickerwork, the limbs of which they fill with living men; they are then set on fire, and the victims burnt to death. They think that the gods prefer the execution of men taken in the act of theft or brigandage, or guilty of some other offence; but when

they run short of criminals, they do not hesitate to make up with innocent men.

From this passage derive the shudders of Charles Dickens and, ultimately, the deranged glee of *The Wicker Man* – the classic 1973 horror film.

The historian Tacitus, writing around a hundred and twenty years after Caesar, gave a vivid account of druids as part of his description of a Roman attack on Anglesey, off the coast of Wales, in the first century. The island had become a refuge for those fleeing the occupation of Britain, perhaps some sort of rebel base. Tacitus, from the invader's perspective, pens a portrait of native anger: 'The enemy lined the shore in a dense armed mass. Among them were black-robed women with dishevelled hair, like Furies, brandishing torches. Close by stood Druids, raising their hands to heaven and screaming dreadful curses.'

Infantry crossed from the mainland in flat-bottomed boats, while cavalrymen swam beside their horses. Arriving on the opposite shore, the troops were stunned into inaction by the 'weird spectacle' of the women and druids, but soon rallied and took the island. The empire, it is said, was tolerant of the beliefs of the conquered peoples brought within its purple cloak, but that seems not to have been the case on Anglesey, which the Romans knew as Mona. The victorious governor Suetonius Paulinus proved merciless, destroying the island's sacred places in seeming revulsion at native ritual: 'For it was their religion to drench their altars in the blood of prisoners and consult their gods by means of human entrails.'

Tacitus was not an eyewitness to these events, though his father-in-law, the general Agricola, may have been. What the historian leaves to us is an idea of druids as anti-authoritarian, as members of a resistance, and it is this aspect that has often characterised their modern relationship with Stonehenge. The druids that he and Caesar wrote about were figures from the Iron Age. Stonehenge was already very old by their day, so they certainly did not build it, and there is no evidence that they used it as a temple. Their modern-day equivalents have made themselves part of its story by insisting on their right to be there.

In the years following the mass gathering of 1905, revivalist druids of one order or another – and crowds of interested spectators – began to assemble at Stonehenge for the summer solstice. The debate over right to access has at times grown heated. In 1901, following the collapse of an upright and lintel, the landowner Sir Edmund Antrobus had fenced off the stones and started to charge for admission; in 1913 he forbade the use of the circle for religious meetings. This led to crowd trouble and police involvement. In 1925, around a hundred people stormed the site without paying. There were further clashes in the 1950s: on one side, the druids and their followers; on the other, soldiers based on Salisbury Plain who found them contemptible and ridiculous. The solstice was becoming an unpleasant spectacle, synonymous with noise and trouble. According to Ronald Hutton: 'Two musical bands, playing the latest teenage craze of skiffle, competed with each other from opposite sides of the monument. When the Druids sounded a horn to greet the sunrise, a jeer went up from the crowd.'

To read archive coverage of the solstice rituals is to chart the development of youth culture: skiffle, mod, rock, rave. 'An atmosphere reminiscent of Blackpool beach spread over the roadways leading to the ruin,' one journalist reported in 1930. 'Girls and boys danced by the lights of motor-cars, which lined the roads, to the music of gramophones and a complete jazz band.'

During the 1960s and 70s, as Stonehenge became associated with the alternative society, security grew correspondingly tight. Newspaper reports feature barbed wire, floodlights, dog patrols and military police. The problem seems not to have been the solstice-worshippers themselves, more the crowds drawn by the prospect of hedonism and gawpery. The druids, 'standing charismatically within the Stonehenge horseshoe', were, in the opinion of the archaeologist Stuart Piggott, 'a compelling magnet for many a psychological misfit and lonely crank'. Meanwhile, the Chief Constable of Wiltshire declared in 1962 that, 'so long as there were Druids about, there would be a substantial body of weirdies making a thundering nuisance of themselves'.

The Stonehenge Free Festival, an outdoor music event at which the rock band Hawkwind were a fixture, began in 1974 and ran close by the stones for eleven years. One reveller remembered 'Tolkien-esque wanderings through woods', another that 'the fire brigade sprayed water for the hippies to dance and play in and around the stones'. The poster for the 1975 festival promised harmony, music and freedom. This bucolic vision came to an end in 1985 with the infamous Battle of the Beanfield, when riot police fought with New Age travellers who were heading, in convoy, to the festival site. The Beanfield has become a byword for police brutality and led to the introduction of an annual four-mile exclusion zone around Stonehenge at the summer solstice. The days of watching the sun rise from the circle, indeed anywhere near it, were over.

Or that was the idea.

Enter King Arthur.

He was among those who refused to accept that Stonehenge was off-limits. For the rest of the 1980s and 90s, protestors attempted to access the circle for the summer solstice, leading to confrontations with hundreds of officers, multiple arrests and court cases, and even – in Arthur's case – a couple of broken ribs. 'Every year I'd get arrested, thrown in the cells, and let out the next morning without charges,' he had told me. 'It was like my yearly pilgrimage. I saw it as my duty. And I thought: "One day,

I'm going to get in."' In 1995, on trial in Salisbury, he was found not guilty of trespassory assembly. His lawyer, one Keir Starmer, later recalled that he had to persuade court staff to allow the druid to unsheathe his sword in order to swear the oath.

A 1999 ruling by the House of Lords resulted in the lifting of the exclusion zone, but in any case the situation was unsustainable and absurd, this annual cat-and-mouse between protestors and police played out in the Wiltshire countryside. So, on 21 June 2000, the monument was opened for public access at the solstice for the first time since 1984. It is now one of the communal pleasures of the English summer: Stonehenge, Glastonbury, Wimbledon, the Last Night of the Proms. 'This is no longer counterculture. This is just culture,' as the *Times* journalist Hugo Rifkind wrote of his own solstice trip. Not that these gatherings have become consumer experiences empty of meaning. The stones will not allow it. Those great silent blocks still call out to people and seem to expect an answer.

'Do you feel,' I had asked King Arthur, 'that Stonehenge belongs to you, or that you belong to it?'

'Symbiotic,' he replied. 'I'm a child of Stonehenge. I moved to Salisbury to be closer to Stonehenge. I feel drawn to Stonehenge, but I feel Stonehenge is drawn to me, in a strange way, as well. I was destined to fight for it, to celebrate there, to be part of its tribe.'

Stonehenge is a contested space. Who owns it; who has the right to be there, and when; who built it and to what purpose; what it now means – all of these questions have been, over decades and centuries, disputed and debated. It is a blank screen on which individuals and societies project their beliefs and values; literally so in the case of the many photographs of the Queen which, in 2022, were beamed on to the stones to mark the Platinum Jubilee. Some saw that as a kind of vulgar blasphemy, at once sentimental and sinister, but perhaps it makes a kind of sense: the megaliths of Stonehenge could be interpreted as an expression of wealth and authority, given the people and resources necessary for their creation. There is, too, a strong link between Stonehenge and royalty. Henry VIII owned it; James I's interest prompted the first excavation and the first book that sought to explain its origins; Charles II, following defeat by Oliver Cromwell at the Battle of Worcester, hid within the circle while trying to escape England for France.

If Stonehenge is disputed territory, caught in a tug-of-war between the establishment and the people, for some creatures it is simply home. It seems to be important to hares. They often go there to die. They also choose to have their young within the embrace of the stones. English Heritage staff, checking the site in the early morning, sometimes notice newborn leverets – hushed and brindled clods – crouched by the base of certain megaliths, left in this place of shelter and safety while the mother is off foraging. Foxes, it is said, shun the circle and keep to the outlying fields, rejecting easy pickings for reasons of their own. In Constable's celebrated 1835 watercolour, a hare runs for the cover of the frame, its long, fleet body an image of transience in contrast with the eternal stones.

Stonehenge has emblematic birds, too. The best known is the great bustard, which looks a bit like a large goose and is thought to be the heaviest flying bird on earth. They can be seen passing over the monument in seventeenth-century engravings, but were hunted to extinction in Britain in the nineteenth century. The taxidermied carcass of one of the last is on display in Salisbury Museum. 'It was served at a dinner for ten people,' says the information panel, where it was described by a guest as 'extremely tender, the breast like plover, and the thigh not unlike pheasant'. The species was reintroduced to Salisbury Plain in 2004 and a population of around a hundred is established and self-sustaining. Nobody eats bustards now, and especially not the hen known to the reintroduction project as T5, who has become such a frequent visitor to the stones each spring that she has been given a name – Gertrude.

The birds of Stonehenge have delighted visitors for a long time. On 8 October 1768, the parson and naturalist Gilbert White penned a letter to his regular correspondent, the zoologist Thomas Pennant, informing him of a pleasing fact – that jackdaws breed among the megaliths. 'These birds,' he wrote, 'deposit their nests in the interstices between the upright and impost stones of that amazing work of antiquity: which circumstance alone speaks the prodigious height of the upright stones, that they should be tall enough to secure those nests from the annoyance of shepherd-boys, who are always idling round that place.'

Those shepherd-boys may be gone, but the jackdaws remain – and are not idle. Carol Druce, who lives nearby and retired recently after nearly thirty years as a guide at Stonehenge, considers these busy birds with their silvery cowls to be guardians of the stones. 'They probably know all the secrets,' she had laughed when we spoke on the phone. 'Birds have been around for a lot longer than people. The stones, with holes and niches caused by natural weathering, make ideal nesting places, and they've no doubt enjoyed it ever since those stones were first put up. They probably watched the stones being put in place.'

Jackdaws, as Gilbert White observed, nest in the trilithons, high up in gaps where the uprights meet the lintels. The most Carol has ever seen are eight nesting pairs, a small clifftop village. Their nests are messes of twigs, moss, mud, feathers, baler twine, bits of tissue and tourist rubbish. 'They bring lambs' tails when the lambs' tails are chopped,' she said. 'You sometimes see one hanging down on the stones where they haven't quite got it into the nest.' The jackdaws have their chicks in May, and always fledge the week before the summer solstice: 'As though they know the people are coming and they've got to get out fast!'

Rooks are Stonehenge's other corvids. They do not live among the stones, they fly in from rookeries in trees on a nearby farm. They come for food and perhaps for human company. Some will sit and take snacks from your hand. The first to do this, according to Carol, was a rook called Joe. 'He knew the times that the shop opened and shut. It was the sampling biscuits that he came for, really. He'd sit by the ticket box and watch people going in and out, and he always seemed to know when somebody had food.'

A rook will often hide its food in small holes in the ground, covering it with turf for later. Archaeologists find it difficult to get permission to excavate at Stonehenge, but rooks dig wherever they please. Who can blame them for making this place their larder? They are quite at home. This is a place of their ancestors. It is often said that the building of megalithic sites became possible – and desirable – as the population of nomadic hunter-gatherers were replaced by incoming farmers. Only in communities with abundant food and manpower would there be sufficient resources to erect such structures, and only when people put down roots in one place would there arise a desire to leave a permanent mark on the landscape. If the development of agriculture led to the raising of the stones, it also gave rise to the rooks. The species likely moved into Britain with the westward spread of farming culture; open ground broken and worked for crops meant access to grubs and grain. Stonehenge and the rooks, then, are shadows of each other. It seems apt that when the birds gather in parliaments to discuss grave matters, they form large black circles on the earth.

*

The formal part of the ritual over, I left the stones, passing beneath a lintel of the outer ring. Loads of people were doing the same, flooding out into the wider site. Security in hi-vis checked their watches. It was well after eight and English Heritage had granted access until ten, so the pagans and other revellers wanted to make the most of the time. Druids were stopped for photographs every few seconds by tourists from Australia, Colombia, Japan and goodness knows where else. There was lots of chanting, lots of mantras, but one six-word phrase was heard again and again: 'I've never seen it so busy.'

Although the circular ditch surrounding the stones isn't very wide or deep, it's big enough for children's games. Kids ran laughing down one side and up the other, or else just lay down and rolled. A few family groups had the bright idea of using it to eat breakfast, getting as low as possible out of the wind. This was the ditch where several cremation burials had been excavated, as well as the skeleton of the so-called Stonehenge Archer – he was in his mid-twenties at the time of his death around 2300 BC, shot with arrows, the stone tips of which were found with the body. He may have been executed, or it could have been some sort of ritual killing, nobody knows. What had been a grave was now a picnic spot. One mum cut up mango, another spread chocolate on bread.

There is a jolly history of picnics at Stonehenge.

William Stukeley, having come round from his ecstatic reverie, enjoyed a meal on top of one of the trilithons with his friend and patron Lord Winchelsea, the two gentlemen leaving their after-dinner pipes on top of the lintel. This act of whimsy may seem disrespectful and even reckless to us now, but Stukeley could have gone further. The stone was, he judged, of sufficient size for anyone with 'a steady head and nimble heels to dance a minuet on'.

Charles Darwin picnicked at Stonehenge in June 1877, making his way by horse and carriage from Salisbury with his wife Emma and son George. Darwin, then sixty-eight, was there to investigate the action of earthworms in causing stones to sink. The custodian of the stone circle, an old soldier, was reading a religious text when the Darwins arrived. 'He was quite agreeable to any amount of digging,' Emma recalled, 'but sometimes visitors came who were troublesome, and once a man came with a sledge-hammer who was very difficult to manage.'

The idea that the stones, though great in size and weight, were also vulnerable and in need of care did not find much purchase until the late 1800s. The public seemed to feel they could treat the monument as they liked.

This became especially problematic with the coming of the railway; a direct service from London to Salisbury was introduced in 1857, allowing for ever greater numbers of visitors. You could even buy a chisel and take a little bit of Stonehenge back home. So many souvenir pieces have been chipped from the more accessible parts of the monument that it looks softer and less geometric than it probably did when first built.

The situation was then made worse by the development of the motor car. One travel writer, visiting at the end of the nineteenth century, noted that 'although there is no occasion for such insane fury, the picnic parties generally contrive to smash beer and lemonade bottles against the stones until the turf is thickly strewn with broken glass'. On Easter Saturday 1899, he noted, members of the Automobile Club, out on a jaunt, had themselves photographed beside the stones, taking pleasure in the contrast between the megaliths and their shining new vehicles.

But it was still possible to find serenity at Stonehenge. One hot day in August 1903, Virginia Woolf – twenty-one and on holiday – travelled there with her sister Vanessa. They had caught the train from Waterloo and made the rest of the journey by pony and trap. Now, they sat with their backs to the stones and ate sandwiches; thus fortified, they could better enjoy the mystery. 'The singular, & intoxicating charm of Stonehenge to me', Woolf wrote in her diary, 'is that no one in the world can tell you anything about it.' It was, she felt, 'a piece of wreckage washed up from Oblivion' and 'a more deeply impressive temple of religion' than nearby Salisbury Cathedral. Returning on the morning of 5 September, the weather having turned to showers, they found they were the only visitors and so sat down within the circle. 'One can imagine why this spot was chosen by the Druids – or whoever they were – for their Temple to the Sun,' she wrote. 'It is a kind of altar made of earth, on which the whole world might do sacrifice.'

Woolf had brought with her to Wiltshire some holiday reading: *Tess of the D'Urbervilles*, which she admired but did not enjoy. It contains the best-known depiction of Stonehenge in fiction. As the novel nears its climax, Tess is on the run for the murder of Alec d'Urberville; she and Angel Clare cross Salisbury Plain by night and find themselves among the stones – 'solemn and lonely' – where, exhausted, she lies down to sleep on a fallen sarsen, saying, 'So now I am at home.'

The book's author, Thomas Hardy, had a passion for archaeology, which was still, in his day, a fledgling science. He made several research trips to Stonehenge, by bicycle, when preparing to write *Tess*. In 1899, as a famous writer whose opinions carried weight, he gave a newspaper interview in which he argued that the monument – 'a national relic . . . a sacred possession' – should become the property of the nation. This happened, eventually, in 1918.

Like Woolf, I had brought my copy of the book to Wiltshire, and Hardy's words were much in my mind as I stood within the circle at dawn. This is what Angel Clare observes as Tess sleeps and the men who will take her to the gallows make their silent approach:

> In the far north-east sky he could see between the pillars a level streak of light. The uniform concavity of black cloud was lifting bodily like the lid of a pot, letting in at the earth's edge the coming day, against which the towering monoliths and trilithons began to be blackly defined . . . The band of silver paleness along the east horizon made even the distant parts of the Great Plain appear dark and near; and the whole landscape bore that impress of reserve, taciturnity, and hesitation that is usual just before day.

Hardy went to Darwin's funeral; Woolf attended Hardy's. All three had, in their lives, known peace at Stonehenge, this beautiful place of the dead.

*

I wandered over to the Heel Stone – a huge, craggy sarsen not far from the circle – and watched King Arthur perform a handfasting for a couple from London. Maxine, the bride, was wearing a bright-blue dress. Alan, the groom, had taken a more pragmatic approach: woolly hat and wellies. The druid wrapped their hands together with cord and said that he bound them for a year and a day, for eternity, or for however long their love may last. Then they jumped over a wooden staff – and that was it, they were handfasted. 'It's always been a dream to get married here,' Maxine said afterwards. 'It's so spiritual. When you touch the stones you can feel vibrations and energy.'

Everyone was touching the stones. Everyone was leaving offerings. There were rowan berries, holly and mistletoe at the foot of the Heel Stone. Into one of the deep hollows someone had pushed a crow feather. In another, someone had placed a banana skin – a sacrifice, no doubt, to the gods of slapstick.

I headed back towards the centre. A newspaper report would later say that politics was kept out of the solstice celebrations, but that wasn't quite true. A group of protestors unfurled a banner and waved Palestinian flags as a piper played 'Amazing Grace'. Mostly, though, the feeling was that there were thousands of personal rituals going on at once, everyone doing their own thing. Often, that thing involved percussion. There were djembes and bodhráns, shamanic drummers and jingle-jangle tambourine men.

All this noise was helpful in a way. It crowded out one's own thoughts, making it possible to appreciate the stones without overanalysing. A former guide, whom I'd met the day before, had offered advice about how to act within the circle. 'It's best experienced without thinking too much,' he'd said. 'Put your camera down and go round once without taking pictures. Just look. Just feel. And it will speak to you. Stonehenge is trying to tell us something. The builders were leaving a message. But we don't know what that was.'

The construction of the monument, the gathering of the stone, the shaping and setting into place is an exemplar of human ingenuity and will. It is a moon landing, a split atom. It says: *this is what we can do.* The sarsens, many of them weighing twenty tons or more, were most likely dragged on wooden sledges – from West Woods, near modern-day Marlborough. These were shaped on site using stone mauls, and finally raised and secured in sockets dug into the chalk with deer-antler picks; the lintels may have been lifted by means of a platform of timbers built layer by layer against the uprights. The archaeologist Barney Harris has estimated that it would have taken more than 4.5 million hours of labour to move and erect the sarsens. The smaller stones, the so-called bluestones, were quarried in south-west

Wales, around a hundred and eighty miles from Stonehenge. It is possible that they made part of the journey by boat, along the Bristol Channel and the River Avon, but the current thinking is that it is more likely they were brought by land.

The so-called Altar Stone, which lies half-buried and covered by two fallen sarsens at the centre of the circle, had the furthest distance to travel – its six tons were brought all the way from Scotland's far north-east. 'The journey would allow people to take part, celebrate, create memories and show loyalty to the authority behind the idea,' the archaeologist Mike Pitts has written. 'Stonehenge was not just a sacred monument: it was about people. Transport and construction, expressing power and control, were key parts of its purpose and identity.'

Such colossal effort indicates, too, that these stones were not simply building materials; they must have been heavy with meaning. There is a theory that the bluestones, of which there were at least eighty, were thought to have the power to heal, or that they embodied the ancestors of the people who raised them – and that when the builders moved from Wales to Wiltshire they brought the stones with them, carrying their past to the place where they saw their future.

Whatever reasons they had for building Stonehenge can only be speculation, but the extraordinary fact of its presence on Salisbury Plain has prompted outlandish conjecture. Jennifer Wexler finds this frustrating. 'It's fascinating enough that *people* built it,' she had told me. 'It's such a disservice to humanity to say, "Oh, aliens built it." These were sophisticated human beings.' She switched to the present tense, as archaeologists often do when their subjects feel too real and present to be confined to the past. 'These are people who are climbing to the top of high mountains to extract special stone to make axes. They are putting in a lot of effort on lots of levels to create their world. They are literally transforming the earth: to deforest, to cut down thousands, possibly millions of trees; to create fields – that's a huge amount of work. They are building monuments for over a thousand years before they build Stonehenge, and we have a good understanding of the tools and technologies that they used.'

'How do those people strike you?' I asked her. 'It sounds like you admire them?'

'You have to admire people who lived in such a harsh reality and still wanted to create beautiful things. Their life was really hard and yet they still put in the effort to build these magical places.'

'Was beauty an object they had in mind?'

'Why would they not? I think it's inherent in human nature to produce art and beautiful things. They are going out of their way to get materials that are gorgeous. Some of their axes are aesthetically stunning. They had sophisticated thoughts and skills and ways of doing things. And they had a deeper connection with nature and the landscape than we have in our modern world.'

Up close, the stones *are* beautiful. The solstice-worshippers pressing hands and faces against them, hungry for intimate contact, no doubt had deep reasons for doing so. But you might also do this for the same reason you stand in a gallery and gaze into the depths of an oil painting – to experience the pleasurable dissolve of form into abstract.

The closer you get to the megaliths, the bigger they appear, and yet proximity also provides a gateway to a miniature realm, the world of lichen. Picking my way through the crowd, I found a spot next to a trilithon and leaned in to inspect one of the uprights. The stone was a Jackson Pollock canvas, thick with spatters of pale grey and streaks of vivid yellow. Higher up, towards the lintel, the trilithon seemed to wear a silvery-green pelt. Stonehenge is home to around eighty lichen species, some

of them rare and mysterious in that they are usually found on coastal cliffs and certainly not this far inland. That shaggy covering on the lintel is a variety known as sea ivory.

Lichenologist Oliver Green spent a day surveying Stonehenge in the early summer of 2003 and later wrote that 'lichens are what make the stones look old. If they were not there the henge would be visually far duller. Lichens are nature's paint, emphasising every change in slope and aspect, picking out the underhangs with different colours and textures, giving the structure depth and creating an appearance of ruggedness that would otherwise be missing'.

A lichen is a composite, a coming together of unrelated organisms – a fungus, an alga and sometimes a bacterium. The word 'symbiosis' – that King Arthur had used to describe his relationship with Stonehenge – was coined in 1877 to describe the nature of lichens, the same year that Darwin picnicked at the stones. Survival of the fittest? That's not what lichens are about. They are an expression of mutual dependence.

So there's something fitting about lichens growing here. This is a monument that seems to have relied for its construction upon the gathering and cooperation of people from different places in Britain. And it's a site that we now understand and appreciate by bringing together elements of archaeology, history, architecture, folklore, religion, geology, ecology and other disciplines of the mind. It is rooted in the idea of complexity and multiplicity, and therefore lichens – this hybrid lifeform – are a living metaphor for Stonehenge.

Lichens can live for a long time, thousands of years in some cases, which means it is possible that some have been growing on the monument since it was built. Even if none are quite so ancient, they will likely be the descendants of the first to settle. A lichenologist called Mark Powell told me that within a decade of the circle being built it would already have had a noticeable covering. He and a colleague carried out the most recent survey at Stonehenge, asked by English Heritage to explain why some of the lichen colonies were turning blood red after solstice events. 'We came up with a plausible hypothesis,' he explained, 'that it was a chemical reaction caused by people urinating on the stones.'

Some folk will always take the piss, of course, but most of those gathered for the winter solstice seemed to me respectful of their surroundings. Actually, respectful isn't quite the word. The feeling in the air was wonder, excitement, awe and the just-rightness of being exactly where one ought to be. 'Stonehenge is part of the British psyche, no matter how you look at it,' King Arthur had said as the bus growled through the dark. So, to be in this place on this day at this time – well, what could be better?

The drumming in the centre circle was growing louder and faster, louder and faster, the dancers ever more frenzied. There was a sense of approaching climax as 10 a.m. – chucking-out time – approached. Finally, at five minutes to go, there was a great cheering and whooping as the sun at last broke through, shining into the circle and on to the tops of the megaliths so that they appeared burnished, stone become bronze. The effect only lasted a few seconds before the light disappeared once more behind the clouds, but this was the moment of transcendence that everyone had felt coming.

William Stukeley wrote in 1740 that Stonehenge 'pleases like a magical spell' and here, now, in this land of stone and glory, was pleasure and enchantment both.

*

To reach Sighthill from the city centre you're best to walk. Pass the train station and the bus station and patches of waste ground until you come to the footbridge over the motorway, where dense and slender railings of brown steel curve above head height; it feels like squeezing along the gills of a mushroom. The drivers, below, following exit signs, will likely not glance to their right and see, up on the hill, Glasgow's only stone circle.

'There it is,' said Stuart. 'I love that it's here.'

Stuart Braithwaite plays guitar in the rock band Mogwai. Their music has a drama and sublimity that makes it the ideal soundtrack to visiting such places. But that was not why he had come along today. This was a family matter. Stuart's late father, John Braithwaite, a maker of telescopes, was one of two men who, in the late 1970s, created the circle for Sighthill, a large housing estate in the north of the city.

'To me, it feels almost like a monument to my dad,' Stuart explained. 'He was very proud of this. He was obsessed with

astronomy and Neolithic stones and community, and all sorts of things that this place embodies. So it holds a lot for me emotionally, but even just as a Glaswegian, I think it's great. Weird things like the standing stones give the city its soul.'

The circle is a ring of sixteen stones, unevenly spaced, and a seventeenth in the centre. The tallest looks about six feet. Some are marked with old graffiti: a few Chinese characters and fading declarations of love. They sit on top of a steep grassy mound, right next to new housing: low-rise flats of brown brick. I could see people through their windows – vacuuming, typing on laptops, talking on the phone. They seemed quite used to having a stone circle as a neighbour.

You might think that it would feel out of place and out of time in Scotland's biggest city. In fact, the circle sits beautifully within a vertical landscape. Tower blocks, the cathedral spire and hospital chimney, the obelisks of the Victorian cemetery, even the wind turbines on surrounding hills – all seem to mirror the stones.

I had been here before. Sort of.

The Sighthill circle was erected on the spring equinox, 1979, the stones having been quarried in Kilsyth, east of Glasgow, and lowered into place by a Royal Navy helicopter, an operation codenamed Megalithic Lift. It had come about as part of the Callaghan government's job creation scheme; money was given to the local authority to create a number of temporary posts, the idea being to get Glaswegians off the dole and doing interesting and useful work.

A young science and sci-fi writer named Duncan Lunan had been put in charge of the Parks Department's Astronomy Project, in which role he hit upon a plan to create a contemporary equivalent of Callanish or Stonehenge: standing stones aligned with the sun and moon and thus able to mark the passing seasons. It would be the first such structure to be built in Britain for three thousand five hundred years. He was given a map, an official car and a giant brass compass – and went off to find a suitable site. Trudging through gales and rain, through the winter of discontent, he visited Priesthill, Ruchill, Maryhill, Castlemilk and the Cathkin Braes before settling on Sighthill, impressed by the sweeping vista of the skyline. Lunan's friend John Braithwaite, with his astronomical expertise and optics skills, became the project's technical supervisor.

The Sighthill housing estate, or 'scheme' as we say in Scotland, was built in the 1960s, constructed on what had been factory and railway land. The waste products of industrial history seeped into stories children told each other about this new place where they lived. A sulphurous pool of chemical effluent? That was the Stinky Ocean. A high, steep bing, said to be made from heaped bone and slag, was Jack's Mountain. It was much favoured as a playground, though you had to watch out; everyone knew that the devil lived on top. A stone circle in such a place was just another tale. Indeed, the circle was given its own local nickname. It was the Cuddies. No one seems to know why. But cuddy is the Scots word for horse, so it may come from cowboy games, with kids 'riding' on the stones.

Storytelling like this is a way of interpreting a place that you do not understand and making it your own. It has a long history. Think of the names given by Christian societies to pre-Christian sites. The Devil's Arrows in Yorkshire; Long Meg and Her Daughters in Cumbria. The Cuddies is part of that tradition.

As the years passed, the backstory of the Sighthill stones was forgotten. Government cutbacks (Margaret Thatcher is said to have loathed the circle and all it stood for) meant that there was never any signage explaining when and why it was created, and many assumed that the stones really were ancient. An easy mistake. Untethered from its origins, invisible even from nearby paths, the site drifted into obscurity. The park in which it had been built grew wild; long grass, self-seeded bushes, hawks and owls and deer. The circle, hidden in this urban jungle, was a good place to start fires, listen to music and get drunk. But some people still found it special. The stones became a family shrine to a local woman – a mother and grandmother – whose ashes were scattered there. They also became significant for pagans. One midsummer evening, more than a decade ago, I attended a solstice ritual at the circle. The air was heavy with incense, lit to welcome the ancestral spirits, and citronella – to deter midges.

'I know they are not ancient stones, but to us they mean a hell of a lot,' a woman in a scarlet cloak told me after the ceremony. 'We could make a temple anywhere, but this circle speaks to us. It should be left alone. Let it grow as old as Stone-henge. It would break my heart to see it moved.'

Heartbreak seemed likely. Sighthill was to be redeveloped. Already many of the high-rise flats – deemed a failed experi-ment, though there were those who loved living there – had been demolished. The land around the stone circle needed to be made level in order to build new housing. The stones would have to be dug out, the site flattened. The circle would cease to exist.

A campaign to save the stones attracted support from many who felt that something of Glasgow's widdershins spirit would be lost if the circle was destroyed. Among them was Stuart Braithwaite, who organised an awareness-raising concert. The idea of the stones being chucked in a skip was especially hurtful as his father had died just the year before. He said he would chain himself to a bulldozer if need be.

For Duncan Lunan, the circle's designer, the proposed demolition felt personal. 'They say in your life you should love somebody and build something,' he told me at the time. 'Well, I have done both. That circle is mine and it's not a trivial thing. I feel I carved it out of the air. You would have thought that unless the glaciers came back nothing could harm it, but I wasn't thinking in terms of deliberate destruction by the council for whom it was originally created.'

In the end, a compromise was reached. The stones were dug out and the ground landscaped. However, the City Council, recognising the strength of public feeling, agreed that the circle could be reconstructed, using the original stones, at a new location close by – and that Duncan Lunan would be tasked with ensuring that the megaliths were placed in positions marking the summer and winter solstices and other astronomical events. That is why I say I had been there before, *sort of.* The Sighthill circle I visited with Stuart Braithwaite both was and was not the Sighthill circle built in 1979. The stones were the same, and their arrangement worked in the same way, but it was not the same, not quite. Here was a twenty-first-century structure based on a twentieth-century structure based on a prehistoric idea. It had, as the archaeologist Kenny Brophy observed, 'a fascinating complicated temporality, which is an academic way of saying it's totally fucked up'.

Brophy, a lecturer at Glasgow University, styles himself the Urban Prehistorian. He's interested in prehistoric sites found in non-rural contexts – such as Balfarg Henge, a Neolithic enclosure excavated in the late 1970s and then repurposed as green space in a suburb of Glenrothes, Fife. Wooden posts marking the circumference of a prehistoric circle are now used by local kids playing football. 'Wear patterns caused by a relentlessly diving keeper are often evident between these uprights,' Brophy has written. I think we can trust his interpretation of the physical evidence; he supports Hamilton Accies – not one of Scotland's glamour teams – and thus knows all about a goalie being kept busy.

We met at the Sighthill stones a few weeks after my visit with Stuart Braithwaite. It was a very cold morning in January, but he had got there early and was busy taking pictures. I don't think it would be going too far to say he has fallen for the place.

'Sighthill was ignored by archaeologists for a long time because it's too recent,' he said as we did our best to huddle out of the wind. 'But it's absolutely of interest to us because it's a stone circle. It doesn't matter if it was made last week, or a hundred years ago, or five thousand years ago – it's a stone circle and that's cool.'

Brophy has been observing the circle since 2013, applying formal archaeological methods just as he would to an ancient site. On the day after the final equinox celebration before the circle was dismantled, he documented the ashes of fires, pieces of charred wood, scraps of newspaper, empty crisp bags and the cap from a bottle of Buckfast, the fortified wine totemic among al fresco drinkers in the west of Scotland. He noted, too, that some of the stones were marked with handprints left by people who had, for some reason, first covered their palms with wet clay. 'I could have, had I wanted, taken fingerprints,' he wrote on his blog. 'I could have, had I wanted, sampled for DNA.'

The last time Brophy had been at the Cuddies was the winter solstice. He was there – 'Just me and the rain and the clouds' – while I was with the gathered thousands at Stonehenge. He had also been there for the summer solstice, watching the sun rise over the stone positioned to mark that event. 'That was awesome, incredible, a really special moment. I was surprised how emotional I felt.'

I was curious about that reaction. If you witness a sunrise at Stonehenge or Avebury, there's a history of awe baked into those places; people expect to have their minds blown and would be disappointed if they were not. But that's hardly the case in Glasgow, and still less with a stone circle that's effectively new. So why, I asked Brophy, did he feel so strongly as the day grew light?

'I don't know,' he replied. 'As an archaeologist, you're not really supposed to have empathy for the prehistoric people. But that connection of stone and sun felt deeply connected to human practices. It was primal, I suppose.

'Despite the fact that I know the stones were only put there in 2019 and they are set in concrete and came from a quarry in Kilsyth, everything about the sunrise was powerful. Duncan has created something magical here. This place really works. And it doesn't just work in an archaeo-astronomical sense, it works at a deep-rooted human emotional level. Nothing about this is authentic, it doesn't make any sense as a prehistoric monument, but it makes sense as a place to create magical experiences – and there's nothing wrong with that.'

*

Stone circles are not a thing of the past. There are approximately 1,300 prehistoric circles in Britain, Ireland and Brittany, but hundreds of further circles and related monuments have been built in more recent times. These range from the Druid's Temple – a folly built around 1800 in the Yorkshire Dales – to the Gurdy Stone, a Welsh slate megalith erected in East Sussex in 2023 by Jem Finer of The Pogues and Jimmy Cauty of The KLF. The raising of that stone made the papers: 'Yellow smoke flares fill the air and a sound system blasts out the duo's music, which combines Finer's manic, droning hurdy-gurdy and Cauty's breakbeats, sirens and bloodcurdling screams.'

Although megalithic structures are still made now, only a handful of people have the skills, knowledge and necessary passion. Perhaps it was always like that. Perhaps they were the work of acknowledged experts travelling the country, like the master masons of our great cathedrals, setting stone upon stone, putting on to the earth and into the air monuments that would outlive them and everyone they knew. It is no doubt foolish to apply modern psychological concepts to the old builders, but surely it required humility, pride and generosity. Humility because human life was so short in comparison with the stones being erected; pride because it was a mark left on the land, proof of a meaningful existence; generosity because these places have bequeathed to us a legacy of mystery and wonder.

On a showery day towards the end of winter, I travelled to the Kent coast and called upon Dominic Ropner, stone-hunter.

Dom is in his mid-fifties with longish hair and a calm manner. 'I build stone circles because, uh, it's difficult to explain,' he said. 'It's almost a compulsion.'

He has megalithomania, a condition identified by the writer John Michell as a kind of contagion of the imagination, causing the infected individual to feel endless curiosity about these ancient places. It's more than mere inquisitiveness, though, I think, that draws certain people to these sites; not just the mind's desire but some obligation of the soul.

We got into Dom's vehicle; Albus the Jackapoo, his stalwart travelling companion, lay down on the back seat – and we were off.

Dom wanted to show me a few favourite sites, prehistoric and contemporary. We'd talk about his own work, too. He runs a business, Time Circles, using natural, non-quarried stones to create features for clients – everything from a circle to a headstone. It's how he makes a living, but money is not his motivation.

'My inspiration at the beginning was building a stone circle as a memorial to my sister,' he explained. 'Carey died when she was thirty-nine. She was buried up in North Yorkshire, I was living in the south, so I wanted some memorial closer to me. I think it's really helped us as a family.'

He built that first circle in 1997 and has since made around fifty more, often with the help of his wife Abigail and their children Daisy, Inigo and Willow. 'It feels like a contemporary Neolithic family, which is exciting – and lovely to know it will carry on when I am gone.' Building takes place when the weather is better, the ground firmer. In winter, he hunts stone. The hedges and trees are bare, the grass short – 'It is the best time of year to see lost stones.' He spots them lying in fields as he walks and drives around: the Cornish granites, Welsh bluestones and big Wiltshire sarsens. He is particular; wants the types of rock used by the prehistoric builders, as if trying to compensate for temporal distance by working the same material. He carries a logbook and camera, talks with farmers, negotiates price per ton. He raises stones from where they have lain for tens of thousands of years and hauls them back home through the night. He has a feeling for stone, its look and texture, its surprising warmth, and understands which should be placed next to which, creating energy, rhythm and mood. The circles he builds are not some cover version of what people used to do, they *are* what people used to do: arranging stone meaningfully, creating sacred space – sometimes as a way of remembering the dead.

'On our islands we've been doing this for a very long time,' he said. 'It's in us all.'

We had been on the road for half an hour when Dom pulled into a lay-by. We got out and walked through a strip of woodland, ducking beneath a fallen elder, serpentine with ivy, that had blocked the path. The dog ran ahead, scanning the undergrowth for treasure; if Dom is a stone-hunter, Albus is a stick-hunter and, like his master, takes great joy in each discovery.

Before long we emerged on to a grassy ridge with long views across a river valley to the North Downs. Just ahead was an odd little building. There was something cartoonish about it, like a Stone Age bus shelter. You could imagine Fred Flintstone standing beneath the capstone on his morning commute.

In fact, we had arrived at Kit's Coty House, which is not actually a house (or bus stop) but a burial chamber from the beginning of the Neolithic period. It is one of the Medway Megaliths, the name given to a cluster of sites considered to be among the earliest monuments in Britain. 'These were the first farmers,' said Dom. 'They came over from Europe over a thousand years before Stonehenge.' We could regard this place, therefore, as something like the tomb of our pilgrim fathers. Not that it has always been treated with respect. Nineteenth-century graffiti, carved into one of the uprights, is clearly visible – a habit that explains why, since 1885, it has been protected by a tight square of iron railings. The charisma of this place has long drawn sightseers.

George Orwell visited in the afternoon of 21 August 1938, the weather being fine, while a patient at Preston Hall, a nearby sanatorium where he was being treated for bleeding in his left

lung. He considered it 'a druidical altar or something of the kind' and sketched it in his diary. 'The stones are on top of a high hill,' he observed, 'and it appears they belong to quite another part of the country.'

Charles Dickens knew the place and mentioned it in *A Child's History.* 'I should not wonder if the Druids . . . kept the people out of sight while they made these buildings, and then pretended that they built them by magic.' He enjoyed calling at the tomb while travelling between Maidstone and Rochester, 'one of the most beautiful walks in all England'.

Samuel Pepys came to Kit's Coty, which he took to be 'a Saxon monument', on 23 March 1669; being Pepys, a multi-tasker, he fitted it between a visit to church and a sexual encounter with the wife of a naval officer.

'It's annoying that we can't get to it,' said Dom, tutting at the railings. He likes to touch stones he admires, by way of saying hello.

I mentioned that I'd been reading *Stig of the Dump*, a novel I'd loved as a child. The book is about Barney, a boy who befriends a caveman, Stig, whom he discovers living in an old chalk pit near his granny's home in Kent. Towards the end of the story, Barney and his sister Lou sneak out of the house one night and – it being midsummer and moonlit – find they have slipped back in time to the Neolithic. They encounter Stig and his tribe using wooden poles and animal-hide straps to lift and drag a slab of rock along a mound towards three uprights. The children lend a hand and the capstone falls into position just as the sun rises over the horizon. Barney wakes to find the tribe and their camp gone: 'But one thing had not changed. The three stones with the great slab on top were still before his eyes – weathered now, with grey lichen growing on them. The mound was not there, but the stones stood just as they had done when he had let go the last of the rope.' The author Clive King doesn't name the place, but it is surely Kit's Coty House.

'Yes, that's probably how they would have done it,' Dom said, considering the building method described in *Stig*. 'I think that's probably how they built the big ones at Stonehenge, too – a ramp to get the stones into position.'

We walked back to the car and drove west to Surrey. Dom wanted to show me a stone circle that he had seen made. We passed a field of white deer and turned up a farm track. The circle was on land belonging to the writer Eleanor Anstruther. She answered the door and said, yes, it was fine to go and look. 'Ivan's up there,' she added.

Ivan McBeth built the circle. He called it the Dragon Circle, but it is known as the Hascombe Stones. He died in 2016 at the age of sixty-three, but is present in his creation, Eleanor feels. 'He's here. I know he's here. He *is* the stones.'

McBeth was a huge figure, literally so, but also in terms of his impact and influence. Bear-like, barrel-bellied, wearing a green velvet top hat over wild hair, he was a trucker who became a stone circle guru. His oeuvre includes the Swan Circle on the Glastonbury festival site. He was part of Club Meg, a loose group of megalithic enthusiasts of which Dom was also a member, all of whom had a deep interest in how the ancient structures were built and how best to do so today.

'Like some ancient chieftain,' is how Dom remembers him.

'Obelix made real,' is Eleanor's take.

She got to know him when he was living at Longleat, sleeping in the woods in a bender tent and designing a stone circle for Lord Bath. She'd just gone through a bad break-up. 'So I went to stay with Ivan to mend my broken heart.' Later, after a time in a squat in Ealing, she came to live on this farm in Surrey. One day, soon after moving in, she found herself standing at the kitchen sink looking over the fields to a hilltop. 'And it just seemed completely obvious that we needed to build a stone circle and Ivan was going to do it. That was all the thought I gave it. I was only twenty-three.'

Ivan, she knew, had always wanted to build a stone circle by hand, following the old ways. This was his chance. But it was also, perhaps, a duty. 'I build stone circles because that's what I do, and that's what I believe the land has entrusted me to do,' he once said. 'And so I wait, and from time to time the land gets in touch, usually by way of its guardians, the people who actually live there.'

Albus led the way to the stones, Dom following. I brought up the rear in a pair of borrowed wellies. The circle was on the crest of a hill, framed by trees and looking out over the Weald. There were nineteen limestones, eighteen in the circle and one in the centre, grey and weathered. They looked settled, like they were in the right place and knew it. Dom walked the circle clockwise, touching each. 'Look at the shells in this one,' he said, pointing to a cluster of fossils. 'Isn't that wonderful?'

Anyone might suppose that the circle had stood for thousands of years. But there were clues to suggest otherwise – a couple of stones bore the drill scars of modern quarrying – and in any case I knew that this place had been built towards the end of the twentieth century. It took about eighteen months, beginning one Beltane and ending at the following years' midsummer.

The stones, which weigh up to around ten tons, were erected without machinery and amid an atmosphere of revelry and ritual. The farm was run as a commune, with something like twenty permanent residents, but there were loads of other people coming through all the time, drawn to help with the circle and celebrate the pagan festivals, of which there are eight in a year. It was a sort of Merrie England work camp: Maypoles and May Queens, druids and dancing, a hot tub always steaming, a kettle always on the boil.

'The atmosphere was kind of timeless and wild,' Eleanor recalled. 'We were all smoking a lot of pot. I think there was probably quite a lot of ecstasy being taken. I can't believe we got away with it. And this is *Surrey*. Now you cannot move for somebody saying you've got to get a permit and health and safety assessment, but we were five hundred naked people on a hill, dancing about and slaughtering rabbits on the central stone and playing drums at dawn. I don't think any one of us ever doubted our right or ability to build the circle. We embodied a sense of unquestioning right to do as we pleased and live how we wanted. And we did.'

Each day began with McBeth playing the flute, a hippy reveille. Depending on size and weight, the stones were lifted on to tree-trunk rollers or tracks and pulled by rope or levered towards their positions, before sliding down a ramp into the socket hole and adjusted until vertical. This was slow work, awkward and exhausting, but it felt authentic, real *Stig of the Dump* stuff. It has been suggested that for the prehistoric communities who built the old stones, what mattered even more than the finished monuments was the bond created by working together on the long and difficult business of their creation.

Is that what she found, I asked Eleanor – that the experience of building the circle was as important as the circle itself?

'Yes. We felt we were right on the tip of the arrow. We were doing something extraordinary – building this by hand. Once upon a time it was day one of Stonehenge; well, I've witnessed day one of a stone circle that will be here for thousands of years.'

It was time to go. The cattle that use the stones as scratching posts decided we'd had enough time on their patch. They came lumbering back, asserting their rights.

Just as we were leaving, the noise of an engine, a wartime sound, made us look up. A Spitfire was roaring overhead, the roundels on the underside of its wings mirroring the ring on the ground. The plane must have taken off from the nearby aerodrome, perhaps in preparation for a forthcoming air show, but its sudden appearance intensified the uncanny feeling of being in several time periods at once. It was 2024 and 1941 and 2400 BC. The pilot, looking out from the cockpit, would see the stone circle below – just as RAF observers in the 1920s, using reconnaissance techniques developed during the war, discovered many archaeological features invisible from the ground, including the lost eastern avenue between Stonehenge and the River Avon. There were, it seemed, ghosts in the fields of England.

'Imagine the last time Ivan left this circle,' Dom said, in the quiet after the Spitfire's passing. 'He probably didn't know that he would never be back.'

*

What was the urge that first drove humans to build circles and tombs, to put up standing stones?

Jacquetta Hawkes believed that it was to do with revival and renewal:

> I do not think it is allowing the imagination too great liberty to say that the faith, for it is very truly a faith, which made the New Stone Age communities labour to drag, raise, pile thousands of tons of stone and earth, was in resurrection, the resurrection of their corn and beasts, of themselves. They laid their dead in the dark, earth-enclosed chamber with something of the same conviction with which they cast the seed corn into the soil.

We still feel that, don't we? A hope, at least a hope, that the end is not the end.

I wanted to see one of Dom Ropner's own stone circles, so travelled to Somerset to meet Ben Goldsmith, the environmentalist and financier.

He wasn't at home, but I found him sloshing through a watery area of his farm, explaining to a small group of friends that this wetland was the work of beavers: 'It's like a garden made by a non-human consciousness. We also have otters here. We have polecats, pine martens, weasels, stoats, wild boar.' In a moment, he said, he'd show us the wildcat pens.

Ben is a campaigner for rewilding, the restoration of rural landscape to how it was before intensive agriculture depleted ecosystems. He has started on his own land but has a radical national vision – far more trees, far fewer sheep, bring back the wolf.

He is in his mid-forties, but seemed at once younger and older, boyish and bruised. After his friends had gone, we walked down the lane from the farmhouse and there was the circle: a ring of eight stones, in height between six and thirteen feet, with a further four lying in the centre, and a large, flat stone a little beyond the perimeter. We sat side by side on one of the stones in the middle, looking into the ashes of a firepit. Ben's lurchers, Pickle and Elvis, lay on the grass and dozed.

'What is this place for you?' I asked.

'Today, now?' he replied.

I nodded.

'First and foremost a place I can come and reflect upon my own loss and upon my relationship with Iris. It's a kind of ritual. This is the place where she died, and it's set right in the middle of the place she loved, where she grew up and lived. It's a sort of grave.'

His daughter Iris was killed, aged fifteen, when a farm vehicle she was driving overturned. 'That's the spot where it happened,' he said, pointing to the flat stone just outside the circle. Someone, perhaps one of the other children, had arranged a love heart of pebbles on top. He'd had the circle built in his daughter's memory, but it had become more than a memorial. It was a place of ongoing connection.

'We know that circles have been meaningful throughout the ages,' he said, 'and we assume that in some way it's about communication with the beyond. Wherever my Iris is, perhaps a stone circle is a way for me to get closer to her. But it may just be that I have a place that's quiet, which feels profound because of these big and brooding stones. It might be that. Yet there are times when the hairs go up on the back of my neck and I conjure Iris in a way that feels near and vivid. It's a place beyond thought. It's a place of feeling. I'll miss her terribly, I'll be in tears, and I'll feel a sense of powerful love. I feel like I find her here.

'Another element is the permanence of the stones,' he continued. 'One of the most painful things about losing a child is the sense that they were unable to live the number of years that should, by rights, be allotted to a human being. She should have had eighty, ninety years and instead she got fifteen; that's terribly difficult to accept. So anything which somehow erodes that stark fact is comforting. What's fifteen years as compared with eighty, ninety years when you start to think about deep time? Long after we're all gone, people might stumble across this stone circle and won't know what it's all about.'

Iris died in July 2019. Dominic Ropner built the circle that September. The stones are Cornish granite from a farm just east of Bodmin Moor. It was an important point of connection for Ben, in his moment of most intense grief, that the man doing this work had known loss – the death of a sister – and had raised stones in her memory. That in itself was a circle of sorts, with Iris, Carey, Ben and Dom all points on the circumference.

Dom and I had spoken about this place. He'd been here recently. He was working nearby and called round, but there was no one at the house so he walked to the circle to see how it had settled. 'She was beautifully calm and took my breath away,' he said, 'but I can imagine she's not always as calm.' He wasn't sure why he was referring to the circle as 'she' but it was probably, he thought, because of the association with Iris.

'I love that,' Ben said when I told him. 'There's no doubt there's an energy here which is ineffable. Sometimes I sit here and it's like the whole landscape is on fire. On an autumn evening with a breeze and a vivid pink and orange sunset, and all of the leaves vivid reds and yellows and the ground all browns and yellows, the place just glows. It glows the colour of Iris. So I understand completely what he means by the mood of the circle. On a summer's afternoon the stones seem so benevolent – you can push your cheek against them and they're smooth and warm and the children hide behind them and it's fun to be here, a place of real happy celebration. So it does change, that's true.'

The colour of Iris. She had ginger hair and blue eyes, an autumnal girl.

The family planted irises at the foot of the stones, but wild boar rooted the bulbs.

Her name is inscribed on the largest stone, but moss will soon cover it.

What I find remarkable is that Ben didn't sell the property after the accident. He didn't try to put distance between himself and the place of pain. Instead, he transformed it – first with the circle and then through his other interventions, the change of use from a traditional farm to an increasingly wild landscape.

'It was a decision that came from the belly, not the mind,' he explained. 'I felt held by nature. Even in the very early days after Iris died, I drew comfort from the birdsong and in swimming in the pond and walking in the woods. It seemed to be absolutely essential to my survival that I be here. What came over me was a powerful sense that I would be here forever.'

'So you won't move now?'

'No. It would feel like leaving Iris behind. She's so woven into the fabric of the place and the stone circle consolidates that. And rewilding the landscape is sort of an expression of Iris in the land. It's to honour her.'

He brought out his phone. 'I'd like to show you this.'

It was a short clip, just a few seconds. Iris's voice, breathless with excitement, as she films what she can see.

'Dad, I'm right by the starlings, I'll get them to fly. Now look, they're going up!'

A cloud of birds in the air. Thousands, tens of thousands, rising, circling, twisting in the blue. Then, once again, the unseen girl's voice as she marvels at the size of the murmuration – 'Look how giant that is! I was right next to them!'

It's strange to consider that stone circles might corral the energy of the dead, some trace of identity and spirit, like data on a phone. Many would dismiss that as nonsense, or rationalise such beliefs as a form of self-soothing. And perhaps it is nonsense. Perhaps it is consoling fantasy. Sitting there, though, listening – in the company of her father – to a lost child's captured wonder, I could just about understand it. Stone circles are enclosing spaces, but they are also open, and so they seem to speak of both absence and presence, holding on and letting go.

Look how giant they are. Look how solemn. Listen to the ghosts in the fields.

HENGE

SILBURY HILL is an act of madness.

It was Jennifer Wexler, the English Heritage historian, who had said so. We were sitting in the café at Stonehenge. Christmas songs were playing: Mariah Carey, The Pogues. I wrote down her words and they came back to me when, a few days later, I visited the hill for myself.

'It's just, like, *why?*' she had continued. 'Why build a giant mound? It has no purpose. It's a very strange and evocative place; the closest thing we have to a pyramid.'

Silbury Hill is the largest prehistoric mound in Europe. Conical, with a flat top, it was constructed in phases between around 2400 and 2300 BC as the Neolithic shaded into the Bronze Age. It 'riseth to a considerable height,' as William Camden put it in 1586, 'and seemeth, by the fashion of it, and by the sliding down of the earth about it, to be cast up by men's hands.' More than a hundred feet high and five hundred wide, it was made from enormous quantities of chalk quarried from surrounding ditches. On completion it would have been white as snow, an Alp in Wiltshire; and although now grassed-over, it does not look at ease in the landscape. It sits beside the A4, providing a moment of awe and mystery for those travelling between Marlborough and Bath.

'There it stands,' Jacquetta Hawkes has written, 'a challenge to science, and a proof that faith can build mountains with the help of no more than bone shovels and antler picks.'

The first time I visited Silbury it was early in the morning, late in the year. The hill was surrounded by a moat, fed by a winterbourne, and sat on top of its own reflection. There seemed no way to get near, and anyway I was trying to drive home to Scotland in the day's little light, so took a few quick pictures and left, promising myself I'd return.

I did not know much about Silbury then. Did not know that it was the reputed tomb of the legendary King Sil, who, according to folklore, was buried on horseback in golden armour. Did not know that a real king, Charles II, had climbed it in 1663, with his brother the Duke of York – later James II – who was much taken with the snails, 'no bigger than small pinnes heads', that he found on top. I *did* know, because I remembered it happening, that in the early summer of 2000 a great hole, wide and deep, had opened up on the summit; a further collapse that year led to works to stabilise the hill and, while they were at it, an archaeological investigation.

Jim Leary led the excavation. He spent the best part of a year working inside the hill, oxygen canister and mask attached to his belt in case the tunnel should come down around him. 'It was like going into a mine,' he recalled when I phoned him at the University of York, where he is a lecturer. 'It was enveloping and at times suffocating. Trying to record archaeology in a small, hot, sweaty environment was very challenging. You could hear thundering as chalk lumps fell through the voids and on to the roof. I never felt in danger; our team trusted the miners and engineers who were in there with us. But I could always sense the monument around us, its importance and power. It embodies the experience of the late Neolithic period, and I felt the weight of the past bearing down.

'I remember right at the end,' he continued, 'when we'd recorded everything and taken all of our samples, we were collecting up our stuff and the engineers were taking out the light systems. I went down one of the side chambers, where it was completely pitch black. I couldn't see my hand a millimetre from my eyes. I sat in there, knowing that there was no way I'd ever come back into the middle of this mound, and nobody else would for a few generations at least. That overwhelmed me and I'm not afraid to say that I shed a tear.'

And what, if it's not too daft a question, did it *smell* like down there in the dark?

'Like the centre of the world.'

Silbury has been excavated four times – the first in 1776, burrowing into prehistory some decades before that word, prehistoric, came into use. It was these earlier shafts and tunnels, inadequately backfilled and collapsing, that resulted in the sinkhole at the summit, an old wound reopened. Yet despite repeated investigations by antiquarians and archaeologists, no body has ever been found. No King Sil, no king at all. This is not a grave. The only thing inside Silbury is Silbury.

It began as a mound of gravel, golden and sticky, around three feet high and thirty across. At some later point, a wider area around the gravel was defined by a ring of stakes and within this were piled further heaps of earth and turves. These were so well preserved that when Jim Leary saw them, deep within the hill, the grass was still green, though flattened and yellowing, as if, he thought, a camper had just lifted their tent. In this way, basket-load by basket-load, Silbury grew. Boulders were added, like coins in a Christmas pudding, and chalk banks swelled the sides.

The materials were brought from different environments – woodland for one of the inner mounds, grassland for another, and gravel perhaps from the river. This mingling may have been symbolic, different groups bearing soil and stone from their own particular territory, the hill becoming a form of memoir. 'By incorporating a patch of home turf in the mound they created an enduring link with the monument,' Leary has written, 'claiming or reaffirming family rights to live in the area through the creation of a communal monument; or renewing the mythic connections that bound these people to this part of the land.'

Silbury: a folk tale written in chalk.

'It is from a time when the Neolithic world was possibly starting to fall apart,' Jennifer Wexler had suggested. 'New people were coming, new ideas, beliefs, technology. I sometimes wonder if it was a last gasp of the Neolithic – a cry to the gods, perhaps, or to rally the people one last time to build something monumental.'

*

The most pleasurable way to approach, I think, is to walk from the village of Avebury along the West Kennet Avenue, a double line of standing stones, and then follow the fingerpost to the right, up and over Waden Hill.

Silbury appears to emerge out of the crest as you climb and then, as you go down, to rise until its top is level with the horizon. The landscape seen thus has a picture-book quality, a painted innocence: a little red tractor gathers hay bales; a swallow swoops out from a long barrow; a fox pursues a rabbit through a ploughed field, strumming the furrows, kicking dust with each evasive jink. The animals are too far away to feel their terror and hunger; all you can do is enjoy the speed and urgent grace.

It was now summer. The moat that I had seen around Silbury was gone. The stream that feeds it had dried up, as it does seasonally, its banks thick with bindweed trumpets and drumsticks of wild teasel. The ground was dry. It appeared cracked and crusty where visible through the grass.

There was barbed wire around the base of the hill. In one place the fence was about six feet high, but mostly a good bit lower, with No Entry signs here and there. These explained that Silbury is a Scheduled Ancient Monument and Site of Special Scientific Interest: 'The steep, slippery and irregular surfaces make it unsafe to allow public access and such access would damage the protected grassland and archaeology of the monument.'

Silbury has been closed to the public since 1978, that prohibition becoming more urgent since the collapse and structural works – although it is now considered stable. English Heritage, which manages the site, is very keen that people keep off the hill; even their own facilities coordinator does not set foot on it during her quarterly site checks. 'It's there to be admired from a distance,' she had told me. 'Our job is to look after it and make sure it's around for many, many generations to come.' Nevertheless, people do still climb it – as was clear from paths trod into its sides, desire lines which spark an answering desire in those who see them.

I badly wanted to go up.

On weekends in the 1920s, after church and Sunday school, but before tea and evening service, Avebury children would climb Silbury, 'puffing and pulling ourselves up on the long tufts of grass', according to the reminiscences of Marjorie Rawlins, who had moved to the village from London, aged six, at the end of the Great War. 'There on the top we would sit and watch the cars, not too many yet, of course, trundling along the Marlborough Road and rest before descending. These heavy slow cars looked matchbox size from our viewpoint and were a source of wonder and interest to us.'

In the 1970s, at boarding school nearby, the novelist Adam Thorpe climbed Silbury many times. 'Perhaps,' he has written, 'nothing as spectacular and lovely has ever been created since on our islands – no work of art or architecture or technological achievement – and what we have now is the mere husk.'

Julian Cope, musician and self-styled 'rock 'n' roll antiquary', moved to Wiltshire in the early 1990s, drawn by the megalithic landscape. When I met him some years ago at his home, a converted stables, he stood up from the kitchen table where we were talking, opened the door and pointed to Silbury, saying that he felt connected to her. Cope was wearing a black military cap, a black leather waistcoat and great clomping black boots; his straw-coloured hair hung down to nipple level and he appeared, at six foot two, to be half-scarecrow, half-raven. Still, he did not quite upstage the hill. Who or what could? The mound is a star, a headline act. As Cope observed in *The Modern Antiquarian*, his classic gazetteer of prehistoric sites, 'Seen from afar or grazing the near horizon, appearing out of nowhere to shock the disinterested motorist, there is no archetype more descriptive of British prehistory than the flat-topped sacred hill of Silbury.'

To the extent that it is possible to own such a place, Silbury is in private ownership. It was purchased in 1873 by John Lubbock, the banker, MP and prehistorian, who had coined the terms Neolithic and Palaeolithic (for New Stone Age and Old Stone Age) and who introduced the first legislation to protect ancient monuments. It is still owned by the family, but held in the guardianship of English Heritage. Lubbock also campaigned for the introduction of bank holidays, giving workers more leisure in which to visit marvellous places such as this. He seems to have had a feeling for time, its transience and depth; that it can be both inheritance and gift.

I walked around the base of the hill. Clockwise, as one walks around a church so as not to wake the devil.

It would have been easy enough to go over the fence, through the nettles and up the slope. No one would have known. But I didn't.

There was something about being held at a distance that felt appropriate. Silbury has an inherent authority that makes the No Entry signs redundant. It seems to say, with its blank mass, something like: *You may not approach the throne.*

For centuries, of course, it was a site of convivial gathering;

a place for kings and commoners, whoever had the legs to carry them up. On Palm Sunday, from at least the eighteenth through to the nineteenth century, there was a tradition among local people of coming together on Silbury and eating cakes, figs and sugared spring water. William Stukeley, in July 1723, invited his noble friends and patrons to join him on top of the hill, from where he was making observations of the landscape, and there he treated them to a bowl of punch.

It could be argued that prohibiting access, even with the best of intentions, has turned Silbury from a living thing into a kind of specimen. 'We've killed it,' Jim Leary told me. 'We've pinned it like a precious butterfly.'

But what if, when it was first complete, Silbury was forbidden to all but the elite? Whose feet in ancient times walked upon England's white mountain? Perhaps only a few special people were allowed to ascend to the summit. Exclusion of the public in our own age could be seen, in that context, as an act of cleansing, of re-enchantment, a setting apart once again of a holy place.

To not climb the hill feels like an honouring of that. So I turned and walked back over the fields to Avebury.

*

The village is in some ways typical: church, pub, community shop, people saying good morning as you pass. Anvil Cottage, Carpenters Cottage, Dovecote Cottage, The Old Forge, The Old Bakehouse, The Old Vicarage, everything is pretty, everything bright – climbing roses, pink hollyhocks; an actual working red telephone box.

So far, so ye olde. Yet little clues, here and there, suggest that this place is not quite the stuff of picture postcards. A black pentacle hangs in a window, an elaborately crocheted Green Man scowls bushily from the top of a post box. You might

wonder, too – should you arrive in summer – why it is so busy. There are only thirty or so houses in Avebury, and three hundred thousand annual visitors. That imbalance is what happens when you build a village within and around the biggest stone circle in Britain.

Work began on the Avebury complex in 2600 BC or thereabouts. At its heart is a 'henge', the archaeological term, derived from Stonehenge, for a ditch enclosed by a bank. The Avebury henge has a circumference of around three-quarters of a mile. The ditch, still impressive, would have been thirty feet deep when first dug out of the chalk. The stones followed: a great outer circle just inside the line of the ditch, two inner circles surrounding huge central stones, and two long avenues of sarsens. The West Kennet Avenue ran for more than a mile from the southern entrance of the henge to a hilltop circle known as the Sanctuary, and can still be followed part of the way. The other avenue ran from the west of the henge towards what is now the village of Beckhampton. Two stones are all that remains above ground of this western avenue. Known as Adam and Eve, they stand in a field a mile from the henge, appearing cast out of that prehistoric paradise.

'What makes Avebury so strange,' says John Betjeman in a 1955 advert for Shell, 'is its sinister atmosphere. What did they do here? Who did they worship? You probably don't know any more than I do.'

My first visit to Avebury had been just after the winter solstice. Trees in the windows, holly wreaths on doors. It was bitter, the sun not long up, and I almost had the place to myself. The only other visitor was a woman sitting on the frosty grass, taking photographs. She, like me, had been to Stonehenge the day before. Such places seemed meaningful to her in a way that the festive season didn't. 'I don't celebrate because I don't see my family,' she told me. She was going back home to an empty house and frozen curry, but seemed cheery in the company of megaliths. There is something about standing stones that speaks to those who are alone. They articulate an idea of community, but are themselves solitaries.

'Merry Christmas,' she said, as I went on my way.

I had seen lots of photographs of Avebury, of course, but nothing prepares you for the real thing. The effect is cumulative. Stone after stone after stone after stone. Tom Templar, singer with the heavy metal band Green Lung, had put it well when we spoke about his experience of being here: 'It's like the jaw of a giant coming up through the earth.'

Simile is Avebury's currency. A reflex of the mind makes it impossible not to perceive meaningful shapes in the megaliths: a crown, a heart, the head of a cat, a figure in a cloak. You are a child again, seeing animals in clouds. Little wonder that this place has long fascinated the young. 'I came to love those irregularly shaped silver grey stones,' Marjorie Rawlins remembered of her 1920s childhood. 'I would sit in the one called the Devil's chair, hunt the sabre toothed tiger around them and play at cave women with mother's old frying pan and anything else I could muster.'

The Devil's Chair is a very large stone in the south-east quadrant of the circle; it has a natural ledge, just the right height and width for a nice sit-down. The Swindon Stone, diamond-shaped, is so close to the road that passengers on the 49 bus have the pleasant impression that they could, if they wished, lean out and tap it on their way to Devizes. The Barber Stone is named for the unfortunate individual whose skeleton was discovered beneath it in 1938. Coins in a rotted leather pouch suggest that the man died in the first half of the fourteenth century; he also had a pair of scissors. The story spun from this evidence is that he was an itinerant 'barber-surgeon' roped into helping locals bring down the stones, in the course of which one fell and killed him. But why did the villagers leave him there? Why no decent burial in the churchyard? It is another Avebury mystery.

Alongside puzzlement, what one feels, walking around Avebury, is a strange mingling of scarcity and abundance. There are so many standing stones, many of them impressively large and heavy, including one at a hundred tons that is the heaviest in Britain. But there is also obvious absence. 'Long ago, in the circles, in the avenues, in this megalithic complex there had been well over six hundred stones,' the archaeologist Aubrey Burl wrote in his 1979 book, *Prehistoric Avebury*. 'Today there are seventy-six, and little concrete pyramids stand like Passchendaele memorials for some of the others.'

I had read in the National Trust guidebook that at the time of the Norman conquest most of the stones erected during the Neolithic were probably still standing, but that by the early years of the twentieth century only fifteen remained in the henge and six altogether in the avenues.

There were two periods of stone-felling. The first was during the Middle Ages, when the barber-surgeon met his end. The stones, at that time, were not destroyed but hidden – pulled down and buried in pits. Why? Perhaps because they were regarded as unacceptably heathen, or were obstacles in land that could be farmed. Aubrey Burl, thinking it significant that the stones had been left intact, favoured the former theory: 'They were handled almost with reverence, covered without hurt to the sarsen, doing God's work without upsetting the Devil.'

The second phase of dismantling was not at all reverent. We know this thanks to an eyewitness. William Stukeley made six lengthy visits to the area, drawing the monuments and making plans of the complex. The illustrations in his book *Abury, A Temple of the British Druids*, are delightful. Men in tricorn hats point to stones with walking sticks; women in frocks, carrying fans, visit the burial chamber known as the Devil's Den; a rider on horseback trots past Silbury where the A4 now runs. Yet Stukeley also documented the 'barbarous massacre' of the monuments. A sketch made on 20 May 1724 shows a huge stone being broken by the proven method. It was heated in a pit of burning straw, then doused with cold water, creating areas of weakness that could be smashed with sledgehammers.

For Stukeley, this was a vision of hell: 'The vast cave they dig around it, the hollow under the stone like a glasshouse furnace or baker's oven, the huge chasm made through the body of the stone, the straw, the faggots, the smoak, the prongs, and squallor of the fellows looks like a knot of devils grilling the soul of a sinner.'

In this way, a great many sarsens were destroyed and their fragments used for farm works and housing. Stukeley, in his writing, named and condemned the men who seemed to care only for their 'dirty little profit'. Yet there was nothing he could do to prevent it. Then, as now, money talks and developers must get on.

Much of today's Avebury, even the museum in which the ancient past is illuminated, was built using stones from the circles and avenues. The great temple of the Stone Age people – if a temple is what it was – had 'fallen a sacrifice to the wretched ignorance and avarice of a little village unluckily plac'd within it'.

*

The villagers, these days, look upon the stones with a good deal more affection, even reverence. For some, they were the reason for moving here.

I called upon Henk Vis at his home one warm lunchtime in August. The Archdruid of Avebury was most welcoming.

He fetched me a glass of water and introduced his five cats – Mollie, Belle, Dottie, Gizmo and Be.

Henk is an engineer in his forties. He moved to England from the Netherlands in 2015, but had first come to Avebury in 2003. 'I got out of the bus, put my foot on the ground, and knew I was at home.'

He estimates the population of the village at about a hundred and fifty – of which, he reckons, maybe a fifth are pagans. The relationship between these spiritual seekers and long-established village families appears to be good, although it has taken many years and a great deal of interfaith work to break down barriers.

'When I first came here people used to spit at me because I'm a pagan,' one incomer had told me when I phoned ahead of my journey. 'But now it's a big melting pot.'

Avebury gets crowded at the major festivals, especially summer solstice, but Henk does druidic work of one kind or another most days. Much of it is observational – noting the position of the sun, moon and stars in relation to the stones, and paying attention to where shadows fall. Other rites are more demanding and involved. 'Samhain, our death festival, is emotionally, mentally and physically tough, but very rewarding,' he told me. The ceremony begins at sunset on Hallowe'en and ends at sunrise the following day. At midnight at the Sanctuary, participants are given apples. The belief is that in the course of the ritual these become vessels for the souls of loved ones lost during the year. At first light, everyone walks to the chalk stream which rises at Swallowhead spring, near Silbury. The apples float off on the current, carrying the spirits of the departed to be reborn.

Henk has been Archdruid since the autumn equinox of 2022, taking over from the previous Archdruid, the late Terry

Dobney, who had trained him for the role. His house is, more or less, in the middle of the henge. 'That's very intense,' he said. 'I don't think people were meant to live inside a stone circle. Avebury is a harsh teacher. It's an amplifier and a receiver. If I'm happy, my happiness is amplified. When I feel anger or despair, I really feel it. So it's about managing your emotions and being on guard.'

He is not alone in this; other residents experience it, too. 'It is the energy of the place,' he explained. 'It's a bit like a church. You wouldn't live in a church either, because it's a consecrated area.' Henk is grateful for his home, but has to get out of the village at least once a week, 'even if it's just going to Marlborough to do some shopping'.

Avebury draws strangers. There is a pattern. They encounter the place and are changed.

On Sunday, 7 January 1649, John Aubrey rode into Avebury for the first time. The young gentleman was out hunting with friends when the chase took them to the village and he found himself 'wonderfully surprized at the sight of those vast stones'. Aubrey was from Wiltshire and yet had no idea until that moment that the site existed; an obscurity hard to imagine now.

Seventeenth-century Avebury could have had no visitor better suited to appreciate its bewildering charm. Even the coincidence of their names – Aubrey knew the village as 'Aubury' – suggests an innate sympathy between man and place. 'Although chiefly remembered in connexion with antiquarian research and biographical memoir, there are few persons of whom it would be more true to say that they were interested in everything,' is Anthony Powell's summation. 'Mathematics, painting, music, natural science, horticulture, heraldry, folklore, astrology, occult phenomena were all subjects – with a hundred others – that he was prepared to discuss . . .'

Aubrey is often credited as having discovered the henge,

which is absurd in a sense, because of course the people who lived there knew of its existence. What he did do was recognise its importance. Not the first to see Avebury, he was perhaps the first to truly *see* it, and to say it should be seen. When his remark that Avebury 'did as much excell Stoneheng as a Cathedrall does a Parish church' was brought to the attention of Charles II, the king decided to visit for himself, with Aubrey as his guide – and thus its future fame was set in stone.

John Aubrey was also the first to draw the site. His plans and sketches are important because many more stones were still in place than by the time of Stukeley's arrival in 1719. Archaeologists talk about 'stratigraphy' – the principle that the ground is made of layers of sediment, so that an object found in a deeper layer of an excavation will be older than an object found higher up. Avebury has a visual stratigraphy. Aubrey's work is in the earliest stratum, layered upon which is all that has come after: Stukeley's drawings; Paul Nash's paintings; David Bailey's wonderful portrait of The Rolling Stones walking the West Kennet Avenue; the cult TV series *Children of the Stones*; and of course the hundreds of thousands of photographs uploaded to social media. This imagery is present at Avebury all at once, layer upon layer of perception and depiction, with the result that it is next to impossible for anyone, now, to look upon the place with innocent eyes.

Paul Nash was part of an interwar movement of artists and writers for whom a love of strange old places and lovely old things was not at odds with creative progress. No nostalgist, his great pictures of Avebury, the oil painting 'Equivalents for the Megaliths' and the lithograph 'Landscape of the Megaliths', do not ache for Albion. They are modern, dream-like, visionary, queer. As Myfanwy Evans wrote of Nash in 1937, 'He has no interest in the past as *past*, but the accumulated intenseness of the past as *present* is his special concern and joy.'

The painter came to Avebury in July 1933 while recovering from bronchitis. He found that the stones possessed a 'primal magic', a 'disquieting beauty', and wrote two months later to Henry Moore: 'I've read somewhere that certain primitive peoples coming across a large block of stone in their wanderings could worship it as a god – which is easy to understand, for there's a sense of immense power about a large rough-shaped lump of rock or stone.' The megaliths, he seemed to feel, had a kind of life force. He quoted the art historian Herbert Read: *'the stone itself has its spirit, it is alive.'*

Alive? In a way. Avebury is a virus. Art is its vector. The shapes of those stones, and the patterns they make, were in the imagination of people before they ever stood upright on the land. And the human mind has continued to be their host. If I close my eyes and think about Avebury, I can see certain stones and how they sit with one another. And I can very clearly see Silbury Hill. Not just because I have been to the place, but because so many artists, antiquarians, photographers and film-makers were there before me. Their images live and breed in the memory. You don't go to Avebury, you contract it.

To better understand what it is about this landscape that so readily infects the creative mind, I had a conversation with Daniel & Clara. The Essex-based duo describe themselves as 'two humans, but one artist'; they work and speak as one. They first visited Avebury in the winter of 2017, arriving on the top deck of a bus, right above the driver, the seat favoured by children, peering out through misted windows at the mysterious stones. 'It feels like you're in a labyrinth of a kind,' they recalled. 'It's amazing that something as simple as putting those stones in that configuration can create that experience. Avebury, as a work of art in itself, is fascinating for being such a direct statement, yet it also has these endless possible interpretations.'

The encounter was a revelation. It transformed their work

and life, prompting a move to the UK from Portugal and a new focus on the British countryside. 'Avebury,' they felt, was 'a dream built into the landscape' – and they wanted to continue to dream it. They began to create art about the site, experimental works using video, Polaroids, even miniature railway-style models of the henge and Silbury made entirely from memory. 'Out of everything in Avebury, Silbury Hill had the most impact on us. It reveals what the aesthetic experience is really all about – opening this feeling of awe in you.'

Their work is shaped, perhaps even fuelled, by anxiety around the climate crisis. 'We feel,' they have said of themselves, 'like Adam and Eve at the end of the world.'

Could that anxiety be what lies behind the present cultural fascination with the prehistoric? Unhappy with the present, lacking hope for the future, we seek solace in the ancient past? Perhaps, I suggested to Daniel & Clara, that is why so many people seem to be out at the weekends visiting standing stones.

They nodded. 'That's part of the picture. We've lived through a pandemic, we're constantly aware that there's violence and terror in parts of the world. There's only so much a human can take; we desperately want to live with purpose and meaning. They've seen all sorts of things, those stones. They have witnessed humans come and go, languages change, societies form and unravel. There's something reassuring about that.'

There is. We should take care, though, not to be idealistic about the Neolithic. The temptation is to regard it as an age of innocence, unfallen man at one with nature. Yet what are these great monuments if not our first disobedience, evidence of our apartness? The Neolithic people were farmers; they cleared woods for their beasts and crops. They built henges for reasons we do not understand, but which speak of a questioning restlessness and a relentless imposition of will. A stone circle is an oil rig in embryo. It is a step on the road to our present trouble.

We marvel at such places, we find them beautiful, but perhaps we should regard them as warnings unheeded. They are as much the fruit of our fatal intelligence as the melting glaciers and heating seas.

'We wouldn't have made Avebury if we were in Eden,' is how Daniel & Clara put it.

*

In an upstairs room of the museum, Ros Cleal opened a box and lifted out what lay inside. I was allowed to hold it, which I couldn't quite believe. It was an antler. White with age, about two feet long, still some weight in it.

'This is one of the implements that dug the Avebury ditch,' Ros explained.

'Wow,' I said.

'Yeah,' she replied.

Ros is curator of the Alexander Keiller Museum and has been for thirty years. She is no stranger to handling tools used by people thousands of years ago. Nevertheless she has retained her admiration of such objects, and understands that those of us unused to the privilege of touch may feel a little stunned. So, as I held the antler, she took a moment to point out the burr, the part that would have been closest to the deer's head, the presence of which indicated that it was shed – and then foraged – rather than being cut from a hunted animal.

The tine nearest the burr was worn to a stub where it had been used to prise out chalk, which may then have been shovelled into a basket, using the shoulder blade of an ox, and hauled up from the ditch by ropes. 'And of course we don't know who's doing it,' Ros said. 'It has always been assumed that it was just men, but it may not have been.'

Antler picks of this sort, found at Grime's Graves, a Neolithic flint mine in Norfolk, still carry the fingerprints of the miners; grooves pressed into chalk slurry during a day's work in the time before Christ.

Ros pointed to a small label stuck to the antler I was holding. 'You see that writing there?'

Someone had written in black ink: *PICK, No. 136, AVEBURY FOSSE, CUTTING I, 1909, ON BOTTOM.*

It had been found in 1909, during an excavation led by the archaeologist Harold St George Gray. 'Fosse' means ditch. Cutting I was in the south-west sector of the henge. If the find came from the bottom, that means it was discovered at a depth of around thirty feet. So many antler picks were at or near the deepest part of the ditches, sometimes heaped up, that it is thought their presence is meaningful. They seem not to have been casually dropped. They may be votive offerings of some sort, or simply trophies denoting a hard job well done, similar to the way in which people still sometimes write their names on plaster before covering them with wallpaper. Perhaps the ditch-diggers laid down their tools with the same pride in workmanship felt by the men who dug out the ditches four thousand five hundred years later. One of the most startling Avebury images is a photograph of labourers in cloth caps and waistcoats posing for a moment with their spades as they dig down and down to the bottom of the ditch.

The picture was taken in April 1922, year of *The Waste Land*, and there is indeed something unreal and fearful about it, something stifling and dizzying, something of the Ypres trenches, too. The ditch was far deeper than necessary for the construction of the bank. 'It's as if there's something really important about going down into the earth,' Ros said. It could be that rather than being intended to keep people out, the point of the ditch was to keep something in. Perhaps within that circle was something considered so powerful and dangerous that it had to be confined by a great cut in the chalk.

AVEBURY.
FOSSE. CUTTING IX, 1922.
(THE DEEPEST PART).

Ros put the antler pick back in its box and we went outside to walk the circle. We were joined by her colleague Briony Clifton, an archaeologist. There was some discussion about which route to take. Should we just follow our feet? 'The henge will guide us,' Briony laughed.

It was the sort of sunny day when Avebury becomes a pleasure garden. A couple, lost in kisses, lay on a picnic blanket at the foot of a stone. Kids played chase around another. A sheep scratched its backside on the Barber Stone. A young man with long hair and a Led Zep T-shirt sat cross-legged and sketched the scene.

Avebury, as one sees it now, is quite different from how it had appeared to Paul Nash. In 1944, he looked back on his first visit:

> The great stones were then in their wild state, so to speak. Some were half-covered by the grass, others stood up in cornfields or were entangled and overgrown in the copses, some were buried under the turf. But they were wonderful and disquieting, and as I saw them then, I shall always remember them. Very soon afterwards the big work of reinstating the Circles and Avenues began, so that to a great extent that primal magic of the stones' appearance was lost.

The difference was that Alexander Keiller had arrived. He was, in some ways, another Aubrey – a passionate amateur with a diverse list of interests that included ski-jumping, fast cars, witchcraft, criminology, aerial photography, archaeology and sex. He was married four times and there were lots of other women.

Antonia White, the novelist, summed him up:

> Reputed a sadist: but the most sentimental man I know. Yet I enjoy being with him in spite of egoism, bombast,

self-pity, merciless boredom. Full of vitality: has a definite charm and certainly an element of surprise. *Exaggerated* about everything – feelings, affections, suspicions. Forces everyone to take part in *his* life, whether digging up barrows, collecting cattle or skiing . . . Yet infects one with enthusiasm and obviously inspires passionate devotion in people who work for him.

Their association ended, White told her daughter Lyndall, when she refused to satisfy one of his fantasies: 'He wanted her to climb into a large laundry basket, wearing only a mackintosh, and let him poke her with an umbrella through the wickerwork.'

Unlike Aubrey, beset with money problems, Keiller was very rich. Born in Dundee, heir to a marmalade empire, he came into his inheritance in 1910 and sold his shares eight years later. Wealth allowed him to do as he pleased; what he pleased was to buy up Avebury and set about resurrecting the stones. Between 1934 and the outbreak of the Second World War, he first excavated the West Kennet Avenue and then within the henge itself, locating stones that had been buried and re-erecting them.

'Archaeology and "the Avenue" has now become his religion,' Antonia White wrote in her 1935 diary. 'All the stones are "she". He says the most beautiful music in the world to him is the sound of cement-mixer pounding the cement which will fix the newly unearthed stone in the socket of its stone hole . . . Every time a new stone is excavated a flag is flown and the gang lines up.'

Altogether, in just five years, Keiller increased the number of Avebury stones from twenty-one to more than seventy. He also bought and demolished homes and businesses, considering their encroachment upon the henge 'the national archaeological disgrace of Britain'. Quite right, too, one might say, when walking around and enjoying how Avebury looks today. But some locals at the time thought differently. 'Sadly, we saw the shape and structure of the top of our precious village, with its quaint houses and friendly neighbourly life disappear for ever as cottage after cottage was pulled down,' Marjorie Rawlins remembered. Hers was the first family Keiller persuaded to move out. 'The ancient circle of stones was to be restored to its Neolithic image. So very slowly began the disintegration of our close community and Parish life.'

Keiller saw the work as a duty. If he didn't do it, who would? No one, he was sure, 'with so wholehearted and innate a love of the stones as I, myself, feel'. But by 1939, even his considerable finances were under strain and he was having to sell land in Scotland to pay for work in Wiltshire. His vision for the henge was that '3000 years after I am gone she will still be standing ... and as far as she can see ... green hills ... not a house or a petrol station'. But then came the war, bringing excavation to an end. In 1943 he sold up, and in 1955 he died.

Avebury is his memorial, but it is incomplete. At least eighteen stones are still buried, their positions known, and there are almost certainly more, while a further five are above ground but fallen. This begs a question: should these remaining stones be excavated and re-erected, as Keiller would surely have done had time and money allowed? It would make a huge difference to the appearance of the site, especially in the south-east quadrant of the circle, which would have an arc of megaliths in the outer ring for the first time in seven hundred years. So is there any prospect at all of digging them up?

'It is unlikely,' Briony said. 'But ideas of places like this change over decades and centuries, so for the sake of future archaeologists I would never say no, not a chance.'

The henge is owned by the National Trust. It is a scheduled monument in state guardianship; any alteration would require both government consent and agreement from English Heritage.

It is also a UNESCO World Heritage Site, which adds another layer of protection. Anyone wishing to dig at Avebury would have to have a compelling reason. There would need to be some important research question that could only be answered through excavation. And because plans for further restoration would arouse intense media interest, there would have to be buy-in from the villagers, the archaeological profession and wider public.

In other words, it would be tricky and will probably never happen. But isn't there a good case for it? Henk Vis, when we spoke, thought so: 'The more complete we can make this circle the better. It will teach us more. There are still so many questions about why these stones are here.'

The only reason they aren't standing now is because of human interference. To raise them would be like reintroducing a species that we hunted to extinction. If we can bring back the beaver and the sea eagle, surely we can bring back the Avebury stones?

'But,' Briony said, 'there is a question of authenticity and interpretation as well.'

Yes. Restoring the circle would not be a reversal of time. It would be a radical intervention in a monument that has already been messed about with considerably over the years. It could be argued that the kindest thing one can do for the place is to leave it alone. After all, the result of Keiller's work is that Avebury is simultaneously ancient and a creation of the twentieth century; a 'modern monument to prehistory', as it has been described by the cultural geographer David Matless. You don't want to end up with a theme park.

Then again. Those stones should never have been taken down. One cannot easily make a moral case on an application for scheduled monument consent, but it does seem to me that a wrong was done to this place that could be put right.

HENGE

'I wouldn't necessarily disagree with you,' said Ros.

'It would be *really* cool,' Briony agreed.

I like that response. These women are expert professionals. They see Avebury every day and know it in every detail. Yet they still take pleasure in the place, and want the best for it. As did Stukeley. As did Keiller. I was reminded of something Jennifer Wexler had said when we sat in that café at Stonehenge: 'Most people do archaeology out of love.'

Ros and Briony went back to work, and I took a turn around the stones. One last circuit for old times' sake.

The bank was high and steep. To my left, beyond the ditch, visitors wandered among the megaliths. To my right, through the trees, just on the other side of the bank, was a flat grassy area neatly mown with concentric rings. At first I couldn't work out what it was. Surely not another henge? But then I realised. Of course. What else? A stone circle on one side, a cricket field on the other – here was England in excelsis.

Henk Vis stepped down as Archdruid of Avebury in June 2025 but continues to live and worship in the village.

LOCH

IT'S THE EYES, don't you think? Must be.

A handful of pebbles picked from the shore, a few discarded until the fit was sure, and then the chosen two lodged in gouged hollows as an animating touch.

No accident that one sits higher than the other. She – we can surely say *she* – was carved that way. The lopsided gaze was intended. Maybe the woman being memorialised had a face like that. Or maybe the deity portrayed, if this was a religious idol, was known for uneven features, just as Odin, later, is always shown with one eye, having plucked out the other in return for wisdom.

So: quartz eyes. The cataract white of a winter sky.

'Ballachulish figure,' says the information panel. 'But who she was, or what she represented, is unknown. The figure was found in a bog, covered by the remains of a wickerwork structure. The bog, overlooking the entrance to a sea loch, was probably a sacred place.'

Figure, a neutral term, is inarguable. Goddess, though, as she's known – the Ballachulish Goddess – well, that's a different matter.

'What is she?' I asked Fraser Hunter, as we stood in the National Museum of Scotland, looking at her through glass.

'You're starting with the hardest question,' he replied, 'because a big chunk of my time when talking about Ballachulish is spent disabusing people of the notion that there's a simple answer.'

Fraser is principal curator of prehistoric and Roman archaeology. That's a good job to have if you are at ease with uncertainty.

'She's the only human figure of this date in Scotland,' he continued. That date being around 600 BC. 'So it's very hard to draw comparisons. The easy temptation is to say she's a goddess, and lots of folk have done that. But it can't be proven. We've no sense that people at that time had a concept of deities. And if they did, we've no sense that they conceptualised them in human form.'

He likes to tell the story of Brennus, the Gaulish chieftain, who entered a temple in Rome and laughed at the gods of stone and wood. The idea that you could capture such beings in a statue – that they would look like people – well, that seemed absurd. So Fraser, after Brennus, is cautious: 'There's no need to assume that the depiction of a human figure is a deity. It could be a spirit, it could be an ancestor, it could be a hero, it could be a person lost in the straits.'

Straits? The fast narrows that connect Loch Linnhe with Loch Leven. There's a bridge now, and has been since 1975, but before then all passages on this dangerous water had to be made by boat. That explains Our Lady of the Ferry – a name attached to the figure soon after she was discovered. A strangely Christian label, it doesn't suit her and you don't hear it much these days, but it gets at the idea that she may have stood at the water's edge, conferring protection upon travellers.

She was uncovered on 20 November 1880 by men labouring in the grounds of Ardsheallach House, North Ballachulish, not far from shore. 'This morning a black image about four feet six inches high was found buried deep in the peat moss, where the foundation was being dug for our new dyke,' the Reverend Chinnery-Haldane wrote in his diary. 'It is of black oak, and has evidently been buried for ages. Its eyes are made of white stones fixed into the sockets.'

Those eyes again. It's the eyes that hold you.

The Inverness Courier carried the story on 9 December,

noting that the workmen, Gaelic speakers, referred to the find as the *Ìomhaigh*, or 'Image'. The author of the article, however, used the word 'goddess', so right from the start that was how she was presented to the modern world. The figure had been found face down; above and below her were 'many twigs and branches, woven and interlaced' – suggesting that she may have been inside a wickerwork container. The find was, the report said, 'a strange relic of paganism' and 'the most interesting and curious and puzzling that has ever yet engaged the attention of Scottish archaeologists'.

Within a week of discovery, the figure had been taken to Edinburgh, to be examined by Sir Robert Christison, the eminent physician, a regular visitor to Ballachulish. It went by train; the railway workers, so it's said, were reluctant to handle what they regarded as ungodly – and may not have taken the best care. 'It was thoroughly soaked and softened with peat-water when I first saw it, and the legs had been broken across at the ankles from some rough usage in the transport to Edinburgh,' Sir Robert wrote in a scholarly paper. 'It is well rounded in every part, except that the arms are represented simply by lines carved obliquely across the chest and upper abdomen. It is very slim in figure, but not more so than some young ladies of the present day swathed in the swaddling-clothes now in fashion.'

A photograph, which may have been taken in the study of Sir Robert's home in Moray Place, shows the figure as it appeared at that time. The head is indeed 'well rounded', the hands resting on the belly are clearly defined, the pubic area is prominent and exaggerated, the facial expression benign – she seems, even, to smile.

In those days, though, there was no way of conserving water-logged wood, and the object soon dried, warped and cracked. What we see now, when we visit the museum, is the result.

She is kept downstairs, below Edinburgh's elegant streets;

to come into her presence you must descend to the Early People gallery and then pass down a narrow sloping corridor lined with fragments of skull and stone. She is set into the wall, upright behind glass. Deep brown and slender, she is withered, twisted and split; a wide cleft runs all the way down her body to the vulva which, now, is difficult to discern, in part because it is one of the places where a black metal bracket holds her secure. Spotlights show the detail: head like a broken nail, mouth a black cuticle, eyes that are unseeing yet seem to have seen too much. What is her expression? Anguish, I think. She gives the impression of being in physical and mental torment. Wrenched out of place and time, brought up into the brittling air, she makes her protest through these splintering contortions, disturbing all who see her. A goddess of suffering and self-harm, then, but not without power. Our Lady of the Scars.

The English language is not up to the job of describing her. Scots has a word, 'thrawn', which she seems to embody in both its senses: bent and unbending. Did Robert Louis Stevenson ever see her, I wonder? She reminds me of Thrawn Janet, in his ghost story of that name, 'wi' her neck thrawn, and her heid on ae side, like a body that has been hangit, and a girn on her face like an unstreakit corp'.

I never visit the museum without coming to see the figure. There's some odd sense of duty, a paying of respects. Yet she is the only object in the whole place that I find troubling, that gives me – as Stevenson put it – 'a cauld and deidly grue'. And it's not just me. Lots of people feel the same: at once drawn and repelled. I was curious, though, how the curator felt. What, I asked Fraser, is his visceral response to her?

'Oh,' he laughed, 'I'm trained not to have visceral responses. I find her really interesting and striking. I enjoy coming down here and having a think. We've had her on display for twenty-five years, but, recently, I've been back to look at her again.'

He has been considering those aspects of the figure one might not notice at first, and which haven't been much discussed. The slanting marks across her chest, for instance, which seem to be blows from an axe – perhaps made during a ritual 'killing' before she was laid down at the end of her period of use. Then there is the block of wood at the end of her legs; a rectangular cavity has been made in it, and this, it is thought, likely contained some small but important object. Here we enter the realm of speculation, but if the figure was made as a memorial to a real person then perhaps it enshrined a piece of bone. In any case, that dim little hollow seems to stand for all that we don't know about the figure – which is most things.

What has become known in recent times is that she is not carved from oak, as was long thought, but from alder, a tree of river-edge and bog. This is significant because it is not a durable wood unless kept damp, so there may have always been an intention that she would be deposited in the wet ground – born to die. When alder is cut, the exposed timber turns a reddish-orange; bright and bloody she was delivered into darkness.

The Ballachulish figure has a cultural and aesthetic context. Although unique in Scotland, there are around forty carvings in Britain and Europe that seem to have kinship. Her older cousin Ralaghan Man, dug from an Irish bog in 1908, shares the family trait of uneven features – as can be seen by all who visit him in Dublin. The five Roos Carr figures, discovered in the East Riding of Yorkshire in 1836, are far smaller than Ballachulish, but they too have quartz eyes. And their energy is different. If she is a goddess, they are malevolent sprites – bad little godlings up to no good.

Whenever I see the Ballachulish figure, I think: *who made you?* An ability to work with wood was no doubt fundamental to life in the Early Iron Age. Everyone must have had some level of knowledge and competence. But the making of a meaningful object like this was surely a job for a specialist, a person known for the skill of their hands, the sharpness of their eye.

The figure, as displayed in Edinburgh, is surrounded on three sides by stacked branches of wind-fallen oak; the impression is of peering into a shelter or shrine. The branches were gathered and arranged in the late 1990s by the artist Andy Goldsworthy. They are supposed to suggest the wickerwork within which the figure was laid down. 'It was given a kind of burial,' Goldsworthy said when we met in the museum. 'The idea of it being put into the ground as a memory and potent presence really interests me.'

We stood by the figure and looked at her, separated by glass and time.

'Do you sense,' I asked, 'that this was made by what we would now call an artist?'

'Oh, for sure,' he replied. 'Absolutely. It's not just a work of craft, it's a work of art.'

'Why do you say so?'

'Well, the energy that's in it. This has a very deeply human energy. There is a sense of watchfulness. The impact of this figure must have been tremendous; the power that it would have had in its place. So it's got energy and power. And that's the hand of an artist.'

Watchfulness. That quartzous glare. A sentinel who gazed over hazardous water, what rising fear does she see in our eyes?

CHALK

THREE TEENAGE BOYS in hoodies and joggies lay sprawled between the hind legs of the Uffington White Horse. There was a strong smell of dope as I walked down the slope to meet them.

They'd driven over from Swindon, they said. This is where they come to chill. I had seen them earlier, giving the finger to a paraglider, but now they had settled in the long grass to watch the sky. Their eyes were a little pink, in contrast with the Horse's great white eye, but in sympathy with the sunset.

I explained that I was writing a book.

'Sorry,' one laughed. 'Dunno nuffing about this place.'

'Three thousand years old, they reckon,' I said. 'Centuries before the Romans came, the Horse was here.'

They were impressed.

'No way! This would be a good spot to take mushrooms. You'd see *everyfing.*'

What would you see, I wonder? Perhaps you'd see the Horse being made. Trenches dug deep, then clean white chalk quarried nearby and shovelled in. Perhaps you'd see the design sketched out with a piece of chalk on stone, if that was how it was done, and the man or woman with the vision explain to their people that this is what they must build. Some, in their lost language, would surely ask, 'But *why?*' – just like we do now.

It was getting dark so I said I'd leave the boys to it.

As I walked back up the hill, I could hear them talking.

'Three thousand years! Woah – that is old as *shit.*'

Well, quite. The Uffington White Horse is a geoglyph, or 'earth picture'; a figure carved into a hill – in what is now Oxfordshire – sometime in the late Bronze Age or early Iron Age. It is likely to have been the creation of nearby farming communities, perhaps members of the Dobunni or Atrebates, tribes later named by the Romans. The Horse's origins are a mire of maybes and perhaps, but we can be sure of its present context and impact. It is the dominant feature of a prehistoric landscape that includes the Iron Age hillfort Uffington Castle and the Neolithic long barrow Wayland's Smithy, all of them set along the Ridgeway, the footpath often described, with careless romance, as Britain's oldest road.

These sites, Jacquetta Hawkes has written,

> are invested with a power woven from the memories, the veneration and imaginative life of the nation. There is no doubt that the source of this mist of enchantment which has drifted for so long among the downs is the White Horse . . . So wide is his rule, so great his spell, that this whole stretch of valley has for as long as recorded memory borne the lovely name of the Vale of the White Horse. Like all great enchanters the Horse can assume various guises and is equally himself through them all.

Although known as the Horse, the figure has also been interpreted as a dog, a cat and a dragon, and this shape-shifting is because it does not seem entirely equine. Strangest of all is the so-called 'beak' emerging from one corner of its boxy head. If this is a horse then what is *that?* The figure looks nothing at all like the eight chalk horses of neighbouring Wiltshire, which are far more recent, far smaller, and more obviously horse-like. They are mere nags, mere foals. The Uffington Horse is 374 feet from head to tail and gives the impression of galloping, almost flying across the hillside. Whatever the motivations of its makers, it appears to us now as a beautiful and radical work of art.

'Taint what a horse *looks* like,' says Tiffany Aching, a young witch in Terry Pratchett's *A Hat Full of Sky*. 'It's what a horse *be.*'

*

CHALK

If there was such a thing as the *Ladybird Book of English Villages* then Uffington would surely feature. I had arrived in the early evening and the streets seemed sunk in a dream. Loved-up pigeons crooned from the thatch of chalk-walled cottages. A lorry loaded with straw passed with a contented snore, littering the road with golden strands. I turned right at the village sign – which showed the White Horse – and walked until I came to an old farmhouse of stone and brick with a rose climbing the front and lavender lining the path. This, as a blue plaque attests, was the home of John Betjeman between 1934 and 1945 – 'the furthest place from London I could find,' he wrote in a letter, 'which you could leave and get back to in a day'. He must have been able to see the Horse – about a mile and half away – from his upstairs windows. What a sight when you open your curtains. It would suit a poet.

Or poets. The Betjemans – John and his wife Penelope – made Uffington an unlikely cultural centre. Guests included T. S. Eliot, David Jones, Gertrude Stein, H. G. Wells and Evelyn Waugh. Great names, but also just people getting on with their lives. Having children, or not. Trying to make marriages work. On one occasion John and Penelope, mid-argument, were so carried along by the momentum of their row that they walked into the bathroom where Cyril and Jean Connolly were sharing the tub. The archaeologist Stuart Piggott later recalled his own first visit: he had knocked the front door and started rather tentatively to explain that they had a friend in common. 'For God's sake come in,' Betjeman interrupted, 'we're having a helluva time with the Prime Minister of Nepal.'

They loved their time here, the Betjemans – or that's the impression one gets. And why wouldn't they? 'We used to have moonlit picnics up on White Horse Hill,' their daughter Candida remembered towards the end of her life, 'masses of us, all conveyed by horse and cart.'

There was an exhibition about Betjeman's Uffington years at the local museum, a seventeenth-century building that used to be the village school, so I popped in to have a look. The star exhibit was Archie, the poet's teddy. John was given Archibald Ormsby-Gore, the bear's full name, in 1909 when he was three years old, and it became a constant companion; not just an affectation, a real presence. Archie came with him when he went to Oxford, the inspiration for Sebastian Flyte and Aloysius in *Brideshead Revisited*. To see the teddy now, within a glass case, felt a little like an encounter with one of those rotted martyrs you sometimes find being venerated in European churches. Biscuit-brown, worn and stitched and patched, the bear wore a woollen vest and an expression of fathomless ursine sorrow. Betjeman was holding Archie when he died.

Elsewhere in the museum there was information about the White Horse. Facsimile notices from eighteenth- and nineteenth-century newspapers gave details of the 'Pastime', the revels on White Horse Hill that accompanied the maintenance and renewal of the figure. Many thousands attended these occasions – useful manpower for the care of the Horse – and enjoyed various entertainments such as 'cart-horse racing, donkey racing, running in sacks, female racing, racing after a pig with a soaped tail, jingling matches, climbing for legs of mutton up a pole, back-sword playing, wrestling and other sports'. These other sports included removing a bullet from a tub of flour with the mouth, gurning through a horse-collar, running downhill in pursuit of a cheese, and – my favourite – women smoking pipes, the prize of a gallon of gin going to whichever lady could puff through the most tobacco in an hour. 'The whole will be under the management of respectable yeomen,' the *Reading Mercury* assured its readers in 1838. 'All drunken licentiousness will be discouraged as peace officers will be employed during the time, under the sanction of the magistrates.'

CHALK

The Horse has always relied upon the work of locals for its continuing existence. 'I estimate that if nothing was done it would grass over and be gone in twenty to twenty-five years,' Andy Foley, the National Trust ranger responsible for the figure, had told me on the phone before my visit. Scouring of the Horse takes place in late July and is the traditional name given to weeding the figure – 'But we don't advertise it as weeding because nobody would turn up!' Then, in late August, a new layer of chalk, very thin, is hammered into the outline, leaving it nice and bright for another year.

'Would it be okay,' I had asked Andy, 'if I came along and helped?'

'Of course,' he replied. 'We'll get some work out of you!'

This is what I find mind-blowing about the Horse: not the fact that such a thing was made in the first place, although that is remarkable, but that people have considered it important enough to maintain ever since, despite their very different beliefs, values and understandings of the world. Think of all that has happened. The Roman occupation, the coming of Christianity, the rise of Wessex and other Anglo-Saxon kingdoms, Viking attacks, the Norman conquest, the Reformation, the English Civil War, the Agricultural Revolution, the First and Second World Wars – through all of these, any one of which could have resulted in its destruction, the Horse has survived. The figure that appears in a sixteenth-century map of wool and silk can also be seen on the modern road atlas, tiny and rendered in red, where it seems to canter along the dotted line of the Ridgeway, ducking its head beneath the yellow band of the B4507. If it kept going, it would cross the Thames at Henley and arrive in London by the western approaches. I should very much like to see it in Westminster, nuzzling the bronze war-horses that draw Boudica's chariot.

Apart from everything else, the Horse is an amazing bit

of graphic design. Someone, so long ago, came up with one of the best logos of all time. You see it everywhere locally, including on the badge of Uffington's primary school, but it's also out there in the culture, a signifier of the magical and mysterious past. It appears on the cover of Alan Garner's novel *Treacle Walker* and within the pages as an image scratched into a 'donkey stone' used for whitening doorsteps; the Horse, thus applied, is a talisman protecting against dangerous visitors.

This talismanic, or perhaps better to say *totemic* quality of the Horse is also evident in what is probably its best known usage in popular culture: on the sleeve of *English Settlement*, the classic 1982 album by XTC. The band came from Swindon, a few miles west of the Horse, and so had been familiar with the hill figure since childhood. 'It felt like our badge, our fingerprint,' Andy Partridge, the band's singer and guitarist, told me. It was his idea to use it for the album. 'I mean, I know it's not "English" as such. It's much earlier . . . but it was perfect.'

CHALK

Colin Moulding, XTC's bassist and co-founder, first got to know the Horse when accompanying his father, a grocery delivery man, on his rounds. Later, in his teens, he used to cycle out there and, further afield, to Avebury and the West Kennet Long Barrow, enamoured with the traces of the past all around. 'As soon as I had my Raleigh Roadster, that was it – I was a free boy.' For locals, he explained, the White Horse is associated with home and homecoming; you see it as the train from Paddington begins to slow on its approach to Swindon.

When Andy suggested using the Horse on the sleeve, his bandmate was instantly happy with the idea. It would somehow stand for a feeling they had, he said, of being 'deliciously apart' – as Betjeman describes his boyhood self in *Summoned By Bells*. 'You just want to express your individualism as a band,' Colin added. 'We were always taught, "Don't mention that you come from Swindon!" In the days of punk, when you came up to London, saying you were from Swindon was seen as the kiss of death. But as time went on, we wanted to say: *This is us*. And the Horse was the banner we wanted to use.'

It was, in short, a tribal emblem – just as it may have been at the moment of its creation. I wonder, though, whether it was more than that for XTC. Did the White Horse and surrounding landscape somehow get inside the music they made?

'The chalk hills did,' Colin said. 'London is the clay but Swindon is the chalk.'

'You were a band built on chalk?' I asked.

'Yeah. Family and chalk, that's what holds us here.'

*

On a wall of the room where I write is a reproduction of William Smith's groundbreaking – literally so – 1815 geological map of England and Wales. Scotland features, but only as far as the Firth of Tay. The map was intended to be useful – to help, for example, in the location of coal – but its utility has a happy side-effect: it is beautiful. Each rock layer is represented by a different colour; Jurassic oolite is a yellow flame burning through the Cotswolds; the Carboniferous limestone a plume of blue smoke rising above it. England's chalklands appear not as white but green.

The chalk of England was formed sixty-five to a hundred million years ago. Chalk is death; it is made from the dead; from the shells of billions of coccoliths, microscopic marine creatures that drifted lifelessly down to the sea floor – joining the bodies of all those that had gone before and soon covered by the multitude to come.

'I like to think of seas where chalk was forming clouded with white as though from a snow storm – a fall that lasted for thirty million years and lay to a depth of a thousand feet,' Jacquetta Hawkes writes in *A Land*, her classic 1951 book on archaeology, geology and art. 'Without Chalk there could be no Albion, and there would have been no Chalk without the Cretaceous seas.'

The chalklands of Albion. On Smith's map, sweeping upwards from south to east, they look – to my eye – like a mosquito; its wings are the Chilterns, its abdomen and legs the North and South Downs, it sinks its proboscis into Dorset. There is also chalk in Yorkshire, in the Wolds, where the availability of the material has given rise to four of the strangest and most intriguing objects we have from prehistory: small carved cylinders of solid chalk, known as 'drums', three of which were found in Folkton, near Filey, in 1889, and a fourth, near Burton Agnes, in 2015. All were discovered in the graves of children and are around five thousand years old. In the Folkton burial, the child – sex uncertain – had been laid in a crouched position, and the drums placed in size-order along the line of the back, the smallest by the head and the largest below the hips. The Burton Agnes grave, dug in the shape of an arch, contained three children: the younger pair, aged around three and five, were touching or holding hands and were themselves being held –'cuddled' comes to mind – by the eldest child, who is estimated to have been about twelve.

You look at something like this, a jumble of skulls loosed from the earth's jealous grip, and you think – were these siblings, these children of the chalk? Did they play together? Die together? What happened?

The drum was found just above the head of the eldest. It is decorated with elaborate motifs of concentric circles and other geometric shapes; three holes are drilled in the top, perhaps one for each child. The Folkton drums are similar, except those have been carved with what look like eyes, giving them the half-comical, half-eerie appearance of little heads, owlish somehow, as if something is peering at you through the trees. It is thought that they may be talismans – that word again – protecting the children on their journey to whatever idea of the afterlife these people had. I remember seeing the drums at the British Museum's *World of Stonehenge* exhibition, the first time all four had been brought together. In a show full of treasures, these small objects stood out in their inscrutability and aura of grief. It is the business of archaeology to learn about the people of the past through the discovery and study of material they leave behind. That is a noble pursuit, and it was a privilege to be able to examine the drums, but I did wish, standing in that busy room, that they had not been found, that they were still serving their purpose, whatever that was, watching over young bones in the old dark.

*

'The cutting of figures in the turf is an obscure and little-regarded art.' So wrote Morris Marples in his 1949 book *White Horses and Other Hill Figures.*

Little regarded it may have been, at least back in the 1940s, the hill figures having been concealed during the war to prevent German bombers using them as navigational aids, but Marples was in no doubt that it *was* an art, 'a characteristically English art', and one that had been practised for a long time.

The three best-known figures are the Uffington White Horse, the Cerne Abbas Giant and the Long Man of Wilmington. Each is a marvel, although only the Horse is prehistoric. Its origins were not known for certain until advances in technology made dating possible in 1990, but there had long been a belief that the figure was truly ancient. G. K. Chesterton's 1911 poem *The Ballad of the White Horse*, with its cantering rhythm, gets at this nicely:

> Before the gods that made the gods
> Had seen their sunrise pass,
> The White Horse of the White Horse vale
> Was cut out of the grass.

In the National Trust car park near the White Horse, an ice cream van was parked on the verge. The driver stood at the serving hatch, baseball cap backwards, looking glum.

'A cone please,' I said.

He nodded.

'You want a flake?'

I nodded.

'You want the sauce?'

I shook my head.

'Who buys more ice cream round here,' I asked, 'the pagans or the archaeologists?'

'No one buys,' he said. 'Is very quiet today.'

It *was* quiet. For one of the great sights of England, I was surprised how few people were around. 'Police operating drones in this area,' a yellow sign warned.

Just then a man came over and said hello. He was tall and straight-backed, seemed to be in his sixties, and had on a camouflage jacket – from the pocket of which he produced some underwear. 'A pair of frillies in the blue badge car park,' he said. 'With the shopping tag still on.' He dropped them in the bin.

Simon Knapper is retired from a long army career in which he reached the rank of brigadier. He lives in Uffington, volunteers with the National Trust, and has become a sort of guardian of the Horse. His duties include litter-picking. The litter sometimes includes knickers. That's the thing about the Horse, it attracts all sorts. It gives rise to various emotions: pride, wonder and, no doubt, bouts of horniness.

I complimented Simon on his moustache, which was neat and brigadier-ish.

'Thank you,' he said. 'I grew it in the Fijian jungle.'

We talked about the Horse, what it means. 'I'm excited by it,' he said. 'I was brought up a Catholic but I love the idea of pagan symbols. And I like the mystery of it. I like its presence, the way it looks out over the whole area. It's exciting to be part of it. I come up here at all times of year, pick up litter, tell people off for climbing on it.' Sometimes he spends the night by the figure, keeping watch; no tent, just a sleeping bag under the stars. 'It's magical. I'm not a pagan, but I understand its power.'

I got the feeling, from speaking with Simon, that the Horse has given him a mission, that it helps to fill his days. He has other interests, though, including trying to identify the site of the Battle of Ashdown where, in 871, the West Saxons defeated the Vikings. Oh, and teaching himself Old English. 'My father swore blind that crosswords and *Countdown* would save him from dementia. But I can't do crosswords and I don't like *Countdown*, so I thought I'd try to memorise Anglo-Saxon poetry. I started with "Caedmon's Hymn", then "Deor", and I'm now I'm on line fifty-three of "The Wanderer".'

'Do you know any poetry appropriate to the White Horse?' I asked.

'No, but I've got one for Wayland's Smithy,' he said, and went straight into it –

> *Welund him be wurman wræces cunnade,*
> *anhydig eorl earfoþa dreag,*
> *hæfde him to gesiþþe sorge and longaþ,*
> *wintercealde wræce; wean oft onfond*
> *siþþan hine Niðhad on nede ledge,*
> *swoncre seonobende on syllan monn.*
> *þæs ofereode, þisses swa mæg.*

It was from 'Deor', he explained, a poem written in the ninth century, the first two verses of which are about Wayland, the legendary blacksmith.

'Before the Normans arrived in 1066, and began to unravel the English sense of self at the tip of a sword, everyone in the country would have known the story of Wayland the smith.' So says Paul Kingsnorth in his essay 'Oak, Ash and Thorn'.

Wayland, or Weland, or Völundr, is a figure from Norse, Germanic and Anglo-Saxon mythology. His is a story of blood and treasure. The smith's skills, his way with swords and gold, were so famous that King Niðhad, covetous, hobbled and enslaved him – cutting the sinews at the back of his knees and forcing Wayland to work metal for him alone. The smith's vengeance was to murder the king's young sons, fashioning their skulls into silver cups, their teeth into brooches, their eyes into jewels, all of which he presented to the royal family as gifts. He got the king's daughter drunk, made her pregnant – which has been interpreted as rape – and then flew from captivity on mechanical wings.

'The story of Wayland spoke to Old English society of themes at once specific and universal: power misused, leaders blinded by cupidity, ordinary men wronged and out for revenge,' Kingsnorth argues. 'If we were searching for a foundation myth for the English people, the story of Wayland would be a strong contender.'

Wayland's Smithy, which Simon Knapper mentioned, is the name given to a well-known Neolithic tomb. I had visited it the day before, walking along the Ridgeway. It took half an hour at dawdling pace, following the chalk path, wheat to the left, barley the right. A horse ambled past and turned down a bridleway through the fields. This is still horse country; the culture persists in a small way. I had seen a number of people on horseback, all women, going nowhere in particular and in no hurry to get there. A woman in Uffington had told me that whenever one of her dogs and horses dies, she scatters its ashes up by the White Horse. There's a special feeling there, she said; it's a place that animals like.

As I reached the Smithy, a tour group was preparing to leave. Mostly Americans. One of the party wore a T-shirt that asked: 'What were the ancients up to?' Another walked barefoot along the grassy top of the tomb. 'There's a real subtle energy,' he drawled. 'Easier to feel when your shoes are off. And it's respectful to the earth.' Before leaving, he had a respectful pee up against one of the beeches that enclose the site. I was glad when I had the place to myself.

Wayland's Smithy is a long barrow – an elongated chalk mound built over a stone burial chamber – that over five thousand five hundred years ago was used to house the dead. Despite being on a popular walking route, it feels hidden within its grove of trees. It was disappointing but not surprising to learn, as I did later, that it has been used for neo-Nazi rituals. Ancient places offer scenery and setting for their twisted visions of an unspoiled England.

It is the mystery of the far past, the absence of written

evidence, that allows this. Objects and structures left behind – the stones, the bones, the chalk drums – are accelerants to the imagination. Archaeology is experiencing a scientific revolution, with a variety of laboratory techniques enabling an ever greater understanding of ancient people and events. Isotope analysis has made it possible to take a tooth and from it create – not jewellery, as Wayland did – but a story of where that person was born and where in the world they travelled. But even with such developments, the creative mind remains crucial. That is why archaeology is both science and art. The facts are not enough; a narrative must be woven around them.

So, as that T-shirt put it, what *were* the ancients up to? Excavation at Wayland's Smithy has revealed that the earliest structure was a lidded wooden box on a stone pavement with split tree trunks placed upright at each end. Radiocarbon dating of the bones suggests that the remains of fourteen people – eleven men, two women and child – were deposited in this box over a period of no more than fifteen years, and possibly a much shorter interval; they may have died in just one year. Three flint arrowheads were found in the grave, all missing their tips, and the tip of an arrow was discovered embedded in a pelvis, having entered the body through the abdomen. Two of the males had been partially scavenged by animals before burial. Weave a story around all that, if you will. Some atrocity, some massacre; a hail of arrows; survivors flee; when they return to bury the dead, wolves have eaten their fill.

The tomb of timber and stone was covered eventually by a small oval mound of chalk rubble and earth, then later encased within a much larger structure, the long barrow that can be seen today. It is trapezoid in shape and about a hundred and eighty feet long, the front dominated by four massive sarsens. The stone to the left of the entrance is much pitted – dark little nooks with, I noticed, a gleam of silver within. Up close, the source of the gleam became clear: visitors had left an offering of coins.

There is a legend that if you tether your horse and place some small payment in the stone, you will find the animal shod on your return. This seems rather lowly work for Wayland, but perhaps – coming to ground here after his flight from Niðhad's court – he was in the mood for a quieter life. Clearly, the building is much older than its name. The site enters the written record as 'welandes smiððan' in the year 955, though it could be that this is how it was known much earlier; the people of that time, seeking to understand this strange and unsettling place, may well have made a connection with the nearby hill figure. After all, who better to shoe a giant chalk horse than the great and terrible smith of the old stories?

Later, I asked Andy Foley, the National Trust ranger, about the coins that people leave. What happens to them?

'We give some to the local cattery, treat ourselves to ice cream, and use the odd pound for a shopping trolley.'

*

A pleasing paradox: the Uffington White Horse is highly visible but hard to see; a landmark that never quite fills the eye.

Aerial photographs offer the familiar view – the Horse stretched out across the hill, so white and so green, like a beast on a flag, or a constellation tumbled from the sky. But this is a false impression. Pictures from the air flatten the land; in fact the figure lies on a considerable slope. Some parts, especially the tail and neck, are on very steep ground; others, such as the back and belly, have a much more gentle gradient. It took me five minutes to walk around the outline, starting from the tip of the tail, up around the ears and beak, then round its forelegs, round its hind legs, and back to the tail again. It felt like walking a chalk path, the Ridgeway in miniature, and at times I was panting with the climb. Even the head, perhaps a dozen steps wide, is uneven – flat as a putting green in the part that contains the eye, then dropping sharply to the beak.

The result of all this is that the Horse is elusive. Standing by the head, you cannot see the rest of the body. From the picnic area near the car park, you can see the neck but not the tail. Approaching from directly below, you can see the trunk, all four legs, the tail, the neck . . . but not the head. I spent an enjoyably frustrating evening driving around the countryside, trying to find a decent viewpoint, peering over hedges and churchyard walls. I ended up miles out, so started heading back, but that was worse. The closer you get, the more the figure recedes. The Horse spooks, it shies away.

This skittish quality is captured in a watercolour by the artist Eric Ravilious. The Uffington figure is in the background, head and dock disappearing over the brow of the hill, as if off on some horsey business of its own. *The Vale of the White Horse* is one of a number of pictures of chalk figures Ravilious made for a planned children's book, to be published by Puffin, the idea being that it would give evacuees a better understanding of the countryside. His paintings of the Uffington Horse, Westbury Horse, Long Man of Wilmington and the Cerne Abbas Giant were all done in 1939, but he then found work as a war artist, which took his attention away from the book. It was unfinished at the time of his death in 1942. He was a passenger on a search-and-rescue mission off the coast of Iceland when the plane he was in went down. He was thirty-nine. His body was not recovered, which feels apposite – an absence of people, a cold vacancy, is characteristic of his work. 'I find it hard to say what it is to be English, but Ravilious is part of it,' Alan Bennett observes in a documentary, *Eric Ravilious: Drawn To War.* An enigmatic artist for an enigmatic Horse; his works ache with ambiguity. His paintings have some riddle in them, some hidden meaning, but the closer you get the further away the answer seems.

The Ravilious watercolour also conveys the unreality of the landscape around the Horse. In my few days there, I could never shake the feeling that the whole place, not just the chalk figure, was an invention. It seemed almost too dramatic, like a child's idea of downland, a Minecraft pastoral. There is, for instance, the Manger, a grassy amphitheatre, rippling and furrowed, that appears to have been scooped out of the scarp. Then there is Dragon Hill, a natural outcrop with a flat top and a great white scar in the centre, like the neck-stump of some titan, beheaded just as it was rising from the earth.

I met Andy Foley on White Horse Hill. He was wearing jeans, boots and a National Trust polo-shirt, and had an easy manner. He has worked here as a ranger since 2010 and has spent more time in the company of the Horse, worrying about it and caring for it, than anyone else alive. He is, essentially, its groom, and laughed when I said so. 'I suppose that's right. I do think about it a lot. When we get a heavy rain in the middle of the night, it wakes me up and my first thought is: the Horse!'

He showed me the spade that he uses for the figure. There were words on the wooden shaft: Horse Edger – Not For Another Use.

'You do all the edging yourself?' I asked.

'Yeah. I wouldn't let anybody else do it.'

'Why?'

'Pride of the job. Think of all those people who have looked after the Horse over the years, and I'm the latest custodian. We use a lot of volunteers, but some jobs I consider mine.'

We ducked under the blue rope that is intended to dis-suade the public from walking on the figure and sat down to talk within the outline of the head, just to the left of the eye.

The long view north was lovely; a motley of fields. I could see Betjeman's house and the thatched roofs of Uffington. Andy pointed out the airbase from where the spy planes take off, and the spot on the steep road below where, a few years ago, a man drove his car off the edge. 'You get good things and bad things here,' he said.

I asked whether he feels protective of the Horse, and he mentioned the time, not long after he started in the job, when the bookmaker Paddy Power used the figure in a publicity stunt, adding white canvas to make it appear as if a jockey was on its back.

'That was wrong,' he said.

'Why?' I asked.

'Because it's desecration of a scheduled ancient monument for the purposes of gambling.'

Desecration is a strong word. It suggests that there's something sacred about the Horse.

'It's a very spiritual place. A place of fertility as well, I think.'

'Why do you say that?'

'I've seen examples of it in real life. Even in my own life. I'm fifty-plus, my daughter's ten. I wasn't planning on having any children, but – hey presto. She's a child of the White Horse, I guess.'

Emily has been helping out with the chalking of the Horse since she was an infant. Andy has some hopes that she might take over the job from him one day.

We had been sitting so still and talking so quietly that we attracted the attention of a red kite. It hovered twenty feet above, giving us proper consideration.

'Blimey,' said Andy. 'I'm not dead. You can't eat me.'

The bird, taking him at his word, flew off.

Later, as I walked up Dragon Hill, I saw the kite again:

riding the thermals, tail notched like an arrow, the only creature to see the Horse entire.

*

The day of the weeding – sorry, *scouring* – was very wet. I had agreed to help set up and so found myself engaged in that most English of summer pastimes, putting up a gazebo in the driving rain. This was unpleasant but necessary, lest the kids from the Young Archaeologists Club perish while eating their sandwiches.

They had come to lend a hand. Everyone is welcome. It's such a big job; Andy needs all the volunteers he can get.

Simon Knapper was there, of course, press-ganging the public. 'The Horse has been here for three thousand years,' he explained to a young family who were walking the Ridgeway, 'and in all that time people have looked after it by scouring it of weeds and pounding new chalk into it. So –' he said, addressing the children, 'if you want to be part of the tradition you can come back in sixty years with your grandchildren and tell them that once long ago, before they were born, you helped care for the Horse.'

They were given trowels and assigned an area. We all were. I knelt down on a hind leg and got to work. Some of the wild flowers growing up through the chalk were pretty. Lady's bedstraw was a froth of yellow, and it seemed a shame to take it out, but it had to go. Really, this was just like weeding the garden, except that it was an ancient monument and you had to remember that. 'You're only going to the depth of a fingernail,' Andy warned, 'just so you can get underneath and get it out.'

The chalk is piled in layers up to a metre deep. This was what allowed the Horse to be dated, using a technique called optically stimulated luminescence. Samples were taken from the deepest – and therefore oldest – part of the belly, and work was done in the laboratory to establish when they had last seen the light. This gave a range of 1380–550 BC for construction of the figure; it is hoped that improvements in technology will soon allow the dating to be refined. The Horse's outline, as well as being deep, is very wide in places, although it has narrowed in the post-war years as a result of encroachment by grass. During the Covid pandemic, scouring did not take place and it is possible that the Horse lost a little width at that time, making it unique in Britain in becoming slimmer during lockdown.

'Look,' said Lisa, a woman working near me on the leg. She had trowelled out a plant with long narrow leaves. 'Plantain. I'm going to take this home and add it to some oil that I'm infusing. It's really good for healing the skin.'

She and her husband Adam, a carpenter, had travelled from their home near Glastonbury. 'I've always wanted to do this,' Adam said. 'I grew up around here and used to fly kites off the hill. I remember my dad here. He's gone on now, a couple of years. There's a feeling of belonging, knowing the land well enough to say, "This is my patch." It's the epitome of England.'

It was tipping down now. Adam's flat cap was sodden. The rain was soaking the chalk; everyone's hands and clothes looked like they'd been spattered with emulsion. We were becoming a public spectacle. A terribly posh chap stopped to have a look, leaning on walking poles and addressing the scourers like an admiral from the bridge: 'How heroic to come out in this frightful weather to look after the Horse! Well done! I congratulate you!'

They must have had this, the people who made the Horse, wet days when the job was a slog, fingers slick and cold and white – and all without proper waterproofs or the consoling promise of a cup of tea. Nothing but chat to keep you going, and of course the importance of the work itself.

CHALK

But why was it important? The present thinking is that the figure is a 'sun-horse' – created to give the impression of pulling the rising sun westwards across the sky, which it does most strikingly at midwinter when viewed from the platform-like top of Dragon Hill. It isn't possible to speak with certainty about prehistoric belief systems, but archaeological discoveries suggest that the sun was important within Bronze Age religion; that it was understood to be pulled by a horse in the day and then, during the hours of darkness, that it travelled by ship through the underworld. In Denmark's National Museum there is the Trundholm Sun Chariot, a rather toy-like sculpture discovered during ploughing in 1902. A bronze horse mounted on wheels pulls behind it a circular disc, one side of which is covered in gold foil and decorated with spirals; it is thought to have been used during rituals, wheeled along by someone – who we might now call a priest – to demonstrate the journey of the sun through the heavens.

The Uffington Horse, considered in this context, can be regarded not as a marker of territory or identity, but rather a sort of prayer in chalk. Hallowed be thy mane.

'The Horse is magical,' another volunteer, Sarah, told me. 'There's an almost mystical sense that our ancestors are around us. I get that same sort of tingle as when I'm at Avebury.'

Sarah is in her sixties and has been helping to look after the figure for a dozen or so years. The chalking is done, she explained, by hammering chunks into a powder until the surface is firm and smooth. 'Some people will work for half a day and in that time they'll do a foot square – absolutely perfectly. Then there's others who will bash and bash and bash, letting their anger loose on the chalk. Me, I'm the mindful kind. You just drift away as you tap, tap, tap.'

'What do you think about as you do it?' I asked.

'Nothing. And everything.'

That sound, that rhythm, hammer on chalk, must have been heard in this place for a very long time.

'Yes. When you have hundreds of people hammering it sounds like horses galloping across the hill. Hoofbeats.'

The scouring was done and people were packing up. The wind blew hard across the figure. The ear was a billowing sail, the neck a milky wake.

It was time to go. Back in the car, back on the road. The real world beckoned, as it always does. But it had been pleasant to spend a few days deliciously apart – upon a white horse.

*

May Day in Cerne Abbas. The Dorset village was in darkness. At half past four, the dawn chorus awaiting its cue, the only sound was water chuckling in a roadside stream; then, as we left the streets for the woods, the banshee scream of owls.

I followed the vicar through the trees and up the hill. He was familiar with the ground and needed no torch. I did. The thin chalk path, worn by feet, was bright in its beam.

To our left, I knew but could not see, was the Giant – longing, like the rest of us, for the sun.

The hill, not high, was steep. At the top we went through a farm gate and walked to a flat area a bit bigger than a tennis court. There was a ribbon of pale light to the east. Though still too dark to make out faces, we noticed a couple sitting on a corner of the grassy bank that encloses the Trendle – as this part of the hill is known. They were sharing a flask and watching the land emerge from the night. The hills across the valley were still a black swell, but soon we'd see the yellow on the gorse.

'Good morning,' said the vicar.

'Morning Jonathan,' they replied.

He introduced them as John and Prue. They had retired to Cerne Abbas seven years ago.

'We do feel that the Giant has accepted us,' John said. 'We were told that if you survive Cerne for five years then the Giant must like you.'

'Oh, you're gone in a year if he doesn't like you,' the vicar – Reverend Jonathan Still – laughed. 'After seven you know you're one of his friends.'

There was silence as we considered this. Not perfect silence. The air had begun to fill with song.

'Ah,' said Prue. 'The birds are waking up.'

The Cerne Abbas Giant is a hill figure cut into the chalk. He is a hundred and eighty feet from head to foot. He holds in his right hand a vicious club. His nose is a grassy mound, a mini-Silbury. His erect penis, the feature that attracts most attention and interest, is twenty-six feet long. It used to be a good deal smaller, but in 1908, when the grass was cut and the chalk scoured after a long period of neglect, the belly-button was incorporated into the tip, lengthening it – in human terms

– from six to nine inches. This was done by accident, but there have been no complaints.

Even more than the Uffington Horse, the Giant is difficult to discern when up close. From the official viewpoint, a lay-by at the northern end of the village, he appears foreshortened. You get a fine view of his legs and balls, but everything above disappears over the slope a bit. Men of a certain age and build will recognise this as the opposite of what they see when glancing down in the shower. Go up the hill, though, and he all but vanishes. The National Trust, worried about erosion, has fenced him off, so you find yourself peering over the barbed wire and trying to distinguish arse from elbow.

Not that everyone stays off him. The writer F. J. Harvey Darton, who came to live in Cerne Abbas late in life and is buried in the churchyard, wrote in 1935 of walking across the Giant's eyeballs to the hand that holds the club: 'The almost childish modelling is superbly true. You cannot see that detail of the grip at any distance; but standing upon it you can almost feel the tense muscles.' Eardley Knollys, a gallerist and member of the Bloomsbury group, moved to Dorset during the Second World War and worked for the National Trust, looking after properties. In 1941 he wrote to his lover, the painter Frank Coombs, who had joined the navy: 'You will be glad to hear that I am now responsible for the Cerne Giant and I strolled up and down his cock.' Even now, the people of the village seem to come and go as they please. The Giant is, one local told me with a wink, a popular spot for romance – 'There's quite a few pilgrimages after the pub.'

To get some perspective, though, and study him in all his glory, you're best to take binoculars up a hill across the valley. The Giant, seen in full, seems to combine the styles of Eric Gill and Donald McGill, sculptural meets saucy. His head, a hot-air balloon rising from his shoulders, bears an expression of mingled confusion and surprise – as if he can't quite get over the fact of his own existence, which, to be fair, few can. He is so striking that local businesses and organisations have recruited him for their branding. He advertises Cerne beer and Cerne milk. He holds a bat and ball on the cricket club badge, a fork and rake on the logo of the gardening society. Go to the gents in The Giant Inn and there he is – on a poster for condoms. Go to the gift shop and you can buy a wall-clock in which his penis ticks the seconds away.

The passage of time has been a much-debated issue. Just how old is the Giant? Until recently, there had been two competing theories. The first was that the Giant is prehistoric, perhaps some symbol of tribal belonging. The second hypothesis speculated that he was created in the seventeenth century as a sort of political cartoon, a lampoon of Oliver Cromwell. There is no written record of him until 1694 – and had he been around much before then, the argument goes, someone would surely have mentioned it.

William Stukeley visited the Cerne Giant in the mid-eighteenth century, noting that 'the inhabitants thereabout pretend to know nothing more of it than a traditionary account among them of its being a deity of the ancient Britons'. Stukeley thought him a representation of Hercules, the classical hero, who was often depicted naked and carrying a club. This interpretation continues to find favour, though there is also a folkloric belief that the figure is the outline of a real giant, an apex predator who devoured so many sheep that the valley folk, sick of his plundering, tied him down while he slept, murdered him, and then – as a trophy of their kill – traced the profile of his body into the chalk. I must say I like the idea that there were giants in England, and may be even now. In Jez Butterworth's play *Jerusalem*, Rooster Byron tells a story of travelling through Wiltshire in the small hours, a little drunk, and encountering a giant just off the A14: 'there he was sitting on the bluff. Gazing out over the land, watching the sun rise.' They discuss the weather, and the giant, in passing, mentions that he built Stonehenge – 'See that over there? I done that' – before going on his way in the direction of Swindon.

Butterworth's giant is only ninety feet tall, half the size of his Dorset cousin, but the Cerne Abbas Giant seems to me similarly benign – and more than that, beloved. Were he to rise from his hillside and walk down to the streets, who now would suggest putting him to death? More likely someone would buy him a pint and drink his health. 'He's why we've got three pubs in a village of eight hundred people,' the vicar told me. 'He's why we've got a flourishing shop and visitors. He's why we're on the map. He's part of the substance of the place.'

In the story of one English village through time, the Giant is setting, main character and theme. 'Cerne without the Giant,' a local historian has written, 'is like *Hamlet* without the Prince of Denmark.'

*

The sky was growing lighter, the birdsong louder, but now a new note could be heard on Giant Hill – the doleful clang of a handbell rising from the slope below. The timbre and rhythm suggested a funeral procession. In fact the bell-ringer had a more cheerful duty: heralding the arrival of the ale.

Two barrels of Beltane Brew are carried up the hill each May Day and everyone is offered a drink. It is made by the Cerne Abbas Brewery with additional ingredients – including cleavers, sorrel, nettles, dandelion roots, elder buds and hawthorn buds – collected on a nearby farm. The villagers are old hands and many had brought their own tankards. There were around a hundred of us on the Trendle by now. Danny England, the young brewer, hammered open the first barrel, poured a glass, held it to the sky and took a contemplative sip. 'Perfick,' he announced. 'Come and get it!'

There were whoops and cheers. Nobody needed telling twice. Soon everyone was toasting the day.

A bald man wiped foam from his moustache and spoke to the fellow next to him.

'The doctor says that if I keep drinkin' I'll drop dead of an 'eart attack.'

'Why you up 'ere then?'

'Well, 'e also says I need more exercise.'

Cerne, in the seventeenth and eighteenth centuries, was famous for its beer. It's nice that the tradition has been revived. I had spoken, the day before, with Vic Irvine, co-founder of the brewery. Vic moved to Cerne from Ascot sixteen years ago, he explained, and is familiar with the idea that the Giant is the adjudicator of who stays and who moves on. 'He overlooks us all,' he told me. 'We can see him, he can see us, and you've got to ask acceptance from someone who doesn't have a voice. That's where we get a bit spiritual.'

Vic had become a great champion and defender of the Giant, an outspoken critic of those who alter the figure's appearance in ways that he considers disrespectful. When the Oxford Cheese Company censored the Giant on the packaging of its vintage cheddar he was outraged: 'How would they like it if we went and chopped off the spire of the cathedral in Oxford?' Just as emasculating, as Vic saw it, were the actions of activists who marked International Women's Day by arranging plastic over the erection to make it look like a flower growing from a stem. Vic's response was to 'restore the Giant's manliness' through a landscape intervention of his own; he and a few friends had taken to climbing the hill on the night before May

Day and outlining the genitals in LED lights. 'We don't publicise it, don't take pictures, don't put it on social media. We just do that as a mark of respect for him and his splendour.'

Anyone who has ever struggled with their Christmas tree lights will know that it's a fiddly job; even more so when trying to arrange them around a twenty-six-foot penis on a hill in the dead of night. 'All of a sudden you lose a ball; then, just when you get that back on, the bell-end goes dark. When you get the whole thing illuminated, it's a eureka moment.'

This is knockabout stuff, but Vic was serious about the Giant. In the summer of 2021, aged fifty, he learned he had Stage 4 lung cancer. 'One of the first things I did when I got the diagnosis was went up the hill – puffing a bit – and just sat there and asked, "What we gonna do now, boss?"'

'Do you find the Giant strengthening?' I had asked.

'Oh, yeah. I can't really put into words how I feel about something so powerful. He's very special.'

*

It was, by now, a little after 5 a.m. Villagers stood on the bank around the Trendle; in the middle was a group of men in white shirts, black breeches and straw hats from the back of which hung red and green ribbons. A few held instruments: squeezebox, fiddle, pipe and tabor. Most wore bells below their knees, carried handkerchiefs, and bore on their chests the emblem of a green dragon. These were the Wessex Morris Men.

One of them, the leader – or 'squire', as morris dancers say – rang a bell for attention: 'Good morning and happy May Day to you all!'

They'd do five dances and a song, he said, by which time the sun would have risen. Fair warning: at a certain point they would take a collection. 'If you put some money in a morris man's hat, you get twelve months of good weather and good luck. And if you put a *fiver* in, when you get home your rhubarb sticks will be at least four inches longer.'

The Wessex Morris Men have danced on Giant Hill since 1978, when the Callaghan government created the May Day bank holiday. They used to start at eight, nine in the morning, but when David Chiplen first became squire he insisted they switch to sunrise and honour the season properly. 'This is the beginning of summer,' he had told me over a drink the day before. 'We've been celebrating bringing in the May for hundreds of years. There's something joyous about the fresh green in the hedgerows. I was reading that on TikTok there's 169 million pieces of video about making an egg sandwich, but does anybody take the time to go and smell the blossom of an apple tree at this time of year? It is beautiful. It is spectacular. There's a feeling of hope and promise that heartens you.'

It's fitting that they dance on the Trendle as this is where the Cerne Abbas maypole is said to have stood. H. J. Massingham, a popular writer on rural life, made the case in 1926: 'None but the wilful blind can fail to see a cultural link . . . between the huge naked idol below and the dancing ring above, one the effigy, the other the place of assembly of the sun-worshippers.'

What was true then is true almost a century later. There is a connection between the hill figure and the morris dancers. Nothing explicit. You can't even see the Giant from the Trendle; he's hidden by the gradient of the slope. It's a thing you feel, but struggle to explain. Perhaps it is that both the Giant and the morris men embody some spirit of place. As the name of each dance is announced – 'Shepherd's Hey', 'William and Nancy', 'Jockey to the Fair' – so too is the village where it was created. In this way, the morris men seem to carry with them, in every leap and step, the soul of England's small places. They express that in their movement, as the Giant does in his stillness. They share, too, the kinship of mystery. How exactly did morris dancing get started? None can say. Why was the Giant made? That's another head-scratcher. 'He somehow is meant to be unknowable,' is how one villager put it. The *when* of his creation, though, is becoming clearer.

Martin Papworth, an archaeologist, was one of those who, in 2020, worked to establish the origins of the hill figure. Speaking on the phone before my journey to Cerne Abbas, he explained some of the discussions around the work: 'When we first thought about dating the Giant, the National Trust manager said, "Do we really want to disappoint people by letting them know a date? Why can't people just enjoy him as he is?" But all you have is the science, really.'

Optically stimulated luminescence, the same technique that had been used on the Uffington White Horse, was employed to reveal the figure's provenance. The analysis, when it came back from the lab, surprised everyone. The Giant wasn't prehistoric. But he was a power in the land long before Oliver Cromwell. Soil samples taken from deep in the soles of his feet and crooks of his elbows indicate that he was made between AD 700 and 1100. This result, locating the Giant within what used to be known as the Dark Ages, led to some confused reporting.

'I was furious when the tabloids said he's a pagan Anglo-Saxon giant,' Jonathan Still had told me when we met at his vicarage on the eve of May Day. 'There's a school of belief that he's all about free living without restriction, without Christianity, without faith. But no! He's not Anglo-Saxon and he's not pagan. He's a Catholic boy. He was on land that was owned either by the church or by the royal house. He was put in place by western Catholic civilisation. He is of the essence of that culture.'

CHALK

The vicar regards the Giant as a statement of identity created by the Christian people of the area after the end of Roman rule but before the arrival of Saxons from the east. The figure is, in his view, an answer to the question, 'Who are we now?'

Either that or he belongs to the later period when, as part of the Saxon kingdom of Wessex, what we now call Dorset was being raided by Vikings. In 2009, on the crest of Ridgeway Hill, near Weymouth, the skeletons of around fifty men were found in a pit; all had been decapitated and their heads piled to one side. Chemical analysis of the teeth revealed that the men came from cold regions outside the British isles, notably Scandinavia, and radiocarbon dating placed them within the period when the Giant was cut into the Cerne chalk. If the hill figure was a warning to outsiders that violence would be met in kind, the mass grave suggests that this was no idle threat.

Another intriguing aspect of the Giant's dating is that it indicates a relationship between the figure and Cerne Abbey, which was founded in 987 on the site of an earlier Christian community. The religious house was closed in 1539, during Henry VIII's Dissolution, and by the 1570s much of the stone had been robbed for buildings in the village. Little of the once-substantial abbey is now visible, though recent excavation has uncovered fragments of stonework, painted window glass and decorative floor tiles – hinting at its beauty. The abbey stood at the foot of Giant Hill and the figure must have been familiar to the brethren who lived and worshipped there. It is tempting to express surprise that monks would tolerate an exhibitionist neighbour, but this is perhaps to misunderstand the monastic life and the mindset of the Middle Ages.

'I don't think they had the prudish attitude that we project on to them,' the vicar said. 'They were far more enmeshed in life.'

Just look at medieval manuscripts, added Jane, his wife. 'There's one in which a nun is picking penises off a tree as if they were apples.'

*

Jonathan and Jane Still moved to Cerne Abbas in 2011 when he took up the post of vicar at St Mary's.

Their relationship with the Giant is at once familiar and complex. I suppose it's rather like the connection one can have with a family member: you see them all the time, almost take their presence for granted, and yet also find them stimulating and demanding. So Jane can speak of the Giant with fondness – 'He's like our uncle on the hill' – while also explaining that, starting a few years ago, 'I increasingly felt the Giant challenging me that I had to tell the world something.'

This feeling led her to create the Cerne Giant Festival, an annual series of talks and activities intended to enable people to develop a closer relationship with the landscape and encourage them to live in a more environmentally-friendly way.

Jane grew up in Texas, but never felt that she belonged. In England, she has lived near Reading and in Exeter, Cambridge, Bedford, West Sussex, Shropshire, Herefordshire, Somerset and Surrey, before coming to Dorset. In Surrey, she had cancer and thought, 'I'm *not* going to die here – the ground isn't right.' But the first time she walked in the churchyard at Cerne, she had a different feeling: 'This is where your dust will lie.'

She told me these things in answer to a question about that notion, common in the village, that if the Giant likes you then you'll settle here. Vic had said it. John and Prue had said it. I heard it everywhere, and it seemed to me that what people must be sensing is the soul of the place; some will feel an affinity with that, others not.

Was there, I asked Jane, a moment when she knew she would stay in Cerne?

'I think that probably the tipping point came after our daughter Alice died. I scarcely visit her grave – I don't think of her as there. But she is very much a part of this village and of the countryside around.'

It was the countryside, or rather the water within it, that brought the Stills to Cerne. They felt called by the holy well, a spring in a quiet and secluded spot just beyond the churchyard. It rises cold and clear out of the foot of the hill – 'pellucid as the thoughts of John Clare', wrote H. J. Massingham – and fills a shallow pool overhung by lime trees before flowing down a stone channel, then out into the village and beyond. This spring, not whoever first carved the Giant, is the true shaper of the landscape.

'After the Cretaceous this was a solid plateau of chalk,' Jonathan said, 'and that little stream has eroded all this valley and taken it down to the sea. It's beyond belief.'

Every May Day, after the morris men have finished their dances, the vicar blesses the spring as part of a short celebration of the season – an occasion open to followers of all faiths, including pagan traditions, and none. He thinks of it as an 'intensely feminine' place, a counterweight to the masculinity of the Giant. The spring has long been regarded as a site of miracles and wonder. There is a legend that St Augustine, the so-called 'apostle to the English', eased the thirst of Cerne shepherds by striking the ground with his staff and causing the water to flow. It is also associated with St Eadwold, brother of King Edmund of East Anglia, who fled here around 870 following his brother's death in battle. The story goes that his hermitage stood by the spring and his bones were later brought into the abbey for veneration. It has been speculated that the Giant is a representation of Eadwold, or at least that this was how the figure came to be regarded by monks of the abbey. In this interpretation, the saint is holding not a club but a staff which is said to have sprouted with buds, leaves and blossom when he first came to Cerne and stood on the hill.

There are many superstitions about the water: drinking from it cures infertility; applying it to the eyes relieves soreness. A sign on the churchyard wall advises that 'If you go down to the well at dawn on Easter Day you will see, over your shoulder, and reflected in the water, the faces of those that will die that year.' Ribbons and rags tied to the branches above the water, and coins lying within it, testify to the persistence of folk belief. It is not uncommon to find people collecting the water for their own private needs. Not long ago, the Stills encountered an elderly man who had brought his grandson to be baptised there.

'Whether he was a Christian or something else, it doesn't really matter,' Jane said. 'There was a feeling of meeting at a space that has been sacred for a very long time.'

The Giant, whatever he was, whatever meanings we put on him now, would not exist without the water and the chalk. Jane calls him 'mythology writ large', but he is also a creature of topography and hydrology. He seems to us large and ancient, but to the land he is small, delicate and ephemeral. If not for the hand of man, he would soon fade. This past winter he all but disappeared beneath weeds and moss and muck – and were it not for a few locals who took it upon themselves to cut the grass and clean the chalk, he might well have left the stage. Exit Hamlet.

*

On my first morning in Cerne Abbas I had driven to a farm a little way outside the village. As I approached the farmhouse, a sheep called Violet wandered over to say hello. I patted her head and knocked the door. Eleanor answered, pulled on her boots, and we walked up the hill behind her home.

CHALK

Eleanor Gallia is a medical herbalist and biodynamic farmer, working the land according to the rhythms of the moon. It is Eleanor who provides the wild herbs for the Beltane Brew, collecting them a couple of weeks before May Day. She was born and grew up in the valley. As we climbed, she pointed out the tower of the church at Nether Cerne where she was baptised with water from the river. She has spent time in other places that were important to her – studying for a herbal apprenticeship in Edinburgh and working on a conservation project in Brazil – but this part of England is not just where she lives, it's who she is. Her mother comes from an old Dorset family; her father was Austrian. 'He came over on the Kindertransport in 1939. He was seven. So I really feel the importance of our relationship to the land. I know both sides: deep rootedness and also enforced uprooting.'

We reached the top of the hill and she pointed north. 'There's the Giant. He's looking good. You can't always see him so well.'

The Giant, a mile or so away, was side-on. I could see his outstretched left arm and, above it, the Trendle. That earthwork has never been excavated, but there is a rectangular mound in the centre that has been interpreted as a Romano-British temple. Dorset, like Wiltshire, is a county where one reads the past in the land and every grassy hump prompts a story. The Trendle, known as the Giant's Frying Pan, is where he cooked all those stolen sheep.

We were standing in what had once been an Iron Age farmstead. Gnarled hawthorns, twisted by the wind, grasped the sky. The fairy-tale atmosphere was heightened by the presence of two horses, the smaller of which frisked and tossed his mane. 'Hello, my beauties!' said Eleanor. They were rescue animals, their presence a kind of answered prayer. A few years ago she had made a May Day wish to have horses on the farm, and now here they were, Amber and Del Boy, white horses with a view of the Giant.

'Of course I love the Giant because he's part of the heritage of this place,' Eleanor said. 'But personally, I'm interested in something deeper and older. Look at these shapes in the fields.' She pointed to the phantom furrows of prehistoric agriculture and the remains of a Neolithic long barrow. 'They've been around for thousands of years and they pulse with life still.'

Just as significant as the Giant, she feels, is what she calls 'the sacredness of the landscape'. That is why it is meaningful for her to have been baptised with water from the Cerne. 'That chalk stream is a force of nature. It's not man-made. It's wild and free. The Giant is a friend, yes, but the real healing is in the water – bright, clear and beautiful as it runs through the land.'

*

I wanted to better understand the Dorset countryside and the feeling people have for it, so went for a walk with Virginia Astley.

Her 1983 album *From Gardens Where We Feel Secure* is one of my favourite records. Ambient and pastoral, mostly instrumental, the music is intended to evoke a summer day from dawn to dusk. The instrumentation – piano, flute, guitar, xylophone, auto-harp, clarinet – somehow captures that strange nostalgia you can feel for a moment even as you are living through it. There's an eerie quality in the music, too, a shiver in the sun, but its dominant note is one of sensory pleasure.

'All I wanted to do,' Virginia told me, 'was make something like when you lie back on the grass in summer and you get that blissful feeling.'

One of the ways in which she achieved this was to make field recordings – birds, church bells, an oar in a rowlock, the tick of a clock – and braid them into the compositions. These are not atmospheric extras, they are the essence of the record because they are the essence of place. The songs are reliquaries, the sounds relics.

Virginia lives near Cerne Abbas, so we had met in the village and driven out to the country. We parked up and walked through Thorncombe Wood. Four ponies – two white, two brown – stood just off the path, hooves in a bluebell haze. Heathcroppers, they eat bramble and holly and the like, stopping new growth from getting out of control. They seemed indifferent to our presence, preferring to stand unmoving by an old beech, touching their heads to its mossy trunk.

Later, when we bumped into the ranger, I asked about this strange behaviour. 'Oh yes,' she laughed, 'they love that tree. It is the tree of the horse god. In winter they can be anywhere, but as soon as it gets warm, I don't know what that tree does for them, but it does something. They will spend the next four months praying to it.'

Virginia led the way out of the woods, past a wooden sign pointing to Thomas Hardy's cottage. He was born and grew up in a thatched house that is now a visitor attraction. We were walking through country that he knew from early childhood: the wood and heath and ponies; the pond where he played with his sister Mary. Hardy is important to Virginia. She used to be writer-in-residence at the cottage and has written a musical based on his novel *The Woodlanders*. She and her daughter Florence, a harpist, have often given recitals in Hardy's Dorchester home, Max Gate, and even out here in the countryside he loved.

More than any other writer, the work of Hardy was inspired by and has shaped how we see a particular part of England. He called it Wessex. Dorset was at the heart of it, and the locations in his books are real places renamed. Cerne Abbas becomes Abbot's-Cernel, Dorchester is Casterbridge, and where we were now was one of the areas of heathland that Hardy called

Egdon Heath. We walked for a while along the chalky remains of a Roman road. 'Hardy brought Holst out here,' Virginia said. That was August 1927. Hardy was in the last months of his life. The composer had been commissioned by the New York Symphony Orchestra to write a piece of music, and what he gave them was *Egdon Heath* – inspired by Hardy's novel *The Return of The Native* and by his own experience of being here. 'Hardy died in January 1928 and the first performance was in the February, so he never heard it,' Virginia said. 'But they were like-minded and very similar in nature. Imogen, Holst's daughter, said that they recognised themselves in each other.' Hardy had heard *The Planets* – Holst's best-known work – on a gramophone belonging to T. E. Lawrence.

We turned off the path and walked up rising ground. We were on a burial mound. Its lower slopes were covered in heather and self-seeded holly; at the crown there was a dip – the telltale sign of excavation done long ago. Urns found here in the nineteenth century are now in Dorset County Museum. 'This is Rainbarrow,' said Virginia. 'There's never anyone around. Hardy says that people ought to come out here at dusk. I always want to come and stay the night but I don't think I'd dare on my own.'

We were above the treeline. Drifting rain silvered the sky.

'Imagine Hardy and Holst on this spot,' I said.

'Mmm, I know. That gives me shivers.'

The Return of the Native opens on Egdon Heath, and it is on Rainbarrow that we first meet Eustacia Vye, the novel's tragic heroine. Virginia had brought a copy of the book and read a passage aloud:

> It was at present a place perfectly accordant with man's nature – neither ghastly, hateful, nor ugly: neither commonplace, unmeaning, nor tame; but, like man, slighted

and enduring; and withal singularly colossal and mysterious in its swarthy monotony . . .

Just then, at a sudden unmistakable sound from the trees, she broke off. 'A cuckoo! I've not heard one up here for years. God, that's brilliant. Like magic.'

She returned to Hardy's description of the heath:

As with some persons who have long lived apart, solitude seemed to look out of its countenance. It had a lonely face, suggesting tragical possibilities.

What is it that gives the chalklands their sadness? I think it must be to do with the colour, or lack of it. Coming from Scotland, where we don't have much chalk, I can never get used to those white paths through the grass. There's something unsettling about them, like glimpsing a skull beneath the skin – landscape as vanitas.

Virginia had been thinking, lately, about the poet Edward Thomas and the painter Eric Ravilious. She had read in Robert Macfarlane's book *The Old Ways* that the chalk downlands 'bequeathed to both men shades of melancholy' but didn't quite agree. 'No, it's the other way around,' she said. 'There was something already in *them* that resonated with these melancholy, poignant, beautiful landscapes.'

'And is that something you feel in yourself?' I asked.

'Yeah, I feel it.'

It was her love for Thomas Hardy that brought Virginia to live here. She grew up in Middlesex and South Oxfordshire, but has been in Dorset for almost twenty-five years. Moving to a place that she knew through old books felt like 'a dream state, like I was half in the present and half in the past all the time'.

Hardy knew the Cerne Giant, of course, and made a few brief references to it in his writing. I asked Virginia for her thoughts on the figure.

'I am fond of him. I've had various friends who, when they wanted to try to conceive, have gone and lain on the Giant.'

'Did it work?'

'Yeah! Well, whether it was the Giant or just, y'know . . . But actually I don't think about the Giant much. I feel much more connected to the White Horse because we went there as children and lived relatively near. I remember going to Wayland's Smithy when I was about seven. That's really deep within me.'

There is something about these chalklands, it seems to me, that stands for Englishness, though there's no reason why they should. The red clay of Devon and the Derbyshire limestone are surely every bit as English. And yet when I think of England it is the chalk that comes to mind. The white cliffs and hill figures, the songs of Polly Harvey and the paintings of Paul Nash.

'In your music,' I asked Virginia, 'are you trying to express the English landscape? Is that what you're doing: bringing these places into yourself and alchemising them?'

'Yes,' she said. 'Alchemising is a great way of putting it. Not consciously, but I think that is what I'm doing. We were always outdoor kids; we'd spend all day in the Downs. That's still my dream – taking a backpack and a sandwich and just going out for the day. And so much of my work has started outside.

'Tonight,' she smiled, 'I'm going to a lay-by to record nightingales.'

*

It was quarter to six and the Ooser had arrived on Giant Hill. The crowd parted and he stepped on to the Trendle.

Do you know the Ooser? Silly question. No one really *knows* the Ooser. Like the Giant, he's unknowable. But you would recognise him.

The Dorset Ooser is a horned figure, a sort of Wurzels minotaur, that appears with the morris dancers on only two

occasions each year: May Day and St George's Day. One of the men – at the moment it's the squire, David Chiplen – has the burden and honour of embodying the Ooser, which involves holding up the great head on a wooden pole, as if it were a regimental standard, while concealed within the brown cloak and sackcloth apron that is the creature's clothing. Eyes like teardrops, mouth like a burst zip, the Ooser has goatskin shoulders, sheepskin hair, bullock horns and a beard of cow tails. He stands about ten feet tall and wears an expression of gluttonous despair that brings to mind Goya's painting *Saturn Devouring His Son*. A circular bump above his nose is said to represent a third eye, but when I asked a morris man about this he had no answers, only questions of his own: 'Is he looking into your future? Your past? Your soul?'

Although the Ooser has been the totem of the Wessex Morris Men since 1973, it has a far longer history. Two Victorian photographs show a version of the head even more horrible than the present incarnation. This older Ooser belonged to the Cave family of Holt Farm, Melbury Osmond, a village ten miles from Cerne Abbas. It is said to have been with the Caves 'time out of mind' and was used to scare away trespassers. In 1891 there was an attempt to sell it, hence the photographs, and by the beginning of the new century the head had vanished. Some say it was sold, others that it fell apart. It may be dust, it may be part of someone's secret collection, gloated over in the dark; its fate, like its origins and purpose, is unknown.

There has been speculation that the Ooser has its roots in pagan fertility rituals, or that it was made for use in mummers' plays, or for 'skimmity riding' – an old custom in which villagers guilty of adultery, domestic violence and the like were shamed by means of effigies displayed in public procession. Whatever its beginnings, the Ooser has long been regarded as dreadful and has entered popular culture as a signifier of folk horror. It appears on the cover of the 1973 book *Folklore, Myths and Legends of Britain*, a key text among those with a taste for the shuddery strange. When they play live, the heavy metal band Green Lung – for whom that book is an important influence – share the stage with a giant Ooser head as a sort of mascot. 'No one knows what the fuck it is,' Tom Templar, Green Lung's singer, had told me. 'It could be some sort of relic of an ancient cult, or it could just be that someone made a weird thing in their barn. That ambiguity is what I love.'

While the morris men performed their dances, the Ooser stalked the crowd. It walked slowly around the ring of people, stopping here and there to give a small bow, but didn't dance or speak. David Chiplen likes to preserve the illusion that the Ooser is real, hence his silence while in character, and tries not to be seen getting in and out of costume. 'Everyone knows there's a bloke in there,' he had told me, 'but it's about trying to hold on to the mystery.'

The Ooser has an authentic air of unease. I'd seen lots of photographs, and had thought it looked rather amiable, but now, on the hill, so tall and grim, it felt troubling. Children trembled, dogs did their nut, and I couldn't blame them.

Just then, Jonathan Still touched my arm. 'Chesney Hawkes the pop star is here. Would you like to meet him?' This is the sort of question, when writing a book, that you're very glad to hear.

I followed the vicar and was introduced. Chesney was wearing a tartan tracksuit and trilby. I commended him on his outfit.

'Got to make the effort for the gentleman on the hill,' he said, meaning the Giant.

Vic Irvine had also made the effort. He had on a pink tracksuit. They've been friends since school, but this, Chesney said, was his first May Day on Giant Hill.

'What do you make of it all?' I asked.

'I live in LA,' he replied. 'You don't get *this* on Ventura Boulevard.'

Or anywhere much. You've got to hold on to the mystery, and here we were in the presence of three at once: the Giant, the Morris and the Ooser. Thomas Hardy, I thought, would enjoy this scene. In *The Return of the Native* he had written about a maypole dance:

> The instincts of merry England lingered on here with exceptional vitality, and the symbolic customs which tradition has attached to each season of the year were yet a reality on Egdon. Indeed, the impulses of all such outlandish hamlets are pagan still: in these spots homage to nature, self-adoration, frantic gaieties, fragments of Teutonic rites

to divinities whose names are forgotten, seem in some way or other to have survived mediaeval doctrine.

In this outlandish hamlet, the ritual was coming to an end – at least until next year. We'd had stick dances and handkerchief dances; the beer barrels had been emptied, the money hat filled, and now it was time to head back down past the Giant. The sun was up and the slope, I could now see as we walked, was covered with purple orchids and yellow horseshoe vetch. With every step came the sound of bells. I wonder what is the collective noun for morris dancers? A shame that 'chime' is taken by wrens.

At the bottom of the hill, the dancers gathered elm branches to wave as they processed into the village. There was time for one more song and the Wessex Morris Men gave it their all:

> And now you've seen our garlands
> We must be on our way,
> But remember, lords and ladies,
> It is the first of May!

Vic Irvine passed away on 16 January 2025 at the age of fifty-four. On the night before his funeral, the penis of the Cerne Giant was lit in his honour.

GRAVE

BRITISH MUSEUM object number 1939,1010.228 is housed in a small polystyrene box lined with foam and kept in the collection stores. The item, a male ladybird, is yellow, half a centimetre long, and approximately one thousand four hundred years old. It is thought to have been buried alive, having made its way into the goose-down pillow of a dead king. *Aphidecta obliterata* has a typical lifespan of around twelve months, but this particular beetle has attained immortality by association. It was the only body found in the Sutton Hoo ship burial and so will be forever preserved and protected as if it were ancient gold.

Sutton Hoo! It demands an exclamation mark. It demands a peal of bells. Those two words ring with the same against-the-odds spirit as Dunkirk, Everest and Agincourt. 'We are solemn about archaeology as a science,' Jacquetta Hawkes observed, 'but the discovery at Sutton Hoo was the most glorious demonstration there has ever been in Britain of archaeology as pure romance.'

It was the summer of 1937. Edith Pretty, a wealthy widow, attended the annual flower show in Woodbridge, the Suffolk village near Sutton Hoo House, the grand home she shared with her young son Robert. There, among the smell of cut blooms, she met Vincent Redstone, a history teacher, and they fell into conversation about the prominent mounds on her land. They were marked on old maps as 'tumuli', meaning burial places, but were they really? And if so, who or what was buried there? The mounds were visible from the house – tantalisingly so. How, Pretty wondered, to go about an excavation? Redstone suggested she contact Ipswich Museum, and through them she found her digger: Basil Brown.

He was a self-taught astronomer and excavator who had found it difficult to make a living as a farmer, had been employed for a time as an insurance agent, and was now working casually for Ipswich Museum, taking whatever jobs came up. He had 'gravitated to archaeology without any real training thanks to a quite remarkable flair for smelling out antiquities', a colleague recalled. 'His method was to locate a feature and then pursue it wherever it led, in doing so becoming just like a terrier after a rat.'

Brown, in old photos, appears tweedy and puckish; Mr Tumulus, a faun in a flat cap. He was tiny. He smoked a pipe, rode a bike, and spoke with a strong Suffolk accent which gave his speech a flavour of the earth he knew so well.

He was fifty in 1938 when he arrived at Sutton Hoo, employed by Mrs Pretty at the rate of thirty shillings a week. That first season he excavated what are now known as Mounds 2, 3 and 4, all of which proved to have been robbed at some point in the past. When work resumed in 1939, Pretty asked Brown to investigate Mound 1. This he did, helped by the gardener Jack Jacobs and gamekeeper William Spooner.

At around noon on 11 May, a Thursday, Jacobs called out that he had found a bit of iron. 'I made a rush and pushed him out of the ways,' Brown later recalled. He recognised the find as a ship rivet, and working with a trowel and bare hands soon uncovered five more. They had found what remained of the bow of a large ship – around ninety feet long and fifteen across at its broadest point, or 'wide as our small room at home', as Brown wrote in a letter to his wife May. Even if the burial chamber had been empty, this would have been one of the all-time great archaeological finds, and Brown's delicate and dedicated uncovering of the ship over the course of that miraculous summer has been described as work of genius.

Of course, it wasn't all him. In early June 1939 the excavation was visited by Charles Phillips, a Cambridge history don, who was astonished by his first sight of the ship in the trench: 'Nothing like it had ever been seen in England before.' He later wrote that 'While full of admiration for the way in which Brown had proceeded so far, I knew that a great responsibility rested on anyone who knew of the current Sutton Hoo situation but failed to inform both the British Museum and the Office of Works about it without the absolute minimum of delay.' This he did, and – to his professed surprise – was asked by those authorities to take charge of the excavation. 'It seemed to me that you might have a bash,' he recalled. 'So a bash we had, that's all.'

The dig took on an Evelyn Waugh air. Phillips assembled a team of bright young archaeologists, all of whom would go on to eminence. Among them were Stuart Piggott, who had worked as Alexander Keiller's assistant director at Avebury, and Piggott's wife Peggy, later better known as Margaret Guido. There was also W. F. Grimes, an archaeology officer with the Ordnance Survey, and his boss O. G. S. Crawford – a good deal older than the others – who wrote of the excavation that 'We felt that we were present at the unveiling of history, and that the history of our own country.' Photographs of the dig offer an accidental portrait of the British class system: Brown in his cap; Phillips in his bow tie; Edith Pretty in a basket-chair at the trench edge, observing proceedings through field glasses.

Little wonder that she kept a close eye on things. Archaeology is not treasure-hunting. It is slow, dirty, unglamorous work. Yet here, for once, was a dig done at speed and yielding glories in abundance, as if the earth was purging riches that had lain too long on its belly.

On 21 July, Peggy Piggott found the first of the treasures: a small gold and garnet pyramid, part of the fittings on a scabbard, and from then the finds came fast. A sword, a shield, a sceptre, a great belt buckle decorated with a writhing inter-lace of birds and beasts – all 'resplendently pagan', as a British Museum curator once put it, and strongly suggestive that this was the grave of a warrior-king. Autumn came early to Suffolk that year as gold leaf blew in the wind.

What the finds taught them was that this was an Anglo-Saxon grave, and therefore a few hundred years earlier than they had assumed. The cards that had been sent out inviting guests for sherry and 'to view the remains of the Viking ship burial' could not now be helped, and in any case it was thought better to keep the treasure hush-hush. Basil Brown was given the honour of carrying much of it into Sutton Hoo House, the gamekeeper following with his gun, though whether this was for security or as a kind of honour guard is uncertain. Mrs Pretty, it is said, kept the gold under her bed for safekeeping.

And there was still more to come. On 28 July, the diggers found a cluster of iron fragments, together with pieces of gilt bronze that seemed to be some sort of face mask. This was the now-iconic helmet, which had been smashed into more than five hundred pieces when the burial chamber collapsed under the weight of the mound. The Sutton Hoo story is thrilling, but not without sadness. It seems unjust that Edith Pretty never saw the reconstructed helmet, never looked into those shadow eyes. She died suddenly in 1942 at the age of fifty-nine. Her grave, marked by a low stone cross, is in the churchyard of All Saints, Sutton.

She had a feeling for the dead. In her early life she had visited the pyramids and Taj Mahal, so knew about ostenta-tious memorialisation; the burial mounds must have seemed familiar, a little Egypt. Her husband Frank had died of cancer three years before the dig. He had not known that he was dying; Edith was advised by the doctor that it would be better to keep the knowledge from him, ignorance dispensed like an opiate. She believed in life after death. She was a spiritualist. She encouraged Basil Brown to attend a spiritualist church service, at which the medium told him to 'go on digging and you will find what you are looking for'. That was the evening of 2 July, more than three weeks before news of the excavation reached the newspapers. The headline of the *East Anglian Daily Times* – 'Interesting Find In Suffolk' – was a masterpiece of understatement.

The attention of journalists and their readers was, naturally, elsewhere. 'We were watching the papers every day for news about the war situation, which we felt was imminent,' one of the excavators later recalled. These young archaeologists, who had been children during the last war, now feared 'that the moment it began the sky would be black with planes, obliterating what was left of Sutton Hoo and probably us as well'.

It became a race against time, as the archaeologist Martin Carver has written: 'In an exhilarating seventeen days Phillips's team had emptied the burial chamber of 263 objects of gold, garnet, silver, bronze, enamel, iron, wood, bone, textiles, feathers and fur.' There was also, of course, the shell of that ladybird – which one assumes made its way into the king's pillow while the grave goods were being arranged within the burial chamber. Of the king himself there was no visible sign. Chemical analysis suggests that a body had been present, but that rainwater passing through the mound's sandy soil had collected in the chamber and acted as an acid bath, slowly dissolving flesh and bone. Once the hull had decayed, this would have drained into the ground beneath the ship. Perhaps this explains the rather sombre and haunted atmosphere that can be felt at Sutton Hoo. The king is no skeleton boxed up in museum stores. He is still there, atoms in the sand, part of the land over which he once held dominion.

An inquest held at Sutton village hall to decide who owned the finds determined that they belonged to the landowner rather than the Crown. But Edith Pretty decided to donate everything to the British Museum. For this Winston Churchill offered her a CBE, which she declined.

'How should we see her?' I asked Joshua Ward, a senior member of the National Trust team that looks after Sutton Hoo.

'I think she's a hero,' he said. 'She could have done what she wanted with the treasure. She could have sold it. She could have had it melted down and turned into new jewellery. But she gave it to the nation.'

The finds were placed into whatever came to hand – grocery boxes and tobacco tins lined with newspaper and soft, springy moss from the woods – and sent off to the British Museum under police escort. There they were repacked in protective cases and transported by horse-drawn cart to Aldwych tube station where, in a disused tunnel, they would be safe from bombing. Having been buried for more than a thousand years, they were going back into darkness.

On 3 September, Basil Brown wrote to his wife from Bromeswell, the village where he stayed during the excavation: 'My dear May, hope you are alright in all this bother of war being declared.'

He had been filling his ship with bracken, he said, in an attempt to protect it.

> *Then if war does not last too long, it may come out alright for people to see. If not it must take its chance. I don't know where I am at present. Mrs Pretty even now thinks the war will fizzle out in a short time, but while Hitler is alive anything may happen, and air raids are the danger. They are telling everyone in this village today to take gas masks with them when they go to work or anywhere. This is a worrying time. I may be home any time or*

GRAVE

*perhaps stay here a few days until I know what I am going to do
as everybody's plans are upset. Am sending Postal Orders.*
     Best Love
         Basil

*

Early one morning I arrived at Sutton Hoo and walked out
to the graves. It was November: *blōtmōnaþ* in the Anglo-Saxon
calendar, meaning 'sacrifice month', when livestock was slaughtered and dedicated to the gods.

The upper platform of a viewing tower looked out over flat
country: farms, smoke from a far-off bonfire, pigs snuffling a
frozen field. Closer to hand were great grassy swellings – the
burial mounds. It looked like the land was coming to the boil.

Sutton Hoo has been in the care of the National Trust
since 1998. I was being shown the site by Laura Howarth, the
archaeology and engagement manager. 'We consider this to be
a family burial plot,' she explained as we looked down. 'There
are around eighteen burial mounds, and they are a testament to
this family, this dynasty, in both life and death.'

From this height, above the trees, the River Deben could be
seen. 'That is where we think the ship would have taken its last
journey,' Laura said, 'and then been hauled up the hill from the
water.' It may have been the dead man's warship or something
akin to a royal barge.

'Think about the emotions playing out,' Laura continued.
'Grief for the loss of a loved one, but also – from the family's
perspective – how do we assert ourselves and maintain power?
Holding an elaborate funeral to say, "We are still in control" is
one of the ways of doing that, I think.'

Who was this man? And who were his people? While the
burial was being excavated its occupant was tentatively identified as Rædwald, King of the East Angles, whose reign had

begun in 599 and who died around 625. Evidence from the ship – a mix of carbon-dating and study of coins – supports this theory without putting it beyond doubt. Rædwald was a member of a dynasty known as the Wuffings whose royal residence has, of late, been excavated at Rendlesham, a few miles upstream from Sutton Hoo.

Much of what is known about Rædwald comes from Bede's *Ecclesiastical History of the English People*, written a century or so after the king's death. It is from Bede that we learn that Rædwald ruled all provinces south of the Humber. The monk-historian also tells us that Rædwald underwent Christian baptism in Kent, but, on returning home, his wife and 'certain perverse advisers' persuaded him not to give up the pagan faith. He attempted a compromise and 'had in the same shrine an altar for the holy Sacrifice of Christ side by side with a small altar in which victims were offered to devils' – a fudge that Bede considered more sinful than ever. So Mound 1 may be the grave of an apostate, a king who rejected the king of kings, and his burial place might, therefore, be seen as expressing commitment to the old gods, body and soul.

Martin Carver, who led excavations at Sutton Hoo between 1983 and 1993, has made a case that the burial mounds, as prominent landmarks, may have been intended as statements of political and spiritual dissent. 'Surely,' he writes, 'it could be no coincidence that Augustine had arrived in the late sixth century, and that Kent had become a Christian ally of France by then? The barrows of Sutton Hoo and elsewhere could thus be read as demonstrative protests against the creep of Christianity, monuments of anti-Christian defiance.'

This was before England was England. It was a scatter of kingdoms led by descendants of northern European and Scandinavian colonisers: the Saxons, Angles, Jutes, Franks, Frisians and so on, who had settled and established power bases in a weakened and vulnerable land following the withdrawal of the Roman army early in the fifth century.

'The most common assumption is that all kingdoms probably began as small-scale affairs, and that some had grown larger by bullying others into a state of dependence,' the historian Marc Morris has written. There were, he adds, 'no rules in this game of thrones, and kings did not defer to other kings out of respect for some universally recognised high office. Compulsion through force was all, and subservience was expressed in the form of tribute.'

If your family and followers killed and subjugated enough people, if they hoarded enough land and wealth, then you might, one day, be a powerful enough warlord to merit burial in a ship full of riches. Sutton Hoo is a bloody masterclass in social mobility. Martin Carver detects in the mounds 'the jubilant belligerence of a young aristocracy, the extrovert champions of early England'.

Accepting that Mound 1 is the grave of Rædwald allows speculation about the identities of the people in the other barrows. Mound 5 is thought to be the earliest and could, therefore, be the grave of Wehha or his son Wuffa, the first two kings of the royal dynasty; whoever it is, he died a violent death from several sword blows to the head. Mound 14 is the only grave that has been identified as that of a high-status female, and the temptation is to believe that this was Rædwald's queen, the unnamed woman eloquent in her arguments against God.

The extraordinary Mound 17, excavated in 1991, was found to contain two bodies: a young man laid to rest with his sword and a richly decorated harness; next to him was his horse, the animal having likely been sacrificed to speed its master through the afterlife. Who was this mounted warrior? It is tempting, as with the female burial, to be led by the writing of Bede and believe it to be Rægenhere, son of Rædwald, who, in 616, was killed in battle against the forces of King Æthelfrith of Bernicia.

There is no way of knowing any of this. These may be the graves of other people entirely, their names unknown, but Sutton Hoo encourages, indeed demands, such speculation. It is a landscape for dreamers as well as diggers.

*

In a dim room on the ground floor of the British Library a little boy and his grandmother were looking through the glass of an exhibition case. A book lay open within.

'This is a famous poem,' the grandmother said. 'Can you see when it was written?'

The boy, keen to please, found the information panel. 'Late tenth, early eleventh century,' he read. 'That's a *long* time ago.'

His grandmother nodded. 'Look at the lovely writing.'

The pages were light brown with ragged edges and covered in neat lines of black ink.

'Why can't I read it?' the boy asked.

The woman smiled. 'It's England's old language.' She pointed to a word on the right hand page – *draca*. 'This part is about a battle with a dragon.'

Cotton MS Vitellius A XV, better known as *Beowulf*, is a treasure of the British Library, and indeed European culture. It exists as a single parchment copy, made sometime around the year 1000. The existence of the manuscript is a kind of miracle. Works from that period have not survived in large numbers. The Dissolution of the Monasteries did for a lot of them; others were used to line the covers of early printed books; still others were used, in Tudor England, in the manufacture of soap. By the sixteenth century, most people could not read Old English – the language in which *Beowulf* is written – and therefore texts would have been unintelligible and their value impossible to judge.

Even so, as Julian Harrison, the lead curator of medieval historical and literary manuscripts, told me, 'Somebody somewhere identified it and felt it was worth keeping.'

Somebody. Somewhere. The origins of the manuscript are unknown. Handwriting analysis indicates that it was written by two scribes. They changed shifts, so to speak, mid-sentence, about two-thirds of the way through the poem. This suggests a scene: monks in a scriptorium, copying from some older document now lost. Scholars have argued that the poem was composed in the eighth century and is set in the sixth.

The manuscript is thought to have remained in a monastery – which monastery is, again, unknown – until the Reformation, after which it came into the possession of Lawrence Nowell, an antiquarian, who signed and dated it 1563. It later belonged to Sir Robert Cotton, a collector of old documents. The layout of the room in which he kept his collection is still used in the indexing of Cotton manuscripts in the care of the British Library. *Beowulf* is Cotton MC Vitellius A XV because it was the fifteenth book from the left on the first shelf of the bookcase topped by a bust of the Emperor Vitellius.

In 1702, Cotton's library was gifted to the nation by his grandson, and subsequently moved to a property, near Westminster Abbey, called Ashburnham House. Here was a name that fate could not resist; in 1731 a fire destroyed and damaged many of the manuscripts. *Beowulf* survived, but not unscathed. It had been singed and scorched and, over the years, parts continued to flake off the edges as the parchment was handled; in this way it lost a further three thousand letters until, in the nineteenth century, its leaves were mounted on paper. Now it is subject to every protection. 'It is a precious object,' Julian Harrison said. 'We treat it with great reverence and respect.'

Beowulf is a horror story, a monster movie, a foundational text of fantasy literature. Had it burned up in that fire, we might not have *The Lord of the Rings*, and no Smaug, covetous and coiled. Yet, for all its fantastical elements, one reads it with a sense of recognition. It has an iron-cold Englishness that tastes like blood. 'It was made in this land,' J. R. R. Tolkien has written, 'and moves in our northern world beneath our northern sky.'

The poem is named for its hero: a great warrior of the Geats, the people of what is now southern Sweden. Beowulf, strong and brave and keen to prove it, travels by ship to Denmark and comes to the aid of King Hrothgar, who is sore troubled by a ravening creature called Grendel. This Grendel, according to Seamus Heaney, the poem's most celebrated translator, is 'a kind of dog-breath in the dark'. It is his habit to enter the king's mead-hall at night and gobble up whomever he finds. Tolkien, in his translation, described Grendel's appalling murder of a sleeping guard: 'biting the bone-joints, drinking blood from veins, great gobbets gorging down. Quickly he took all of that lifeless thing to be his food, even feet and hands.'

This world of *Beowulf* is supernatural. Grendel and his demonic mother – whose name, like Rædwald's queen, we are not told – live in a lair beneath a lake. Beowulf, having vanquished both, dies while defending his own land against a fire-breathing serpent. 'Nowhere,' Tolkien writes – and he would know – 'does a dragon come in so precisely where he should.'

However, *Beowulf* is also a realistic world of elite warriors, of feasting in halls and lamenting the noble dead. A dead king is laid out in a ship, his treasure and weapons piled upon him. Beowulf himself is burned on a pyre, his ashes and armour and wealth buried within a high mound – to be seen and admired by those passing on the sea. It is a poem in love with finely wrought objects: swords, shields, spears, lyres, mail-coats, ornate bridles, crested helmets adorned with wild boar.

Sounds familiar? When the Sutton Hoo ship was excavated, it astonished those who knew the poem. Here was *Beowulf* come to life.

The Sutton Hoo helmet and the *Beowulf* manuscript have never, as far as I can establish, been in the same room at the same moment. During the Blitz, when the ship burial treasures were deep in Aldwych Underground, historically important documents were sent out of the capital for safekeeping – to a tunnel below the National Library of Wales in Aberystwyth; it seems likely that *Beowulf* was among them.

It is possible to walk through London from the manuscript to the helmet, from the British Library to the British Museum, in twenty minutes. There is something heart-quickening about these relics of ancient power being in such proximity, but never quite meeting. It is a physical expression of their cultural closeness. The *Beowulf* scholar Sam Newton has suggested that the poem could have been composed in East Anglia, during the reign of King Ælfwald, a later king of the same dynasty as Rædwald. How delicious to think of *Beowulf* performed by a bard in the great hall at Rendlesham, its audience rapt and torchlit as the dragon-felled hero is placed within a burial mound. This was a poem set in the past, in lands across the sea, and yet it must have spoken to those first listeners, as it does to us now, of their own time.

Heaney, in the introduction to his 1999 translation, drew attention to the passage towards the end of the poem, in which a Geat woman cries out in grief for the loss of Beowulf but also in fear of the violence and oppression which her people will suffer now that their defender is dead. It could, he wrote, 'come straight from a late twentieth-century news report, from Rwanda or Kosovo; her keen is a nightmare glimpse into the minds of people who have survived traumatic, even monstrous events and who are now being exposed to a comfortless future'.

Toni Morrison, too, identified within *Beowulf* this resonance with contemporary evils. In a 2002 essay, she wrote of Grendel: 'He is the essence of the one who loathes you, wants you not just dead, but nourishingly so, so that your death provides gain for the slayer: food, lands, wealth, water – whatever. Like genocide, ethnic cleansing, mass murder or individual assault for profit.'

As I write, and perhaps as you read, missiles are striking cities. Underground stations are being readied as shelters. The Sutton Hoo helmet is sometimes said to be the face of the Dark Ages, but I don't know. Those empty black eyes seem to express our present darkness just as well. The world does not lack monsters and anything may happen while they are alive.

*

I have been talking all this time of a ship burial. But what Basil Brown found in 1939 was not a ship. It was a ghost.

All the timber had rotted away. As it decayed, sand moved in to replace it, so that what Brown uncovered was not the vessel itself but a kind of cast in which the planks and frames were visible, the iron rivets corroded but still in position, and there was enough detail to suggest that there had been room for forty oarsmen. The impression was clear enough to reveal that the ship had been repaired, which indicates that it had a working life. That meant it was built for the water, not the earth. Burial, its destiny, had not been its purpose.

It would be fascinating to learn where the ship had been. Was it solely a craft of rivers? Or did it know the salt of the seas? Did the people who buried it believe that it would carry their king to a land of the dead? There were forty gold coins in his purse, enough to pay each member of the revenant crew.

Photographs of the excavation are thrilling and strange. Foreshortened, the ship resembles some fossil reptile, archaeologists crouched in its guts. Much of the public and media focus,

understandably, has been on the finds, especially the helmet, but that shape in the sand has a similar eerie emptiness. In Woodbridge I spoke with a man who, as a child, had played with friends on and around the burial mounds, and had gone on to have a career in social work. The atmosphere at Sutton Hoo, he said, was similar to what he had often felt in the homes of clients who had died: they were still present as memories and stories, their lives lingering in unstirred air.

There is no one left alive to ask what the 1939 dig was like. But the ship was re-excavated in the second half of the 1960s. Angela Care Evans was, at that time, in her twenties. In 1967 she was on her way to dig at Mycenae but first spent ten days working at Sutton Hoo. The summer of *Sgt. Pepper*, and here was a band of archaeologists back inside the ship. 'Oh, it was extraordinary,' Evans remembers. 'The sheer scale of it was mind-blowing. But the other thing was the colour. It was bright yellow. I remember coming from the British Museum hut at the west end of the site and thinking, "Wow!"'

Now in her eighties, she is president of the Sutton Hoo Society and a former curator at the British Museum, where she was responsible for the treasures from the ship burial. She knows them intimately: the weight of the gold buckle, the glint of the garnets. She witnessed the reconstruction of the helmet, shield and lyre.

We met in Woodbridge, in a steel hangar called The Longshed, where a full-size replica of the Sutton Hoo ship was being built by a team of professionals and volunteers using Anglo-Saxon tools and methods. The plan, I was told, is to take it out on the water and so learn how, in the fifth century, it might have been used – for instance, was it only ever rowed or could it be sailed? So far they had finished the keel and about a third of the planking. Already the ship looked huge. The air smelled of caulk – the treacly mix of pine tar, beeswax and beef fat being used for waterproofing – and there was a rhythmic banging from just outside, by the river, where men in blue overalls were driving wedges into the trunk of an oak, splitting it for timber. Across the water, hidden by trees, were the burial mounds. On a wall above the replica ship was a giant poster of the helmet, as if Rædwald himself was keeping a weather eye on the work.

The Sutton Hoo burial ship no longer exists. In the haste of trying to complete the work before war began, the trench had never been backfilled; Basil Brown, remember, had covered it with a thick layer of bracken in an effort to protect it. But the mounds had been used for tank training and mortar practice, and the post-war years passed, and so by the 1960s, when the bracken and silt were taken out, some of the upper parts had crumbled and what was left appeared 'twisted in a bed of agony', as an archaeologist later put it. A decision was made to take a plaster cast of what remained and then to dig through the ship – thus destroying it – to see what lay beneath. Nothing did.

Given that the ship would soon be lost, I asked Angela Evans, did she consider it a privilege to see and touch it?

Yes, she replied, and it was *exciting*. Not only because of the connection to the Anglo-Saxon world, but because it gave her a tangible appreciation of what that previous generation of archaeologists had experienced and achieved. 'All the time you'd be thinking, "Gosh, what was it like in 1939?" When the first jewellery came out it must have been breathtaking. There's no other word for it. The great thing about gold is it doesn't deteriorate. Just brush a bit of sand off and there it is.'

She got to know several of those involved. Stuart and Peggy Piggott. Charles Phillips. W. F. Grimes. Mercie Lack, who, along with her friend Barbara Wagstaff, took such evocative photographs of the 1939 dig. 'Miss Lack was a wonderful old lady. Very stern. One of those amazing pre-war characters. Now, who else was there?'

'Basil Brown,' I said.

'Oh, Basil, yes.' She smiled at the name. 'He was quite remarkable. When I met him, in deep old age, he was very gaunt, but still had these bright sparkling eyes. In his breast pocket was a hearing aid which whistled the whole time. He was charming; so enthusiastic about everything. And he had done such a brilliant job.'

Part of that brilliance was in restraint. On finding the ship, he had not immediately exposed it – even though the desire to do so must have been great. He had instead left a skin of sand over its contours, protecting its fragile structures from any rain and wind until the British Museum team got there. He seems to have been a person in whom passion manifested as caution, and love as patience. He had been given a great gift and would take proper care in its unwrapping.

Brown continued digging in Suffolk until age and poor health made him frail. In 1968, he had a suspected heart attack in the trench of an Anglo-Saxon manor house, which would have been a fitting place to go, but though he survived he never excavated again. He lived to be eighty-nine. The vicar, at his funeral, said that for as long as history was written he would never be forgotten.

'Was he proud to have discovered the Sutton Hoo ship?' I asked Evans.

'I don't think Basil knew what pride was,' she replied. 'He was very *satisfied* with what he'd achieved.'

*

The Egtved Girl lies in a black oak coffin in a low glass case in Room 9 of the National Museum of Denmark. Snow White, Damien Hirst, these thoughts come and go, but she is wonderfully herself and shrugs off comparisons. You stand over her and look down and see – what? A blouse and skirt. A horn comb. A nest of fair hair.

'She was buried on a summer's day in 1370 BC,' says the information panel. 'A small yarrow flower was laid on the edge of the coffin before the lid was placed over it.' It is the flower that reveals she died in summer, the time of its blossoming. Like the Sutton Hoo ladybird, it is a frail traveller bearing knowledge.

They come to us, the returning dead, across a great distance. The Egtved Girl was found in 1921 by a farmer working his land in southern Denmark. There is a black and white photograph of the tree-trunk coffin lying unopened on the earth. It looks like a sleep pod, the technology that in science-fiction films carries astronauts ageless through the stars. She was in her mid to late teens when she died. Analysis of teeth, hair and nails – pretty much all that was left of her body – suggest that she grew up in south-west Germany and made the long journey to Denmark around a year before she died. Yet the laboratory can only take us so far. Wrapped in a piece of cloth by her feet were, and still are, the cremated remains of a child aged five or six. A sacrifice? A sibling? Prehistoric burials sometimes come with grave goods and always come with mysteries. They bequeath us their bodies, but not their biographies, and each is a story prompt.

Denmark is abundant in a particular category of burial: the so-called bog bodies. These are human remains found in wetlands, decomposition slowed by submersion in an environment low in oxygen, rich with tannins and sphagnum moss, so that what emerges – often while peat is being dug for fuel – is not a skeleton but recognisably a person: face, flesh, hair, even fingerprints so well defined that they could be entered into international databases and checked against known crimes.

Were bog bodies executed criminals? That's one theory. Ritual killing is another. Tacitus, writing at the end of the first century AD, noted that human sacrifice was part of the devotional practice of Germanic tribes. The Roman also recorded the system of capital punishment: 'Traitors and deserters are hanged on trees. Cowards, those who will not fight, and those who have defiled their bodies, are plunged into a boggy mire, with a wicker hurdle pressed on top them.'

Defilers of bodies. The Latin original is *corpores infames*, which has been translated in different ways. My old paperback copy says, simply, 'sodomites'. This was the preferred interpretation of the Third Reich, which used it to justify the persecution of homosexuals. Hatred and othering were given a compelling backstory. It was part of the sickness of the Nazi world view that they could look at a bog body and think, 'Quite right, too.'

What might they have made of Tollund Man? The global face of bog bodies was found in the spring of 1950 by two men cutting peat in Bjældskovdal, not far from the town of Silkeborg. His skin was stained deep brown and he wore a sheepskin cap. Eyes closed, lips almost smiling beneath a hawk nose, he lay on his right side – a dreamer reluctant to wake. 'Majesty and gentleness still stamp his features as they did when he was alive,' observed P. V. Glob, the archaeologist who was called to inspect him. The illusion of peaceful sleep was disturbed, however, when peat was removed from the side of his head and revealed a noose around his throat. He had been hanged. As workers raised him from his resting place, straining to lift the heavy crate, one suffered a heart attack. 'The bog claimed a life for a life,' Glob wrote.

In the autumn of 1973, Seamus Heaney visited Tollund Man at Silkeborg Museum. His fascination had begun when he read Glob's *The Bog People*. The book's considerable impact comes, in part, from the eloquent empathy of the writing (translated by Rupert Bruce-Mitford, a noted excavator of Sutton Hoo) but in particular from the black and white photographs. Pictures of items found with the burials – Tollund Man's umbilical noose, Arden Woman's coiled hair, the wooden stakes used to pin down Haraldskær Woman – have the skin-crawling wrongness of surrealist art objects. The bodies themselves are dark fairy tales: Tollund Man crouched and hunched like a fetal troll; Windeby Girl blindfolded and shorn; Grauballe Man a mandrake root pulled groaning from the earth. *Mosefolket*, the Danish title, seems to better express their tenebrous commonwealth. On a flight to Dublin, I kept those pages covered so as not to trouble the passenger in the next seat.

Heaney's bog body poems are among the most studied and praised of his works. He acquired a copy of *The Bog People* in 1971 and the following year wrote to his publisher that he was well advanced with poetry inspired by the body of a woman, a bog queen as he saw her, who had been dug up in County Down in the late eighteenth century. 'She dreams things, in her peaty bower,' he wrote. 'Hopefully, she re-dreams a myth for a new Ireland . . .'

For Heaney, whose first home was Mossbawn, a farm in County Derry, the Irish bog was a site of national identity and mythology, 'a landscape that remembered everything that happened in it and to it'. But it was also a place with strong personal resonance. He was a man with a 'hankering for the underground side of things'. He had felt that way since boyhood when, one summer evening, he and a friend 'stripped to the white country skin and bathed in a moss-hole, treading the liver-thick mud, unsettling a smoky muck off the bottom and coming out smeared and weedy and darkened. We dressed again and went home in our wet clothes, smelling of the ground and the standing pool, somehow initiated.'

He felt himself 'betrothed' to the bog. The smell of it on his skin never faded from his mind, nor did its engulfing threat.

It was a place to play, but you had to mind. Not everything that went into the black water came back out. And some things that did come out were better not encountered. He and the local boys scared each other with stories of 'mankeepers and mosscheepers, creatures uncatalogued by any naturalist, but none the less real for that'. Later, his Grendel would be a 'grim demon/haunting the marches, marauding around the heath and the desolate fens', slaughtering men and taking them back to a 'moor-nest' to devour.

The latent terror of the bogs would also find expression in a poetic connection between the prehistoric bodies and the violence of the Troubles – 'an attempt to rhyme the contemporary with the archaic', as he put it. 'Punishment', to take one example, is a response to the Windeby Girl ('her shaved head/ like a stubble of black corn,/her blindfold a soiled bandage,') but also about the tarring and feathering, blindfolding and cutting off the hair of young Catholic women who had relationships with British soldiers.

Such things were not abstract for Heaney. He had skin in this. His second cousin, Colm McCartney, was murdered in 1975, stopped at a fake roadblock and shot. In a poem written in his memory, Heaney imagines using moss to clean blood and dirt from the young man's face; he picks rushes that return to green life as he braids them into a scapular – a kind of devotional necklace – for Colm to wear over his shroud. This poem, 'The Strand at Lough Beg', is not one of the bog body works, but it recalls Heaney's earlier vision of Tollund Man as a victim sacrificed to the fertility goddess in supplication for the return of spring. Bogs are in-between places, not land or water, womb or grave, cradling bodies neither living nor, it appears, quite dead; and so they are open to conflicting interpretations. Both despair and hope can be seen in those dark pools, for those who care to look.

Bog bodies have been emerging for centuries, no doubt for as long as peat has been dug. Europe's oldest fleshed body is Cashel Man. Found in Ireland in 2011, he is about four thousand years old, which places him in the Bronze Age, but most bog bodies date from the Iron Age. Their uncanny preservation can lead to misidentification. When Grauballe Man was discovered in Denmark in 1952, newspaper reports suggested that he was a local, Red Christian, who had disappeared in 1887, presumed to have fallen, drunk, into the bog; an old woman who had known him as a child claimed to be familiar with his features. This was quite a feat of recognition given that Grauballe Man had died sometime between 400 and 200 BC, his throat cut from ear to ear.

Such errors can have strange consequences. Lindow Woman is the name given to part of a human head discovered in 1983 on Lindow Moss in Cheshire, a year before the better-known Lindow Man, whose leathery corpse is a star sight of the British Museum. Police thought that what had been uncovered were the remains of a woman who had gone missing twenty or so years before and was now the subject of a cold-case investigation. Detectives suspected her husband of murder, but no evidence could be found. Now, when told what had been dug up close to his home, he confessed: 'It has been so long, I thought I would never be found out.' The head, scientists later established, was one thousand seven hundred years old.

Not all bog bodies are prehistoric. In the late 1770s, on the island of Hoy, the second-largest in the Orkney archipelago, there lived a young woman called Betty Corrigall – unmarried and pregnant. Some say the father was a sailor, some say otherwise, but the cold truth is that she was left alone with a bairn in her belly. The shame and the condemnation of the island community being intolerable, Betty walked into the sea. She was rescued, but a few days later took her own life in a sheep shed, the ruins of which still stand. As a suicide, a churchyard

plot was forbidden to her, so she was buried in moorland on the boundary between two parishes.

Time passed and the unmarked grave was forgotten. In 1933, two men found a box while cutting peat. Inside was a woman. The wet ground had preserved her body. Her dark curls, it is said, turned white on exposure to the air, and the rope with which she had hanged herself crumbled to dust. These details sound more like legends than facts. Still, locals tell them even now.

The coffin was reburied, but disturbed again in 1941 and several times after that by soldiers, stationed on Hoy, for whom the body had become a curiosity. Officers, keen to end this outrage, had her moved to a new location forty yards away and a concrete slab placed on top. In 1976, a fibreglass headstone was set up. Both it and the small wooden fence that surrounds the plot were painted white, the brightest thing for miles, and now the grave stands out, in innocent defiance, amid the glowering browns of moor and hill.

John Budge, a Hoy native in his seventies, repaints the headstone every few years; a tender duty. No, he does not think that Betty should be moved to the churchyard, as some have suggested, and given the burial that was denied at the time of her death: 'She's been disturbed enough,' he told me. 'She should be left to rest where she is. And being a special grave, it gives her the respect that the poor creature should always have had.'

Visitors to the island, passing along the quiet coast, cannot fail to notice the headstone a short distance off the road. Many stop and walk out on wooden boards over sodden ground. There, by the grave, they read her name and something of her story, and in the kindly thoughts of strangers the memory of Betty Corrigall is kept from decay.

*

Ned Kelly said to meet him on Kildare Street, at the café opposite the museum. We'd have a cuppa and a blether and then head across.

He was easily spotted, sitting outside with coffee: brown trilby, tartan jacket, big white beard.

Eamonn P. Kelly, known as Ned, is the former Keeper of Irish Antiquities at the National Museum of Ireland in Dublin. He retired from the position in 2014, but when you're a 'keeper' – a word he finds meaningful – I don't suppose you ever do give it up. You can keep things in your heart and in your head, even if you no longer hold the keys.

He had said he'd show me the bog bodies. I wanted to see them through his eyes. The museum has four on display, and others behind the scenes. Actually, 'display' isn't quite right, and 'behind the scenes' is plain wrong. All thoughts of this being a show should be set aside. The *Kingship and Sacrifice* exhibition is about allowing the public to come quietly into the company of the bodies, each of whom is laid out in his own circular enclosure, a sort of curated grave, gently lit. 'They're not treated as objects,' Ned explained. 'This isn't a bronze sword or a stone axe. This is a human being.'

We walked over the road to meet them.

Ireland's National Museum is a grand nineteenth-century building next door to the Irish parliament. You enter through a rotunda and are soon among marvels.

The bodies in the museum are, in order of discovery, Gallagh Man, Baronstown West Man, Clonycavan Man and Oldcroghan Man. Bog bodies, mostly, are named for where they were found, but only when they are removed from that place, which gives them an air of exile as they lie behind glass, unmoored. Their real names, of course, are unknown, and on a molecular level they are unknowable; immersion in a bog saves so much of the body, but the acid destroys the DNA by which we might, otherwise, be able to say more about who they were, where they came from, and how they relate to the present population. Ned has a nice line: 'A bog body is an ambassador from the past who has come to tell us a story.' But the story they tell is incomplete, redacted.

We stopped in first to see Baronstown West Man. He was found in 1953 in County Kildare. Of the four bodies, he is the most skeletal: ribs like untied laces; bat-wing tatters of gauzy flesh. He lies, like all his fellows, in a glass cabinet on an opaque slab. Inside these small rooms, half-mortuary, half-monstrance, there is no information panel, no writing at all. 'The body,' Ned explained, 'makes its own statement.'

The permanent exhibition as a whole gives plenty of context. It articulates a theory that these bodies were tribal kings. 'This isn't just about killing people and throwing them in bogs for casual reasons,' Ned said. 'There's something serious and important going on.' He explained that in the Irish kingship tradition, the land over which a king reigned was personified as a sovereignty goddess to whom he was ritually wedded at his inauguration ceremony. Thus the king became the interface with the 'Otherworld' on behalf of his people and assumed responsibility in the event of any calamity – a poor harvest, say, or a destructive flood, or a spreading sickness. A failed king would be sacrificed and his body placed in the bog as a propitiatory gift to the goddess in hope of better times.

Many objects have been found in bogs: weapons and shields, ploughs and quern stones, harnesses and yokes, expensive garments and jewellery, even firkins of butter, all of which have been interpreted as votive offerings. You give away something it hurts to lose, that seems to be the way of it, and what greater pain than the loss of a life? A person belonging to the community, perhaps an individual of high status, or just ordinary, but *known*, familiar, woven tight into the fabric of the place and not easily unknotted.

As the narrator observes in Sarah Moss's novel *Ghost Wall*,

> the people who come to us now out of the bogs must have been cared for, fed, must have been part of their families and villages until one day they found out that they were no longer like everyone else, that sometime in the night something had changed. No-one knows how far before death that day might have been, whether one morning someone came to wake you carrying a rope, the blades already sharpened and waiting in the heather, or whether you had weeks or months to say your farewells, to get used to your status as a ghost.

We moved on to Gallagh Man. He was discovered long before the others, in 1821, and is likely a bit older than them, having been dated to somewhere between 200 and 400 BC. He was wearing a deerskin cape at the time of his discovery, but is now naked. He looks very dry, like tree bark or flake tobacco. Ned Kelly first made his acquaintance as a boy, visiting the museum in the 1950s. On Sunday afternoons he and his brothers would catch a bus into the city from their home at the foot of the Dublin mountains. 'For a young child this was pretty grisly,' he recalled, 'and there was the fascination that you're actually looking at a dead person.'

He knew about bogs, though. 'We always cut turf when I was a child.' So they were familiar, not forbidding places. His father, who had grown up on a hill farm, had the right to dig for fuel. Digging was a happy family occasion, one Ned continued well into his adult life. 'But in fact,' he said, 'it was a bog body that resulted in us giving up cutting on the bog. My brother went up to open the drains and prepare for cutting, and he found the body of a woman who had been murdered. The body was concealed in a drain that myself and my father had dug.'

She had disappeared from Dublin close to Christmas and was missing for six months before her body was found. The killer has never been identified. 'The murder was such a sad and horrific deed perpetrated on a young mother that we never returned to harvest peat thereafter,' Ned said. His brother planted a pine tree on the site in her memory.

The final two bog bodies, Clonycavan Man and Oldcroghan Man, were found in 2003, three months apart. The former's precise find spot is unknown, as his remains were discovered in a screening machine in a peat extraction works. Pressed roadkill-flat by the weight of the ground, his face is squashed but still legible. His neck is bent in a way that looks sore; you want to reach out and adjust his position, make him more comfortable. Most striking of all is his hair, thick and fox-red, arranged into a sort of pompadour, but shaved at the front, like the tonsure of monks in the early Irish church. He's older than that, of course, pre-Christian; indeed, pre-Christ.

'Now, this unfortunate fella,' Ned said, 'he was first of all struck in the face with a blunt instrument and his nose was broken. That would have knocked him out. And when he went down, he was hit on the head with an axe. Not a nice way to go.' There was something about the way he said this. Not trite. Real sympathy.

'Do you feel sorry for the bog bodies?' I asked.

'Oh yeah. I mean, he's only a young fella. A dapper little fella. He'd be nearer twenty-five than forty.'

Clonycavan Man was five foot nine at most. He had a moustache and goatee beard. He may – this is uncertain – have been disembowelled.

'Was he killed out there on the bog?' I asked.

'I think so. There wasn't an intention to inflict pain. Usually, these people are immediately rendered unconscious or suffer a fatal wound from the outset. Then, whatever else is done is part of the ritual.'

But why bogs? Why use this particular part of the land for sacrifice and deposition? Professor Melanie Giles, in her book on the subject, points out that such places were not remote from the experience of most of the population – as they are now – but were a rich resource that 'could feed larder, medicine cabinet and dyer's vat, supply bedding and roofing and fuel the smith's workshop and hearth'. In other words, people knew them, probably quite well, and would have regarded them as giving places. Yet they were also, perhaps, seen as 'thin places', portals between worlds, where – to quote Giles again – 'the sacred might be touched and the supernatural realm made manifest'. Why were they viewed this way? It must be to do with their appearance and nature: open spaces in a wooded landscape, black water reflecting the sky. Bogs are liminal zones, a soupy limbo, neither solid nor liquid, places where the normal processes of decay are slowed, as if time itself has been dammed and seeps through cracks. The Iron Age people, one suspects, understood the preserving quality of bogs and may have felt that to put someone into that place was to hold on to them at the very moment of giving them away.

Oldcroghan Man now: the best – or worst – saved for last. It was interesting to watch people enter this room and come into his company. They didn't get too near, and they spoke in whispers.

Ned and I sat down and looked.

'Extraordinary,' he said. 'So little of the body, but a great presence.'

Oldcroghan Man was found during the digging of a bog drain. He has no head, and no lower part to his body, having been decapitated and cut in half at the time of his death. On the left-hand side of his chest is a diamond-shaped hole where the killing blade went in.

When he first emerged from the ground he was the colour of dark chocolate, wet and glistening, water pooling in his hollows. He has since been freeze-dried and is a lighter, though not uniform brown – skin like a landscape, like the bog itself.

He was a big man. A little over six feet three inches is the estimate. His arms, even with muscle wastage, suggest great strength. Around his left bicep, loose now, is a leather and metal armband. His perfect hands astonish. Bend close to his right and you can see the contour lines of the thumb, the creases on his palm and at his wrist; his pinky and ring finger are crooked inwards, almost a gesture of benediction. But the left hand is half-clenched, a warning not a blessing. The museum's then head of conservation, transporting the newly found body to Dublin in the back of his estate car, couldn't shake the thought of those powerful arms coming around his neck as he drove.

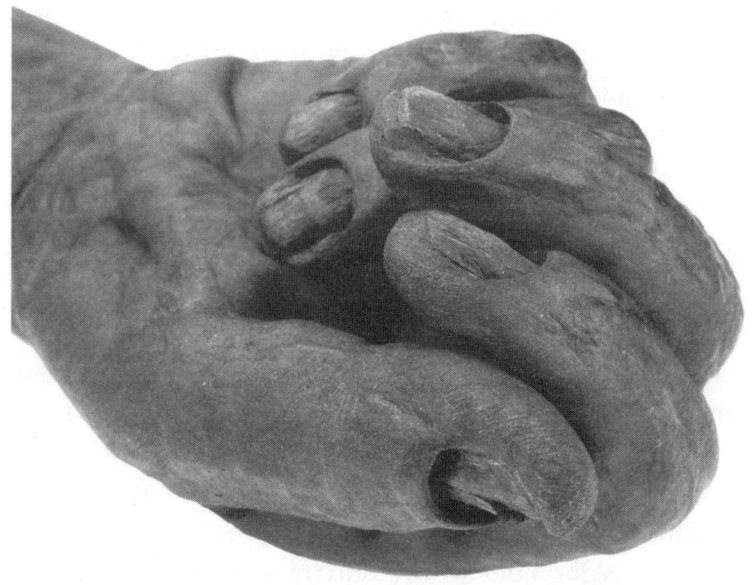

Once in the lab, though, the body seemed more pitiful than threatening. An archaeologist in a white coat reached out and held one of Oldcroghan Man's hands. He had suffered so much, she later said, and this touch was reassurance that they meant him no harm.

I mentioned this to Ned and he nodded. 'The hands are very evocative. This was a young man. He had probably held the hands of his children and embraced his lover. Hands remind you that you are dealing with a human being who had a real life. This is a person who has died in awful circumstances – a real tragedy for the man and the people who loved him, y'know?'

The mutilations of the body seem meaningful, more than mere cruelties. Holes were made in the arms, post-mortem, and hazel ropes – known as withies – pushed through. These appear to be the remains of a form of cattle hobble and may have had ritual significance; they look like broken matchsticks poking through the skin. The nipples had been sliced, as were those of Clonycavan Man, a procedure that has been linked to the symbolic ending of kingship. He was killed sometime between 175 and 362 BC.

Laboratory examination of the hands had revealed no cuts, marks or abrasions. The fingernails were manicured. These were hands of the sort you'd expect to find on a modern office worker. His diet in the final four months of his life was rich in meat, though the last things he ate were ground cereal and buttermilk, which may have been some sort of ritual meal. The stomach contents of bog bodies can be highly suggestive of ceremonial preparations. One Irish body, discovered in 2012, had a last supper of around more than two hundred ripe sloes.

So: Oldcroghan Man. Big and strong. Soft hands. Not engaged in manual labour but eating plenty of good food. What picture emerges? A member of the elite, a warrior, 'the golden boy of his tribe', as he has been described. His remains were found on the boundary of two ancient territories, close to a hill thought to have been used for the inauguration of kings. He may have died within sight of the place where he was once raised up.

Time spent among the dead leads, perhaps inevitably, to consideration of one's own mortality, and Ned had mentioned that he intended, when his day comes, to have his ashes buried on his farm in Connemara; he'd already picked out the spot. To rest easy in your own land, in a place of your choosing, and not to be howked up thereafter – well, that sounds grand, does it not? Preferable to the strange resurrections we had witnessed today. The bog bodies of Dublin, poor souls, are treated with as much dignity and respect as the circumstances of public exhibition allow, but it is not what most of us would want for ourselves, I'm sure, this glassy purgatory.

Still, they could always count on a warm word from their former keeper.

Ned tipped his hat to the headless man. 'Farewell, my old friend,' he said. 'If there is an afterlife, you'll be one of the guys I'll be looking to have a chat to.'

*

IT WAS STILL DARK as I walked the muddy track. My torch picked out flooded potholes and a blackboard on which was chalked, Sheep In Field – Please Close Gate. They were clumped like dandelion seed in the lee of the fence, regarding early-rising humanity with an expression of blank disdain. Can sheep give side-eye? If so, these surely did.

There was a large black shape dead ahead: a whaleback mound breaching the land. I followed its edge and arrived at a doorway, an oblong of flickering light; faint music within.

'Hello?' I called.

'Come in! But mind your head!'

I knew that voice. It was Tim Daw, the farmer who'd had this tomb built on his land in Wiltshire.

He walked down the passageway to greet me. 'Good morning!' Breath clouded his head-torch beam. Woolly hat, heavy jacket, green wellies. It was late December.

I ducked below the sarsen lintel and entered a narrow corridor of rough stone. Dim candlelight showed doorways to left and right.

'The layout is based very loosely on other long barrows,' Tim said. 'We're trying to get at the soul of what they were doing.'

They being the Neolithic people who had constructed structures like this to contain and memorialise their dead. Long barrows – such as Wayland's Smithy on the Ridgeway – are among the most atmospheric places in the British landscape. And if they feel charged to us now, as curious visitors, what must they have meant to those who built and used them?

Tombs, writes the archaeologist Mark Edmonds, 'were where you went to connect the brief span of life to a more profound and persistent order. These were powerful places, enduring in a way that so much of life was not. That made them an appropriate setting in which to congregate with ghosts . . .'

The All Cannings Long Barrow isn't a replica. It's the real thing. Not Neolithic, of course; it was constructed for Tim Daw by Anglesey stonemasons using traditional methods and materials. But it is nevertheless a site of communal burial. There seems to be a demand for such places. Tim sold all the space within the first two years. So far the ashes of forty-five people have been interred. The rest will arrive in due course. There are 340 niches, but each has room for more than one urn.

'Do feel free to come and look.'

He led the way into the side-chambers. There are five of them, circular, with corbel ceilings and stone columns. In some of the occupied niches, objects had been placed next to the urns, giving a sense of who the person had been. 'This lovely woman here,' said Tim, 'her husband and daughters brought her reading glasses and the dog's collar. And this man, they've used a decanter for his ashes. There's all sorts in here.'

A ceramic penguin. A yellow rose. A fishing reel and lures. Glimpses of quiet lives. Leaning against one urn was a blue plaque: 'Quantity Surveyor, Stamp Collector, Grandfather, and all round Top Bloke.' In another niche, a little wooden pyramid bore a brass plate: 'A True Wiltshireman.' We were a long way from Sutton Hoo and its regal opulence, yet if the ship burial expressed the beginnings of national identity then here, modestly, was its latest iteration.

'We are a nation of flower-lovers, but also a nation of stamp-collectors, pigeon-fanciers, amateur carpenters, coupon-snippers, darts-players, crossword-puzzle fans . . .' Who would have guessed that Orwell's idea of Englishness as a cluster of small private enthusiasms would find perfect expression in a prehistoric tomb built in the twenty-first century? Perhaps his old maid biking through the autumn mist was not, after all, heading to Holy Communion, but on her way to commune with the dead in a long barrow. There are worse places to spend a morning, or eternity. And the soundtrack's not bad either.

The music that had been faint earlier, I could hear properly now: Wagner's 'Ride of the Valkyries'.

'Certain music is very powerful in here,' Tim said. 'You know what's really good? "Love To Love You Baby", by Donna Summer. That sounds wonderful, but I don't think it's quite . . .'

The right vibe? Perhaps not. Orgasmic disco has its place. A house of the dead near Devizes is probably not it.

Tim is in his sixties, a second-generation farmer. We had spoken on the phone before I made this trip, and I had begun to understand his perspective. He has an academic rather than spiritual interest in ancient places, but respects and welcomes other points of view. I asked him why he had built the barrow.

'I've lived where I live all my life and was brought up around big ancient monuments. I can walk out on the hills and see long barrows and forts. So I had an inkling that to leave your mark on the landscape was not impossible and might be nice to do. But I'm not an egotist or an eighteenth-century aristocrat raising a monument to my own glory.'

He used to work as a guide at Stonehenge, where he was often asked by visitors whether they could scatter cremated remains among the megaliths. He'd explain that it wasn't possible, but their questions – and the yearning for meaning he sensed behind those questions – gave him an idea. 'Leaving your mum's ashes at the crematorium or something like that is dissatisfying. And a lot of people end up leaving them under the stairs or on the mantelpiece because they don't know what else to do with them. So I thought: can we do something different and better for people? Could we build on an ancient tradition?

'One of the things about memorialising someone is it's got to be beyond the prosaic and the functional. There has to be an element of something more, something special. This mound is seventy metres long. It's *big*. It's a statement. You're saying that your mum, your grandmother, whoever it is, was a person worth remembering.'

While we had been speaking, others had started to arrive, stooping under the lintel – 'Mind your head!' – and walking up the passage to the chambers. It was ten years since the long barrow had opened, and Tim had arranged an anniversary celebration.

'Ten years ago this was just an empty field,' he said. 'Now people come to remember loved ones, but also just to celebrate life.'

We gathered outside to watch the sun come up. The barrow is aligned with the midwinter sunrise, which means that on bright days, at this time of year, the first rays shine down the passageway and strike the back wall – bringing light to the darkness. Today was dull, so the effect wouldn't happen, but nobody seemed fussed. It was enough to be here.

From outside, now that it was light enough to see, the barrow looked much like any of its Neolithic brethren: a wedge-shaped grassy mound set among fields. Visible on a nearby hilltop was the ancient site it most resembles, Adam's Grave.

There were a couple of dozen of us outside the barrow. I had assumed that most would have come to visit loved ones who had passed. I expected a few tears. In fact, the majority seemed to be people who had purchased niches for their own eventual interment, and the atmosphere, far from sad, was festive. Friends exchanged Christmas cards. Someone went round with home baking. 'Would you like some mulled wine? Some stollen? It's very buttery.' The occasion felt like a reunion, but of course it was a *pre*-union. Most of these people would, in time and for all time, be dead together, their ashes on shelves in the neighbourly dark. For now, though, they chatted and laughed, spoke of the journeys they had made to get here, which routes they'd taken, and what ridiculous hour they'd had to get up that morning. We will all one day go into the great silence, so why not moan about the traffic while you can?

There was a short service, bit of chanting, nothing very formal; the wind and the birdsong felt as much a part of it as the words spoken.

Afterwards, as people drifted away, Tim closed up the barrow, pulling the metal gate shut. The design on the iron-work, he explained, was based on a DNA double helix. This seemed fitting, somehow, for a tomb: 'It uses our bodies as vessels. It is the life force that never dies.'

I got talking with a druid couple from Crawley who were walking back to their car. They felt calm, they said, knowing that this beautiful spot is where their ashes will rest.

'But it *is* a long way to come,' the woman laughed, 'so we've said to the kids that if they don't want to drive down, just FedEx us and Tim will pop us in there.'

*

'Croeso i Ynys Môn' said the road sign. *Welcome to Anglesey.*

I had taken the bridge over the Menai Strait and arrived on the island they call Môn Mam Cymru, the Mother of Wales. The masons who built Tim Daw's long barrow travelled from here and spoke Welsh as they shaped the stones. Now, I was on my way to see the work of their ancestors. I was driving to Barclodiad y Gawres, a passage grave, where I had arranged to meet a woman with a great fondness for such places.

Passage graves are a type of chambered tomb. They come

later in the Neolithic than the long barrows and are distinguished from them by their round shape. A narrow passage leads to a central space from which, often, burial recesses extend in three directions. The architecture of these tombs – the dead carried up a tunnel into a chamber within a swollen mound – suggests ideas of birth and rebirth. 'The nature of Neolithic society in Britain has been forgotten for all time,' Jacquetta Hawkes has written, 'but I myself do not doubt that whether or no it can properly be called matriarchal, the women were its foundation. It rested on their earthiness, their interest in fecundity and physical creation . . .'

The symbolism of the tombs, their association with renewal, is emphasised in some cases by their construction on solar alignments that allow them to function as markers of seasonal change. The All Cannings Long Barrow works in that way, but it is an ancient tradition. The best-known passage grave in Britain and Ireland is Newgrange, one of a cluster in the Boyne Valley, County Meath, where, at midwinter, for about twenty minutes, the rising sun shines through a small aperture above the entrance, travels as a narrow beam up the floor of the sixty-two-foot passageway and makes the walls glow. Every year there are around twenty thousand entrants in a worldwide lottery for a place in the chamber on the winter solstice. Eight are chosen, each of whom is permitted to bring a guest, so sixteen people are privileged witnesses to the light – or not, if clouds refuse to rouse themselves from the skyline.

Despite its popularity and fame, Newgrange is not universally admired. Its reconstruction in the 1960s and 70s with a steep wall of quartz and granite continues to provoke strong feelings. The archaeologist Francis Pryor has written that the mound now 'resembles a chirpy pillbox hat with a bright white hatband – something Aer Lingus might one day adapt for its stewardesses'. Modern interventions are always tricky.

GRAVE

I remember, as a boy, visiting Maeshowe, a passage grave in Orkney, and being struck by the stark white ugliness of the nineteenth-century ceiling.

Since childhood I have been drawn to tombs and suchlike places. I love their dank old names – howes, cairns, fogous, souterrains – and seek them out whenever I can.

While in Hoy to visit the grave of Betty Corrigall, I had taken time to walk out to the Dwarfie Stane. It is in a heathery valley, not far from the foot of a cliff-face called the Dwarfie Hamars, and reached by a footpath leading off the road. Often described as Britain's only rock-cut Neolithic tomb, it's a block of grey sandstone, about thirty feet long and fifteen wide, a glacial erratic, small change dropped by careless ice. There is a low and narrow entrance on the west face. The interior was hollowed by people who had no metal tools, a job so hard and slow that it must have been very important to them. There is a fair bit of historic graffiti carved into the stone, inside and out, including a line of lovely Persian calligraphy, the translation of which is 'I have sat two nights and so learned patience.' That was the work, in 1850, of Major William Mounsey, a soldier and spy whose antiquarian interests led him to chisel his name on various sites around Britain that would have been better left alone.

I went on hands and knees into the Dwarfie Stane on a dull morning when it seemed as if there was no one around for miles. There is an Orcadian tradition that places of ancient burial are occupied by a *hogboon*, a guardian who must be placated by offerings of food and drink. You don't have to believe that to feel unease. I never forget, when going into such places, that I am entering a grave.

There wasn't much room to move. The place wasn't meant for things that move. Yet against the back wall, set down just so, was a posy of cornflowers. Two cells were separated from the central area by low sills; the one on the right, the better-carved, featured what looked like a stone pillow. Within these cramped little cribs the dead had been laid. I couldn't bring myself to crawl into them. I let my torch do the exploring. The floor of the cell with the pillow was covered in straw, quite fresh but pressed flat. Someone had been sleeping there, had brought straw bedding for the purpose, and perhaps intended to return. I did not much want to make their acquaintance, so backed out of the entrance and went on my way.

Now, in Anglesey, the prospect of entering a tomb in company seemed much more pleasant than going into it alone. Especially with such an expert guide. Dr Ffion Reynolds is an archaeologist working for Cadw, the government department responsible for the historic places of Wales. Non-speakers of Welsh sometimes assume that 'Cadw' is an acronym, but in fact it's a verb, meaning to keep or to protect. That sense of active caring suits Ffion, who seems to have a strong feeling of mission as regards the monuments in her charge. Like Ned Kelly, she is a keeper in its widest sense: a key holder who also, one feels, could at any moment unlock the true meaning and purpose of these mysterious sites. Interested in what other cultures may be able to teach us about the beliefs and practices of our past, she has studied shamanism, totemism and animism, and worked with the Shipibo tribe of the Amazon rainforest in Peru.

We met on a bright, windy morning in early October. The Porth Trecastell car park was busy with a party of women who had been swimming in the bay and were now swaddled in big coats and bobble hats. Someone rang a hand-bell to announce that tots of sherry were being served.

Ffion parked up, said hello, and gave the waves an appraising glance. 'Wow, look at that sea. I haven't seen it looking that rough in ages.' She is in her early forties. She was wearing an 'I ♥ Stones' T-shirt and a pair of black trousers embroidered with fly agaric mushrooms. She is a devotee of mushrooms, and loves to go out and find them, the more weird and wonderful the better. She is writing a book exploring the uses of fungi in prehistory.

Mushrooms, being organic, do not much appear in the archaeological record. But intriguing survivals suggest a culture of use. Ötzi The Iceman, a five thousand-year-old body found emerging from a melting glacier in the Tyrolean Alps, was carrying mushrooms at the time of his death – two pieces of birch polypore threaded on leather strips, and a piece of hoof fungus in a pouch.

Ffion and I walked out to the tomb. It is right on the headland, saucer-ish and sleek. You could prise it from the earth and skim it across the Irish Sea, to clatter against its kin in the Boyne Valley.

'These tombs are incredible feats of engineering, beautiful places,' Ffion said. 'I find them beguiling. I want to know *more*.'

I love that 'beguiling'. She meant charming and intriguing, I think. But the word also contains the idea of deception, as if these trickster tombs give a false account of themselves, which perhaps they do. 'Archaeology is a form of storytelling,' Ffion said. 'What I'm telling you about these sites is just one idea. You don't have to believe me, or agree with me. The beauty of archaeology is we'll never know.'

A wedge-like modern entranceway ended in a locked gate. A security camera watched as we approached. Dim solar lights clicked on as Ffion opened up and we went in.

Barclodiad y Gawres, she explained, means 'The Giantess's Apronful', which speaks to its creation myth: that a giant walking along the coast spilled some of the rocks she was carrying. The name suggests something of its appearance before excavation in the early 1950s. The grassy mound that covers it is a reconstruction. It looks real enough from outside, but inside is a concrete dome with the feel of a Cold War bunker.

What it protects appeared to be, when we first entered, a chaotic scatter of rock. The only feature that seemed the obvious work of human hands was the entrance to one of the burial chambers, topped by a large tilting capstone. But as my eyes adjusted to the low light, I began to make out the tomb's real treasure: a number of megaliths decorated during the Neolithic with patterns typical of that period.

'Can you see the way that they've been created?' Ffion asked. 'Rather than being scratched, they've been *pecked* – and that's the style of megalithic art you find in Ireland and Scotland. Passage tombs occur along the Irish seaboard. So this art is a tradition, I would say, of seafarers.'

We were looking at a stone near the entrance. It was about five feet tall with a pattern of diamonds surrounded by zigzags. Just a little further into the tomb was a low stone covered in spirals. As Ffion said, the designs had been 'pecked' – created by striking the surface with a tool, creating many little hollows which, together, give the desired motif. Our phone torches, held at an angle, picked the details out. Once upon a time – a fairy-tale phrase that does just as well for the Neolithic – these shapes had flickered in firelight. There had been a hearth in the central chamber. People weren't using this place just to dispose of remains; they were in here long enough and often enough to need warmth and light. Where better than a fireside for the telling of stories? And where better than a tomb to tell stories of ancestors? Bones do not survive well in the acidic soil of Wales, but there is good evidence from elsewhere that people interacted with their dead, arranging and mingling skeletal remains in a way that suggests that the physical integrity of the individual was not as important as the presence, in the tomb, of the collective.

'The relationship between the dead and the living was really close and visceral in the Neolithic,' Ffion said. 'They were

kind of obsessed with death. They tried every different way of burying. When somebody passed away they didn't put the body straight into the chamber. They would build an excarnation platform. They would put the person on the top of it, would let the body rot, collect the bones, clean them, and then put them inside the chamber – to stop disease from spreading, to keep it all nice and clean inside. What we've lost in our contemporary society is that connection with the dead. As soon as somebody close to us dies, they get taken away. We don't have that close relationship with bodies any more.'

But what about those patterned stones? What was their purpose in all this?

'A lot of people think that they might be maps, or they are telling you something about the relationship between human beings and the sky. But I tend to think that they're entoptic.'

Entoptic phenomena are visual effects that originate within the eye. When you are in bed at night and rub your eyes or close them tight, those bright shapes moving through the darkness are entoptic. The shapes can also be seen during altered states such as drug hallucinations.

Ffion thinks it probable that hallucinogens, such as henbane and psilocybin mushrooms, were used in prehistory as part of ritual activity. She mentioned a study that had shown a close likeness between the rock art of Irish passage graves and the shapes seen by research subjects under the influence of mescaline. It could be, therefore, that the sort of art we see in these tombs – the spirals and zigzags and so on – represent visions experienced during ceremonies. These occasions may also have included chanting, drumming, incense, firelight, the consumption of food and drink, and, of course, the watchful presence of the dead.

If that sounds fanciful, consider the discovery at Star Carr in Yorkshire of thirty-three headdresses or masks, known as frontlets, made from the skulls and antlers of red deer. These have been interpreted as having been worn during shamanic dances. Star Carr is Mesolithic, so we're talking about hunter-gatherers living around six thousand years earlier than the settled people who built the passage graves, but the point is that prehistoric ritual could have been as performative and dramatic as we allow ourselves to imagine.

And we must allow it. Imagination is fundamental to thinking about ancient people. It is one of the things that links us and them. Just as we have the same bodies and can therefore appreciate the development of their tools and technologies, the things they made and did with their hands, so too do we have the same brains – and our thoughts, dreams, ideas, fantasies, perceptions, emotions and imaginings must surely be similar. Modern human consciousness cannot be the same as during prehistory; we are separated by millennia of cultural and intellectual development, not least of which is writing, but our minds are as like theirs as an oak is to the sapling from which it grew. They are *in* us, and we draw from the same deep roots.

Towards the end of our time together, I asked Ffion a question I have found it fruitful to ask archaeologists: why does she do this work?

'I'm adopted,' she replied, 'and I think archaeology, in a strange way, is a way of connecting with my past. I don't really know who my ancestors are. But archaeology provides a connection to Wales and a deep connection to the land. The ancestors, the people in the past, I feel I can just about touch them.'

*

IF ARCHAEOLOGY IS a form of storytelling, storytelling is a kind of archaeology. You dig down, through the layers and years, until you find an expressive piece of evidence, some revealed truth. My story – one of them – begins with a tooth.

I remember, or think I remember, the way it felt: smooth, hard and dry in my small, soft palm.

I had thought it an incisor, but it turns out that's a false memory. It was a molar. I know that now for certain, having read the analysis of bones recovered from the burial. Three pieces of skull, part of the sacrum, five fragments of rib, three radii, two ulnae, portions of the left and right femur, two tibiae, four fibulae, a bone of the ankle and a bone of the heel. The legs allowed for estimates of height (five foot eight or perhaps a little more) and age: about eighteen years old, slightly younger if the individual was female, which was not determined then, in 1984, and cannot be now as the bones have been lost.

I myself was ten years old. Small, dark, shy, full of solemn excitement. I would not have been able to explain why it felt that way to hold the tooth. But it was surely to do with the abstract made physical. Here was death in the form of bone. Here, too, was time. This person lived and died in the Bronze Age, I was told, and had been one of the Beaker People, named for the clay pots they buried with their dead – just like the one we, my grandparents and I, found.

Let me dig down.

Here's the way I heard the story: Friday evening, the Red Lion in Stirling; a quarryman at the bar, a few drams to the good. Not sufficient to stop his hands trembling, but enough to make his voice loud enough to overhear. He'd had a shock. He'd been working the excavator, digging into a bank of earth, when – 'Christ!' – a skull came tumbling out. His first thought was there'd been a murder, but no, it couldn't be that. Whatever this was, it was really old.

My grandfather, Grumps to his grandkids, was a coach-builder. That was how he earned a wage, building buses in a factory, but archaeology was what he loved. He would have been in his early sixties that summer, approaching retirement I suppose, and had stopped in for a pint after work. He spoke with the quarryman about what he had found, then came straight back to the flat to pick us up, Gran and me, and we drove off to see what, if anything, we could see.

The sand and gravel quarry was a few miles north-west of Stirling, between a turreted Victorian mansion and the River Teith. I remember, sort of, walking out to the spot. It was late July, fine weather, a light evening. Two heavy slabs jutted from the top of the quarry face, well above head height, forming a V; the wide end hung in the air, but the narrow part was still mostly buried. On the ground were further slabs. These had fallen when the bucket of the excavator bit into the face, smashing open a grave that had been undisturbed for approximately four thousand years.

My grandparents recognised the big flat stones for what they were: broken remnants of a cist burial, a cist being a box or chest. This one would have been almost five feet long in its perfect state. The skeleton would have lain in a crouched position, the body having been placed into the cist on its side, arms and legs drawn close, as if in the womb. The beaker, which may well have been intact until the grave was damaged, would have been shaped like an inverted bell and had probably been set down beside the head.

Beaker People, or Bell-Beaker Folk as they are sometimes known, were migrants. They started to come to Britain from the European mainland about four thousand five hundred years ago; DNA studies suggest that within around five hundred years they had almost entirely replaced the existing population. Analysis of people buried with beakers has shown that they have a different genetic signature, different ancestry, from those who were buried in the Neolithic long barrows and passage graves.

These newcomers looked different: lighter skin, lighter hair, blue eyes becoming more common. They brought with them new technology – the ability to work metal; copper at first and then bronze. They also brought a new cultural practice: burying their dead singly, not in communal tombs, and placing beside them those decorated pots for which they are named. At least some beakers held liquid, possibly alcoholic.

Burial alone, the body left intact and undisturbed, accompanied by what seems to be a drinking vessel. What does this suggest? A concept of life after death different from whatever the Neolithic people, with their communal tombs and cremations, believed. It could be that the Beaker folk thought the individual passed into some other world, where they would need their whole selves. Such a journey would make anyone thirsty, and so they would have to be provisioned with something to drink. We talk about the *Bronze* Age because their metal items have survived, but perhaps it would be as well to talk of the Afterlife Age, the Faith Age. The trouble is that all we have are the bones and grave goods. You can't dig up a person's spirituality. You can't take a trowel to the soul.

My grandparents had their trowels with them that evening, and spent the next hour or so, while light allowed, examining the broken mess on the ground for anything fragile that could be rescued: bits of beaker, bits of bone, gathering them in a plastic lunchbox. Was it then that we found the tooth? My memory of that time in my life is imperfect, a jumble of sherds.

On the Monday morning – so the documents suggest – they contacted Lorna Main, an archaeologist working for the regional council, who came out to the quarry and made everything official. My recollection is that we spent the next few days digging the site. I was given the job of writing it up for *Discovery and Excavation in Scotland*, the archaeology journal. This was a case of adults humouring a keen child, but I took it seriously, clanking out a report on an old manual typewriter fetched down from the attic. It was the first time I had ever tried to write for publication, and my first experience of being rewritten by an editor. The bland facts of the official record – 'Salvage excavation produced human skeletal remains and fragments of a beaker' – do not convey what the experience meant to me, and still does.

In any case, my attention was soon elsewhere and I didn't think about the dig for a long time. All those activities – the trowelling, the typing, the days spent with my grandparents – were, I now think, intended to keep me busy and give my mother a break. Her belly had swollen with new life that summer, and a week after we first went to the quarry my brother Liam was born.

He lived fourteen months and was buried in the autumn. From the cist of her body to the cist of the ground, not long.

*

My grandfather, Eric Ross, was born in 1921, the son of a game-keeper. He joined the RAF in 1941 and became a flight mechanic with 651 Squadron, working on Austers, the observation planes used for reconnaissance and to assist in directing artillery. He and his crew drove around in trucks with an Auster in the back, putting its wings on as required, so that it could take off from any suitable bit of straight road – or so I'm told.

I have three exercise books he kept during training, full of neat handwritten instructions, calculations and diagrams pertaining to the operation, maintenance and repair of aircraft. He used colour pencil to illustrate the correct painting of camouflage and insignia; there is something of the child's drawing about the pictures, a reminder of how young these men were and how little of the world most of them would have seen before they were sent off to save it.

He served in North Africa, Italy and Palestine, and was released from service in September 1946. He married Susan – my grandmother – four days before Christmas and they settled down to a long life together. In wedding photographs, taken at the Miners' Welfare in Stirling, he is in uniform and she is wearing a shining dress, almost sci-fi, with sharp shoulders and collar, and a tall bridal crown of white doves.

My grandfather's interest in archaeology may have begun during the war. 'Eric was the only man I knew who had actually used a genuine working Roman bath,' one of his friends has told me. 'Just before the Victory Parade in Tunis, his squad was given a few minutes in the still-operational baths fed from the hot springs that the Romans had used. Eric said the bath was pretty full of sand by the time they got there, but at least they were all slightly cleaner for the parade.'

So, washing the desert from his body in Roman ruins is how ancient history got under his skin? I hope this is true. I like it very much as an origin story. I wish I could have asked him about this, and about his experience of the war, but of course it is too late. People slip away before we are ready to hear their stories.

However it happened, the past became a passion and he took night classes in field archaeology, learning to dig. He shared the knowledge with his wife; and they, in time, shared it with their eldest grandson – me.

A battered leather suitcase that I now have at home contains a few documents relating to his military service, including those exercise books, but much more of it is pamphlets about prehistoric sites, and correspondence with professional archaeologists on whose excavations he and my grandmother volunteered. A letter to Susan from a noted Romanist, written in 1976, advises those coming to dig on the Antonine Wall that they would be billeted in student halls and could expect a daily subsistence payment of sixty pence for lunch; bring your own sleeping bag and mug. There is a roughing-it quality to these letters. You can almost smell the tea urn and damp socks.

Archaeology, in those days, was not as professionalised, and seems to have been a rather roving pursuit, reliant on volunteers with energy, half-decent boots, and some idea of what they were doing. It would suit the hippyish young, and the older crew who had been through the war and austerity. There is a sense, too, of a crew going from dig to dig – a bath-house here, a broch there – spending only the humdrum part of their lives in the present day. A postcard thanking my grandparents for confirming that they would take part in excavation of the Roman fort at Camelon, near Falkirk, concludes with the words, 'A lot of old faces are coming back.'

I can see them, those people, the diggers, with their waterproofs and sandwiches and notebooks and tools and even, in the case of one of my grandparent's cronies, dowsing rods. He was a nuclear engineer and believed it possible to locate ancient structures underground using wire from coathangers held in the casings of ballpoint pens. You'd see him walking the sites, following the swivelling steel. This was on archaeological society field trips to historic monuments. There are many fuzzy photographs of me, as a child, at ruined castles and chambered cairns. My friends would go on holiday and come back with suntans and tales of Tenerife. I felt sorry for their ignorance. What did they know of the recumbent stone circles of Aberdeenshire? The music of those names – Sunhoney, Tyrebagger, Dunnideer – was lost to them.

Language was part of the attraction for me, I think. When we went on digs there was a whole other vocabulary. The talk was of 'postholes' and 'features', 'cuts' and 'fills'. I grew used to stepping down into the trench and being allowed to scrape away the earth in a particular area, probably where I could do least harm. Later, when I was strong enough, I'd push wheel-barrows to the spoil heap. With every load of earth removed, the site was further revealed. This was a barrack-room wall, someone would say; and here was a road on which Roman soldiers had marched. I knew about the Romans. I had a book at home with colourful and rather bloody illustrations of their battles with the Macedonians and Gauls. It was strange to think of them here in the Scottish rain and mud, just as it was hard to picture my gentle grandfather at war in Italy, or anywhere at all.

The attic of my grandparents' flat, a place for tools and fishing gear, was where they kept their excavation kit: trowels, spades and mattocks. I cherish the few things of theirs that I have inherited – a writing desk, a walking stick, Penguins of Tacitus, Plutarch and Pliny – but would give them all up for one of those trowels. I should like to hold it in my hand, its handle worn smooth, and put its edge to the familiar earth. Really, I should have become an archaeologist rather than a writer. Perhaps because most of the people I knew back then were doing it for fun rather than work, I just didn't see it as a job. The joke about a career in archaeology, of course, is that there's no future in it, but that has turned out to be the case with print journalism. We, the Newspaper Folk, are relics; bury us with a beaker of ink.

So whenever I think about my childhood adventures in digging, I have a feeling of a path not taken. This book is an attempt to walk it a little.

*

I had not, as I say, thought much about the cist burial over the years. It would be overly neat to say it was a buried memory, but the mid-1980s was a difficult time for our family. We were too often at the cemetery, burying our own dead, and then trying to live with the losses.

However, as the fortieth anniversary of the discovery approached, I began to wonder what had happened to the things we had found.

Lorna Main, the archaeologist who had taken charge of the dig, has been retired for a number of years. But I contacted her and she replied. 'Looking back,' she wrote, 'it was a dangerous place for us all to be rooting around for bones and pottery with a high, active and probably unstable quarry face above us.' She sent a few black and white photographs. One shows my Gran up on the bank, trowelling the interior of the surviving part of the cist. In another, taken at the foot of the face, I am hefting a heavy rock, wearing a pair of too-large waterproof trousers tucked into wellies, so much younger than I remember being. A few months from my eleventh birthday. A few days from becoming a brother again. A wee boy who would soon have too much to carry.

The bones are gone. They had been sent to Glasgow University for examination, which is when the individual in the grave was determined to have been in their late teens. But what happened after that work was done, nobody seems to know. So I will never hold that tooth again, and we cannot, now, hope to carry out the various analyses that might have told us their sex, something of their diet and the environment in which they lived, if they suffered from disease, and whether they had travelled during their short life. I feel sorry for the person, whoever they were, disturbed in their grave, boxed up and measured, and finally mislaid and forgotten somewhere in the system. We have been careless with them, who were buried with such care.

Not everyone in the Bronze Age was given a formal burial. The numbers suggest that it wasn't standard. Most bodies must have been disposed of in ways that are archaeologically invisible, perhaps cremated and their ashes scattered. The teenager in my cist, if I can call it mine, was 'significant enough in the community to be singled out for special treatment in death' – as an archaeologist has put it to me.

But significant how? Perhaps they were a member of a leading family, or had won honour in battle, or were admired in some way that had nothing to do with martial or social status. Perhaps they had a negative significance; they had committed some misdeed so dreadful that their toxic body must be shuttered within stone.

I think not, though. Some graves reek of rank. The Amesbury Archer, as he is known, was found in in 2002, three miles from Stonehenge, in a grave that had probably been timber-lined. He died around 2300 BC, aged thirty-five to forty-five, and was buried with almost a hundred objects including three copper knives, two gold hair tresses, several flint-tipped arrows, a small stone anvil that may have been used in metalworking, and guards to protect his wrist from the recoil of a bowstring. He also had five beakers; most graves have just one. The Archer has been described as the 'poster boy' for the Beaker culture. Oxygen isotope analysis of his tooth enamel indicates that he lived in central Europe as a child, probably the Swiss Alps; the items found in his grave hint at travel in France and Iberia before his arrival in Britain. It has been suggested that he could be Britain's Prometheus – the smith who brought the new technology to this country. 'Metallurgy has always been a magical and dangerous art,' Alan Garner tells us, 'and its practitioners are magical and dangerous men.'

Our cist burial was nowhere near as grand. Had it been an important discovery, had it even been intact, the beaker would have soon found a place in a museum collection. Instead, like the bones, it vanished in the system. If I hadn't become interested, and if Lorna Main hadn't been able and willing to help, it might have stayed lost. Several months passed with no success, but then a happy email: Trevor Cowie, a curator retired from the National Museum of Scotland, had located the beaker – and would be glad to let me see it.

I met him in Edinburgh, at the museum, with his younger colleague Matt Knight, who is responsible for the prehistory collection. We sat in the café and I told them the story of how the cist was found; then we went upstairs, through security, to where staff worked out of sight of the visiting public.

In a small warm room Matt put an opaque plastic tub on the table.

'That's probably your grandad's lunch box, is it?' Trevor said.

I couldn't believe it. I was ready for the beaker, but not this. As soon as I saw it, I was back there. The neat slabs of chocolatey home-baking that Gran would pack for days out. The steam rising from a flask as we sat out the drizzle in some old ruin or other. This lunch box, stalwart companion on our excursions, had since 1984 held the beaker from the cist.

Matt laid out the pieces. They were biscuit-coloured; about the right size to dunk in tea. A fragment of lip had an orangey stain, which could be from whatever it had once contained, or from the flowers that some archaeologists think were placed in burials. There were more pieces than I had remembered: sixteen, plus a number of tiny fragments.

'Your pot is late in the tradition,' Trevor said. He thought that it had been made sometime between 1750 and 2100 BC. This estimate was based, in part, on the surface pattern. The classic techniques are lines of dots made by combs, and impressions left by twisted cord. Mine didn't feature those. The potter had stabbed a herringbone design into the surface using some sort of spatula. The beaker would have been built up in rings, the joins smoothed as the vessel grew, and then hardened in an open fire. Quite a skill. Were beakers made by specialists, I wonder, or by people mourning a personal loss? And if the latter, did they think of the person they loved as they shaped and decorated the clay? Perhaps we would identify a residue of grief in every beaker, if only we had equipment to detect it.

'We don't always know the circumstances in which these pots are being made – whether in advance of someone dying or in reaction to somebody dying,' Matt said. 'That puts quite a different impetus on how you make the pot. If somebody dies unexpectedly and you need to build a pot for them, you need to do that as quickly as possible, before the body starts to decay.'

Would it be okay, I asked, to touch the pieces of beaker?

'Please,' said Trevor. 'They're quite robust.'

I put on gloves and, one by one, picked them up. Along the edges, where they had broken, a grey interior was visible. It was strange to hold them again. These little bits of pottery, which once may have contained a 'libation offering for the afterlife', as Matt had put it, also carried stories: of a death and burial thousands of years ago, and that of my own family. This is what happens as objects move through time. They pick up traces of those who come into contact with them. We in the present, trying to fit the past into categories we can understand, privilege the story of an artefact's origin – when it was made, how, why, for whom – but that is just the beginning, not the end of its life. Nor has that life ended now that the beaker has been rediscovered and properly catalogued. Who knows what, and whom, may be in its future; which hands and minds may turn it over? As the archaeologist Mark Edmonds has written of ancient objects, 'if some of them could speak, and if we could understand them, they would probably tell us that we are merely passing through their stories. That the associations that matter so much to us are simply pauses on their longer and more convoluted odysseys.'

A week after her first visit to the quarry, Lorna Main had been called back out – to record a set of slabs from a second cist burial which, she learned, had been destroyed several weeks earlier. More than one grave, then, and a strong possibility that there had been others. What we had chanced upon – thanks to a conversation overheard in a pub – may have been a small cemetery, the burial place of a community. No Bronze Age settlement has been found in the area, but it is reasonable to assume that they lived nearby. There is only so far that you would want to carry a body and the heavy slabs for the grave. The beaker, however, is the only surviving witness.

'Although it's a fragmentary pot,' Trevor said, 'there's still a story to be teased out of it.'

*

It was one of those mornings very late in December when the year seems to be in its final illness. The trees were black lungs, the sky a tubercular grey. There was a sound of gunfire: a pheasant shoot. Ducks rose from the water with an ovation of wingbeats, as if applauding that some other poor birds were getting it and not them.

The loch isn't large. You could walk around it in half an hour. It looked like it had been there forever, fringed by bull-rushes and trees, but I knew better. This was where we found the cist. The quarry had since been flooded as part of land-scaping measures. Where we had dug, where we had found the beaker and bones, was now deep below still water reflecting ashen sky.

There was a feeling, coming here, of things being wound up, squared off. The flat where my grandparents had lived all their married life had lately been sold, passing out of the family. I had gone up to the attic on my last visit and removed from the dusty eaves that leather suitcase full of papers. The military

and archaeological documents, the old photos: babies in white robes and old men in dark suits – I would look after them now.

Some memories you choose to hold; others you are given to carry.

I remember my brother's death, the moment of it. I don't have a clear picture of the funeral, but I can still see the small white coffin, and feel how I hated that such a thing existed, that it was a necessary object in the world. Later, at school, when we studied Seamus Heaney and I read for the first time 'Mid-Term Break', a poem about the loss of his brother, I recognised in the closing line a blunt anger at the obscenity of a child's dying: 'A four foot box, a foot for every year.'

A lot of old faces coming back.

The people of the past, I feel I can just about touch them.

If I had the beaker with me, there at the loch, I'd have cast it in the waters and watched until the ripples reached the shore.

LOUGH

THE LONG HORIZON of the Irish Sea was an altar laid for mass, a pair of lighthouses the candles.

It was a soothing pleasure to be out on the water, noticing such things. The consolations of analogy: this is like that.

Well, why not? The news had been bad, full of blood and fire, and it had seemed a good moment to take a boat and explore an old mystery, leaving present cares behind for a while. There is a sort of cowardice in seeking solace in the past, a desertion of one's post at the front line of history, but sometimes the headlines are too much, and the desire to get away too great to resist.

From the ferry port of Larne, north of Belfast, a hundred-mile drive had brought me to Boa Island in Lower Lough Erne. I say island, but it isn't really, not any more. Road bridges at both ends connect it to the mainland. They were built in the mid-1920s, following partition, allowing drivers to travel through that part of County Fermanagh, so close to the new border, without having to leave the North and stop at customs.

Boa Island is six miles long and a mile wide. It is home to a hundred or so people. More than there used to be (during the Troubles the population dropped to about seventy) but also far fewer – until the Famine there were closer to nine hundred living here. I was told these things by Douglas Rowe, a farmer in his seventies, who owns the land on which we were standing, as his father did before him.

We were in a small graveyard, Caldragh Cemetery, down a single-track road. Mr Rowe is quietly spoken and it was at times difficult to hear him over the sullen drone of cattle. The cows were in a neighbouring field but couldn't be seen; the burial place is enclosed by a thick green wall of thorn bushes and trees. And just over there, the farmer said, just beyond those trees, is the shore of the lough and a landing place for boats. Coffins, in the old days, would come by water.

Many rough stones poked through the grass, crooked mossy nameless stumps; I had read that this was once a *cillín* – a place for children who, unbaptised, had been forbidden burial in consecrated ground; liminal spaces such as small islands, at the threshold of water, land and sky, were one of the places traditionally used for that sad purpose. Among the old graves, a few newer headstones stood brazen and bright. Burials still take place here; the most recent marked by a wooden cross with flowers at its foot.

Mr Rowe stopped by it for a moment. 'This man drowned. A good fella, he was. A good neighbour. An awful shame.'

He sighed, then turned. 'But the main interest in this grave-yard is of course the Janus stone.' A narrow path of flattened grass led the way.

The Janus, also known as the Dreenan Figure, also known – in the title of Seamus Heaney's poem – as the 'January God', is an idol carved from Carboniferous sandstone. It is about two and a half feet tall, but sits on a concrete plinth, lending it stature and aura. It came up to my breastbone and I felt sorry for the height advantage; there is a strong instinct to lower your head in its presence. The idol has two faces, similar but not identical, wide at the crown and narrowing sharply to the chin, a sort of arrowhead shape, a sort of talon. One face, that looking west, appears to have a moustache and protruding tongue. The other face, looking east and the more weathered, has a cleft chin, the furrow green with moss.

Between the faces, cut into the top of the stone, is a small trough or socket a few inches deep. There have been suggestions that this was made to receive blood, but it seems more likely, given the Irish weather, that it was intended for the collection of rain – and that this was in some way made holy by contact with the idol. There is certainly something of the font or stoup about it, although when I dipped my left hand knuckle-deep, I soon wished I hadn't. The water was brown and stank of cow shite. What unchancy baptism might it grace?

Heaney came to this place in the early 1970s, filming a documentary called *The Loughsiders*. In brown leather jacket and black wellies, still baby-faced in his thirties, he sloshes ashore, encounters the idol and gives it voice: 'I am the god of Boa Island. I am the first god of the first people . . . I bury the winter for them. I resurrect the spring. I look after their dead. I look forward to their children. I fear a new god will destroy me.'

How old is the figure? Who were the people that carved it – and why? The first appearance in the historic record is 1841 when the artist George Du Noyer, visiting the island on 4 September of that year, made three pencil sketches of the stone in his sketchbook. The earliest detailed written reference is a paper presented to the Royal Irish Academy in 1933, by Lady Dorothy Lowry-Corry. 'It would seem certain,' she begins, 'that the stone which I am now about to describe is very ancient.'

For most of the time that the stone has been known beyond Boa, it has been assumed to date from before Christianity's dominance of Ireland. *I fear a new god will destroy me.*

St Patrick, writing as an old man, probably in the late fifth century, refers to *idola et immuna* – idols and unclean things – worshipped by the Irish before their conversion. Yet it wouldn't have been a case of one day you're pagan, the next you're not. It is thought that there was a lengthy period of overlap during which public worship of gods by the elite had come to an end but the old ways persisted in ordinary homes and out-of-the-way places. Think of it, perhaps, as a land with two faces – mindful of the past, watchful of the future.

The archaeologist and curator Helen Hickey has written that the 'advent of Christianity is unlikely to have brought about abrupt changes in such isolated areas as Fermanagh . . . the early missionaries do not appear to have penetrated into this part of Ireland, so that Christian beliefs must have percolated slowly into the region. Christian missionaries tended to be tolerant of pagan practices and where possible modified and transmuted rather than destroyed cherished beliefs. The ancient oral learning was written down without excessive censorship, the poetic traditions were allowed to flourish.'

This tolerance could explain why such a figure is found in the context of a Christian place of burial, although there is also the strong possibility that it was present before the ground was consecrated. Equally, though, it may have been moved here, at a time and for a reason unknown, from some other site. That can happen. Next to the Janus in the cemetery is a stone idol removed from a disused graveyard on a nearby island, Lustymore, and brought to Boa in the 1930s. Lustymore Man is smaller, has just the one face and is more crudely carved – inferior in all respects. Still, he's a bit of company, a good neighbour. The figures have been together for almost a century now, a short time in their long lives, and sit in companionable silence among the unknown dead.

A few years ago there was talk of shifting the Janus. Digging the figure out from the graveyard and bringing it to the city, to a museum where it would be safe. No more would rain fill the hole in the head. No more would wind erode the faces. But the islanders would not have it. Will not have it. Raise the idea and you're soon told.

'If anybody tried to move him?' a local told me. 'Well, I'd smash him before that.'

I don't know if he really meant it, that he'd destroy the Janus rather than see it leave the island. But I understand the urge.

LOUGH

The Boa figure is a national treasure, emblematic of Irish history. You'd place it alongside the Book of Kells, the butter-soft palms of Oldcroghan Man. Yet it is also deeply local, a particular thing of these particular shores. *The first god of the first people*, still, even now, watching over the loughsiders.

Hang on, though, what if the Janus isn't pagan at all? In 2001, during foot-and-mouth, that curse on the land, a museum curator was taking pictures of the statue, slides for a lecture, when he noticed through the viewfinder some odd parallel lines on a stone to one side. What was that? A hand? Two hands, in fact. He had found, half-buried in the earth and grass, a good chunk of the missing lower part of the figure. It now leans up against the concrete plinth and you can, if you wish, but not without a shiver, touch your own hands to those root-like fingers so long hidden from sight.

Curiously, there are aspects of this rediscovered part – the crossed arms, certain details of the figure's garment – which, for those who know about such things, suggest a new interpretation: that it may have been made a few centuries later than first thought; early medieval rather than Iron Age, making it the product of a Christian rather than pagan culture. It may have been carved – I'd been told – at much the same time as the figures on White Island, a little way up the lough.

White Island can only be reached by boat, which I did that afternoon; there was a dark swell, a strong wind from the southwest.

'When you take a boat out on the Erne waters you voyage into time,' Heaney says in *The Loughsiders*. 'Populations come and go; the lough goes on forever. The islands lie like stepping stones in the long river of our past . . . Wherever you look or walk or sail, somebody has been there before you. You can take the pulse of Ulster's history in the slap of waves against the boat.'

Lough Erne, its Lower and Upper parts connected by a river, has more than a hundred and fifty islands in its fifty or so miles, most of them uninhabited. The best known is Devenish, with its old round tower, a suitable confinement for some Irish Rapunzel. In the early centuries of Christianity, these waters would have offered a convenient route between monasteries and churches on the islands and shores. White Island is far smaller than Boa, with a thickly wooded edge and grassy interior. No one lives there, but Highland cattle are grazed between Easter and the end of September. They peered through ginger fringes, as best they could, at the small party of tourists who, just as I arrived, had gathered in the ruins of the little church. The roofless building dates from the twelfth century, and to enter you pass through a beautiful arched doorway. The carved figures within are older – ninth- or tenth-century – and were likely part of an earlier monastic church.

There are eight figures, small statues really, mounted on the wall beneath a modern canopy. They are the first thing you see when walking through the arch. They stare at you with impassive faces and blank eyes. It is a cold sort of greeting, but also a challenge. They seem to ask: *who are we?* The figures appear to be Christian – one, hooded, holds a bell and crozier. But while their biblical identity and meaning would presumably have been apparent to the monks and pilgrims who first knew them, the modern visitor struggles. Would many of us realise that the figure raising his left hand to his mouth is thought to be King David, writer and singer of psalms, and that the bag at his waist – hard to make out now – is a reference to the stones he carried into battle against Goliath?

David's Sling. I had heard those words lately. It is the name given to an air defence system, which had been in news reports on violence in the Middle East. Seeing the statue reminded me. So even here, even on a tiny uninhabited island in a quiet

part of Ireland, there was no escaping the horror of the world. But why should there be? We who are not there, our minds and bodies unharmed, it sometimes feels that all we can do is fill our heads with the pictures, the blood, to wound ourselves with awareness, to not turn our faces away.

The White Island figures are wonderful, but do not have quite the same look, and certainly not the same atmosphere, as the Janus. Yes, there are similarities, in particular the prominence of the oversized heads, which has been seen as a stylistic hangover from pre-Christian sculpture. But while the statues are clearly the work of a master, an artist-monk in some long-ago workshop, the Boa idol seems the offspring of the earth. One imagines it slipping the womb of rock and soil, crowning, pushed up and out into the light, pupils dilating in those four stone eyes, a wild god born to witness the sorrow of this world – yes, and the miracles too.

'My eldest boy . . .'

A man was speaking to the tourist group. I had been taking pictures of the church, not even half-listening, but there was something about his tone, and the quality of their attention, that caught my ear. The man was a stranger to them, but – prompted by the statues, their mute testimony – was telling a personal story.

His son, he said, had been born three months premature with blue-ish skin that signifies low levels of oxygen in the blood. He and his wife, fearing for their baby's life, decided that they had better arrange a baptism as soon as possible. They also went to church, to a service for the sick, at which the minister laid on hands and prayed.

'Well,' the man recalled, 'this warm burning sensation went from my head right down to my toes.'

He felt calm after all the worry and knew at once, in his heart, that the child was going to make it.

'But,' he shrugged, 'you have to have the faith.'

The tourists went on their way. I returned to the boat. A curlew, cruciform, blessed the sky.

WEST

IT WAS A WET WINTER morning in Cornwall and I was looking for a film star in the fields.

What made this harder was that the film star is a stone. But I had its name, Boscawen Ros, and an idea of where, roughly, I might find it; and I certainly knew what it looks like, having been to the cinema to admire its eight slender feet of granite.

'Granite is beyond the reach of clocks,' the filmmaker Christopher Morris says in the voiceover for his documentary *A Year in a Field.* The stone had been set up in the early Bronze Age. Morris, who lives about a mile away, walked to the barley field in which it stands and filmed it on most days between the winter solstice of 2020 and that of 2021. This was, he had told me, 'an unnoticed silent tiny act of rebellion'. Rebellion against what? Mankind's greed and folly, I think; our raptorious velocity. We are the hawk that stoops to kill and our squirming prey is ourselves.

The images Morris gathered during his year in the field are gorgeous: an arrowhead of geese shooting over the stone; the arrow-flights of barley waving by its foot; a bullseye of sunlight around its silhouette. Set against this is his narration, in which he intones the latest statistics and incidents of climate breakdown, the fires and floods and targets missed. 'Our annual rhythms are no longer solstice, equinox and season,' he says, 'but want, take and more. We are engaged in the undoing of the world as we know it.'

When we met in Glasgow, following a screening of the film, I had asked Morris which was the dominant emotion behind his work – wonder or despair?

'Oh wonder,' he replied. 'Wonder drives everything.'

Now, a month or so later, I was in Cornwall to meet his stone for myself. But first I would have to find it.

Cornwall is divided into districts known as 'hundreds'. I was in the hundred of Penwith, right down on the western tip of the peninsula, the crooked upper claw of the Cornish pincer. It is sometimes claimed that there are more standing stones here than anywhere else in England – that's if Cornwall *is* England, which some dispute. 'Penwith is a quintessence of all Cornish scenery,' Jacquetta Hawkes wrote, 'so thick with remains that it is difficult to steer a route among them: the traveller consulting the one-inch Ordnance Survey Map will see that the whole region is grey with Gothic type.'

I couldn't get my map out. It was pouring. But I had planned a day's exploring and would just have to remember the way. The idea was to follow field paths, visit a number of sites and end up at Boscawen Ros.

I'd been reading *The Living Stones*, a book by the surrealist artist and occultist Ithell Colquhoun, who moved to Penwith from London at the end of the 1940s and lived there, off and on, until her death in 1988. 'The whole of Cornwall, and Penwith in particular, needs to be walked over, strolled over, mooned over many times before it can be known,' was her advice. 'Even a bicycle is a hindrance to such communion of person and place . . . The landscape is intensely varied and can change completely in the space of a few paces; and for this reason those who tear through it miss most of its beauty.'

So I was going on foot. Taking it slow. Getting wet. As well as Colquhoun's book, I had been looking at one of her paintings from the 1950s. *Landscape with Antiquities* offers a semi-aerial view of the area, including a number of standing stones. It is somewhere between a map and a dreamscape. Now, in Penwith, I felt I was walking through this picture; the mud under my boots was oil paint newly applied.

The high roadside hedges were full of fruitless brambles and cadmium spatters of late gorse. There was a sense of things hidden away. The trick was to stop at every farm gate and look into the fields. That's how I found Gun Rith, a standing stone more than ten feet tall. It is known as the Fiddler, so you might think it would be the life and soul, but it was backed into a hedge like a shy guest at a party. The Pipers, a pair of enormous stones in neighbouring fields, were more convivial, leaning in to chat over a boundary of red rowans. The Fiddler and Pipers are, according to legend, musicians turned to stone for the sin of playing at a dance on the Sabbath. The dancers themselves, a party of young women who were having such a good time one Saturday night that they did not notice midnight strike, were also petrified – and are now the Merry Maidens, Cornwall's best-known stone circle. Such cautionary tales are common. I had heard the same story at Kiss-in-the-Ring, a circle in Devon. But the Penwith megaliths do have some strange quality that suggests an unceasing consciousness. Ithell Colquhoun had it about right: 'Stones that whisper, stones that dance, that play on pipe or fiddle, that tremble at cock-crow, that eat and drink, stones that march as an army – these unhewn slabs of granite hold the secret of the country's inner life.'

Following the field paths was a romantic idea, and would have been lovely in summer, but my waterproofs were soon slick with farm muck. A white horse leaned over a wall, its neck and body swathed in a heavy brown blanket; it looked like a skull, a Mari Lwyd come galloping down from Wales. Christianity, rather sportingly, had provided a landmark to help me find my way to the pagan places on my list: the church tower of St Buryan periscoped on the horizon as the land rose and fell. Still, I had a job reaching Boscawen-Ûn, a circle of nineteen stones and a twentieth tilted over in the middle, pointing like one hand of a clock. It was here, in September 1928, that the first gathering of the Gorsedh of Cornish bards was held. They wore blue robes, processed from the nearby farm to the circle, and sang 'Land Of My Fathers'. It being a Friday, not Sunday, the Penzance Silver Band was quite safe and no one was turned to granite by an offended God.

The day was wearing on when I came at last to Boscawen Ros. It had stopped raining. I had hardly seen another person since setting out at first light, unless you count the stones. They do feel very much like proxy humans, especially when one comes into their company by oneself. And surely they have always seemed that way, even to those who first set them up? We see ourselves in them and them in us. Anyone who has ever been lonely, or in need of time alone; anyone who has ever felt that life is long, yet short; anyone who has wished to be silent and still – will find those feelings reflected in a standing stone.

Boscawen Ros is in a field off the B3315. If you are heading west, and have gone a little way past the Merry Maidens, the single-track road to St Buryan will be on your right; just before it, on the left, is a lay-by with space for three or four cars, beside which is the Boskenna Cross. Find that and you're almost there.

The Boskenna Cross is lord knows how old. Centuries and centuries. There are many such wayside crosses in Cornwall, vigilants of the verges, censed by exhaust fumes. The Boskenna example is typical: granite with a round head. Facing the road is a crucifixion, carved in relief, the figure lichened and badly worn. A herd of tiny snails, I noticed, were cooried into Christ's body, as if for shelter. It had been sketched in November 1870 by the artist and antiquarian John Thomas Blight, who took a particular interest in the old stone crosses. He was, at that time, struggling badly, and a few months later was committed to St Lawrence's Hospital, the asylum at Bodmin, where he spent the rest of his life, dying in 1911. He has no known grave, and so the ancient places of Cornwall that he loved must stand, collectively, as his monument.

I passed behind the Cross and over a stile; a few rough stone steps through a hedge and into a field. Following the edge around the far end, I came to a second stile. This led into a corner of Longstone Field, as it is known, where Boscawen Ros stands.

'Boscawen' means 'the place of the elder', but there are no trees now. The field was stubble, little brown stalks of harvested barley. It made a popcorny noise as the wind blew. The farmer had worked around the stone, leaving an area of yellowish grass in the approximate shape of a ship, twenty paces from bow to stern. The stone's upper part was covered in a brittle pelt of pale lichen. Beyond the field was a glittering band of silver-blue: the first I'd seen of the sea all day. 'That's its spell,' Christopher Morris had told me. Sparrows chittered round. Crows smutted the sky. The stone did not seem to resent the presence of one drawn by its recent fame. So I sat down, leaned against its comfortable bulk, and poured a cup of tea.

I was thinking about what megaliths can mean to people. For Ithell Colquhoun they were, in some sense, alive. Barbara Hepworth thought Cornwall's prehistoric landscape 'Unconquerable and strange, and my God how sculptural.' Katherine Mansfield, writing to a friend from Penwith in the summer of 1916, complained that 'I am very much alone here. It is not really a nice place. It is so full of huge stones . . .'

Christopher Morris had found Boscawen Ros by accident, out walking very early one morning, having moved to Cornwall from his native Wales a short time before. He was lost, and there it was, a native greeting a newcomer. They are now on intimate terms. Having filmed it for a year and taken countless photographs before and since, he knows every granite inch. As to *why* it has become so important to him, that is more complicated.

'In a destabilised world, everybody is desperate for an anchor point,' he had told me.

He walks to the stone when life feels dark. When the world is beset by pain, and politics seems not just ineffectual but actively cruel. Which is to say: quite often.

'What are you seeking?' I had asked him. 'Consolation? Comfort?'

No, that wasn't quite it.

'The stone,' he replied, 'has been there for so long that it's seen it all come and go. And somehow I do find it cathartic to visit. In the same way, even though I'm not religious, I find that to sit silently in a church is similar to what I experience at these ancient places.'

Old churches, old stones. There has been a surge of interest in archaeology, folklore and faith in the last few years; in the arts this has found expression in the vogue for nature writing and folk horror. It is tempting to regard this as a form of escapism, a desire to retreat from a difficult present, to sit on the couch, turn off the news and relax with *Digging for Britain*. But I suspect it's a bit more complicated.

Tom Templar of Green Lung believes that it is to do with a post-Brexit crisis in national identity. 'Why does English culture have to be Winston Churchill?' he had said when we spoke. 'It can be whatever you want it to be. For me, this kind of stuff is the most compelling way to explore Britishness.' Nostalgia can be toxic; prehistory offers detox.

I had recently gone online and watched a lecture titled 'Prehistory for Antifascists'. Dr Ben Pitcher of the University of Westminster argued that in 'a historical moment when it is easier to imagine the end of the world than the end of capitalism, we are turning to the distant human past to explore those really big existential questions about who we are, where we came from, and what we are like'.

'So, what do *you* think is going on?' I had asked Christopher Morris. 'What's behind the current fascination with our ancient ancestors and their monuments?'

He considered this. 'Is it simply because, faced with something as overwhelming as climate change, we are desperate to find the old ways?'

'Maybe,' I said. 'But for most people that won't be conscious. It's more of a feeling, surely?'

'Yes,' he replied. 'A feeling lots of us are having. The key is that it's *pre*history – an unwritten time that leaves a lot of room for personal connection and understanding. Mystery is so important in a world where everything is on your phone.'

A stone is the opposite of a screen. You can't swipe limestone or doom-scroll granite. We spend so much of our lives online that there is a great need, I think, for the tangible – for the feeling of rock under the fingers, earth under the feet. And yes, not knowing all the answers about these places may be healthy, too. A necessary humbling.

When Daniel Defoe came to Cornwall in the early eighteenth century, he visited the circle of Boscawen-Ûn and later set down his impression of the stones. All that can be learned of them, he wrote, is that here they are.

*

The following morning I was on the road again. Driving inland from Lamorna, where Ithell Colquhoun had lived and died, to the high moors between Madron and Morvah.

Every road sign was a treat. In Penwith, almost all place names are Cornish. The Cornish language Kernewek, now experiencing a revival, derives from the same linguistic root as Welsh and Breton. That ancient tongue, which language scholars call Common Brythonic, was also spoken in those parts of northern England and southern Scotland sometimes referred to as Yr Hen Ogledd, the Old North – and probably by the Picts, a tribal people further north in Scotland. Kernewek had died out as a native language by the beginning of the nineteenth century, but persists in the place names, so the traveller in Cornwall has a strong feeling of passing through a landscape that was known and named long ago. You can just about hear the voices. Jacquetta Hawkes, writing in *A Land*, saw the evolution of place names as a geological process, a kind of erosion:

> As the generations pass on these names from one to the other, successive tongues wear away the syllables just as water and wind smooth the rocks; so they become rounded, slip more easily from tongue to tongue, perhaps lose their meaning, yet grow more and more closely attached to the land itself. So closely, indeed, that often place names outlast the language that made them, remaining as evidence of the former presence of dispossessed or submerged peoples.

I pulled into a small car park off a single-track road. I had arranged to meet the founders of Stone Club, and they – Matthew Shaw and Lally MacBeth – arrived before long. It was wet and windy and the ground was boggy, but they were undaunted. 'This weather is *good*,' Lally said. 'We might have Mên-an-Tol to ourselves.'

That was our destination. Mên-an-Tol, which means 'holed stone', is probably Cornwall's best-known prehistoric monument. Two uprights flank a round central stone with a hole in the middle. It looks like a piece of binary code, or as if a Barbara Hepworth sculpture had fallen from its plinth and rolled here from St Ives.

The hole, believed to be natural, is close to the ground and a foot and half or so in diameter, allowing those who are willing and able to crawl right through. It is thought to have been set up somewhere between the late Neolithic and middle Bronze Age; its purpose, like its date, is uncertain. Some speculate that it was once part of a stone circle, others that the holed stone formed the entrance to a tomb. Mysterious and Instagrammable, it's a very Stone Club sort of place.

Stone Club has four rules:

1) The first rule of Stone Club is to tell everyone about Stone Club.

2) Stone Club is for everyone.

3) Pack a mac and pack a snack.

4) Rules are for breaking.

In observance of the first rule, let me tell you about Stone Club. Anyone who was in the Dennis the Menace Fan Club will recognise the capering spirit. Upon joining, at the cost of a few pounds, you receive a badge, membership card and welcome letter, which explains that 'Stone Club is a place for all stone enthusiasts to congregate, to muse and most importantly to stomp to stones.'

Matthew and Lally founded the club towards the end of 2021, driven by a post-lockdown desire to get out into the light, reconnect with landscape and foster a sense of fellowship and well-being. Do you remember that experience, during the pandemic, of seeing your own patch with clarity and intensity as never before? That feeling for place is what Stone Club taps into. There are regular events, open to everyone, with talks, music, film screenings and so on, as well as occasional 'picnics' – meet-ups at stone circles and other sites. Stone Club, with its strong online presence, is a digital community with a hand-made vibe. There's nothing ironic about it, nothing hipstery try-hard. It's wholesome and sincere; serious in a fun way. There is a 'gentle activism' which finds its most explicit expression in campaigning for the right to access ancient monuments on private land. Rules, remember, are for breaking. But in the end, it's all about the stones: visiting the famous places, tracking down the obscure, planning the next trip – and the next and the next and the next. 'It's a never-ending odyssey,' is how Matthew put it.

Stone Club is for everyone. That's the second rule. The ancient past, in its blankness, offers a more generous space, a neutral space, a time before the kinds of political and religious authority that we now recognise, and certainly before any of our present culture warring around identity, which is made ever more bellicose by social media. Stone Club is about leaving that behind, at least for a while, and sharing the pleasures of the physical world. You don't get much more IRL than a big granite stone.

'When we meet at sites we always encourage people, in a very light way, to go there as those who have something in common,' Matthew said. 'Like, all of us are here today because we want to see Mên-an-Tol. If we start with that, we can come together and share other things along the way. It doesn't matter who you are. These spaces don't care whether I think I'm English or Cornish or Welsh. Mên-an-Tol doesn't care what I am.'

Matthew and Lally are a couple. They met through a shared interest in Ithell Colquhoun. Matthew is an artist, writer and musician with a background in green activism. He has recorded three albums in Boleigh Fogou, an eerie underground passage dating from the Iron Age. 'The third was just the sound of the fogou itself,' he laughed. 'We got really purist.'

His love of old stones began while growing up in Sandbach, Cheshire, informed in part by the Saxon crosses in the market square and partly by childhood reading of Alan Garner, whose imaginative fiefdom, Alderley Edge, was a common place for family walks. *The Weirdstone of Brisingamen*, one of the Garner novels Matthew read as a boy, contains a passage that could almost be the Stone Club creed: 'Rocks are old, stubborn souls; they were here before we came, and they will be here when we are gone. They have all the time there is, and will not be hurried.'

We set off down a track, in no great rush, leaning into the gusts.

The third rule of Stone Club, pack a mac, goes some way to explaining why a little wind and rain doesn't put them off. The club is an all-weather endeavour. That said, Lally in particular does not seem the cagoule sort. She is an artist, writer and curator in her thirties, studied fashion history and theory at Saint Martins college, and had turned up for our walk in a blue dress, green wellies, a bright-yellow corduroy jacket, mulberry beret and a scarlet cupid's bow of lipstick. She has a particular interest in folk custom. The previous evening she had been dancing with the WAD, an all-female morris side based in Falmouth. During performances she wears a wicker dunce's cap and plays The Fool.

It was only a short walk from our cars to the stones. Half a mile or so. Not much chance of getting lost, but then – as Lally said – 'You never get lost in Cornwall, only piskey-led.'

Piskies are the fairy folk who inhabit quiet and lonely places. Nothing gives them greater satisfaction than leading travellers from the right path. Lally's morris side takes its name from Joan the Wad, queen of the piskies in the old Cornish stories.

I once spent a day walking in Devon with a man called Dartmoor Paul. As a child he had been taken every Sunday by his parents to a cave in Sheeps Tor, where they would leave a sixpence and a pin for the piskies known to live there. The pin was so the little people could mend their clothes, the money was – I suppose – a premium against misdirection. I am not saying that those years of insurance payments are why Dartmoor Paul never now gets lost, but he navigates that often featureless landscape without recourse to a map and has done for almost fifty years as a guide. He also shared, during our time together, a tip for what to do if you are being piskey-led: turn your coat inside out. The piskies will no longer recognise you, and you'll find your way back home.

Given the weather, I did not turn my coat inside out on the way to Mên-an-Tol. Besides, I was with people who had walked this route many times. We passed derelict farm buildings and fields enclosed by the heavy stone walls known as Cornish hedges. The drystane dykes of Scotland, which I know so well, are frail in comparison. There was no question that we were in 'the granite kingdom' – as the poet Charles Causley described Cornwall.

We turned off the track and on to a path through heather, leading to the grassy clearing of Mên-an-Tol. Lally had warned

that some people find the stones disappointingly small, but I liked their modesty. The human scale was inviting.

Whatever the intention of its builders, Mên-an-Tol has continued to be used, and in this sense it is a living place. The site has long been associated with healing. Tradition has it that children suffering from tuberculosis and rickets should be passed through the hole three times; adults with spinal problems and other miseries must go through nine times on hands and knees, which can't be much fun with a bad back. According to Daphne du Maurier, to suffer from nightmares was to be 'hilla-ridden' – and Mên-an-Tol could cure that, too. Ithell Colquhoun crawled through the hole in an effort to ease her rheumatism, but declared herself disappointed in the result, 'not knowing that in order to be effective the rite should be performed in a state of nudity'.

The distinctive silhouette of Ding Dong Mine – its ruined engine house and chimney – was visible on the horizon. Such industrial relics, memorials to the strength and courage of miners, are as redolent as the megaliths of a lost past; and of course there would have been no Bronze Age without tin, so it feels appropriate that Ding Dong has a visual relationship with Mên-an-Tol. The mines drew men deep in pursuit of ore; the holed stone offers an intangible resource – lore, the raw material which gives a place its enchantment.

One of Mên-an-Tol's other names, the Devil's Eye, suggests that that the stories about it have not always been benign. Prehistoric structures quite often have names of that sort, indicating that they were seen by communities who lived near them, but did not understand their origins, as supernatural, even diabolical. The Devil's Arrows in Yorkshire, the Devil's Den in Wiltshire, the Devil's Quoits in Oxfordshire. Dartmoor Paul had taken me to Grim's Grave, a Bronze Age cist with a name that may derive from grīma, an Old English word for ghost, or from Grim, thought to have been used as a name for the god Woden. Grime's Graves is a Neolithic flint mine in Norfolk; Grimspound is a Bronze Age settlement in Devon. Carn Kenidjack, not far from the Penwith town of St Just, is Cornish for 'the Hooting Cairn'. It was to this rocky place that the devil led two tin miners one evening to watch a wrestling match between demons; it is said, even now, when the wind catches it right, to echo with the howls of infernal combatants and spectators.

The further west you travel in Cornwall, Daphne du Maurier wrote, the deeper you go into superstition and folk belief: 'Spells, charms, curses, wishes, these things sometimes had more power than prayer.' It was her opinion that the Reformation had an uncommon impact on the Cornish people; with Catholic ritual and imagery forbidden, and certain emotional needs no longer met, they found solace in the old magic – not necessarily as practitioners, of course, but as people who understood themselves to be living in a numinous world, where 'the spirits that were in the sacred wells, on hill-tops and in groves, beneath the stones and in the hollows of the earth, gave an answer to the emptiness within'.

Does any of this feeling persist? There is certainly an atmosphere in Penwith, perhaps better felt in the off-season, an energy that is somehow, I don't know how, bound up with the waves in Lamorna Cove, the bristle of lichen on Boscawen Ros and the spider eggs in Boleigh Fogou, small moons in that vast night. Philip Marsden, in *Rising Ground*, writes about calling in at the Penwith home of his friend, the painter Jeremy Le Grice, who tells him that 'There *is* something about this place. The more I think about it, the less I can really put my finger on it. People talk about the light . . . But that's nonsense. It's something innate. I think of it as a secret buried in the land. It's not something you see – it's something you *feel*.'

Of course, we all went through the stone: first Matthew, then Lally, then me. That meant going on hands and knees through a puddle where the ground dips. I didn't feel reborn, I felt cold and wet, but a moment's discomfort was worth it to join the generations who have crawled the same way. There is something reassuring about the monument and the long tradition attached to it. What was it Christopher Morris had said? Everyone needs an anchor point. Well, here is Mên-an-Tol, a mooring ring offering safe harbour in a stormy time.

Lally put it best, as we turned back to the path through the moor: 'The world is falling apart, but the holed stone is always here.'

*

PENTRE IFAN invites metaphors. It is a church, says a poet. It is a picture frame, says an archaeologist, through which the ancients regarded the landscape. A mathematician might see it as *pi* – by pleasing coincidence, its initial letters – and wonder what strange problem it might solve. Look, though, at how its capstone points over the Pembrokeshire countryside to the blue haze of the sea, as if about to slide down a slipway to the water. 'The megaliths do move,' writes Pamela Petro, an American author with a particular love for this place. 'They're the only ships we've ever built that sail through time.'

The name means 'Ifan's Village', although who Ifan was, and when he lived, and how he came to be associated with the emblematic site of Welsh prehistory is unknown. Pentre Ifan is a dolmen: a type of Neolithic monument – known in Wales as a cromlech and in Cornwall as a quoit – characterised by a huge capstone supported by upright stones. They are often referred to as tombs, and it has been argued that the big stones were the framework for burial mounds that have been lost over time, so what we see now is essentially the skeleton of the building. The

'grand but gentle presence' of Pentre Ifan, Jan Morris believed, 'can only commemorate some kind and useful life, and a calm and hopeful end to it.'

However, excavations of dolmens have found little in the way of human remains, or, in the case of Pentre Ifan, none at all, so it could be that these were not places of the dead, or at least that was not their primary purpose. This is much debated. Maybe they were meant to do what they still do now: blow our minds. They were 'the cathedrals of the Neolithic', Professor Vicki Cummings has written, 'amazing constructions with great importance in people's belief systems'. Just as the medieval cathedrals used technological advances to send their spires soaring heavenwards, so the dolmens can be seen as grand architectural flourishes, demonstrations of human will and skill to some spiritual end. They were, perhaps, a kind of sacralised showing off.

I visited Pentre Ifan in late September. It was a golden afternoon, the sort of light you wish you could cut with a sickle and store over winter.

The monument can be described without difficulty. Here are the bare bones: the capstone is sixteen and a half feet long, weighs around sixteen tons, and is held about eight feet from the ground by three uprights, two at the back and one at the front. These supporting stones taper to points, so the great weight is being kept up by no more than three fingertips. This is what cannot be so easily conveyed – the effect on eye and mind. It looks and feels like a magic trick, a sequinned assistant floating up from a table. It is not like Avebury or Stonehenge, where you can almost smell the toilsome sweat; Pentre Ifan delights rather than awes because it is a hard thing made to look easy. It is elegant, suave, effortless; the Cary Grant of stones.

Set in a rectangle of close-cropped grass fenced off from more rugged farmland, the monument is near a road and, as a result, is never long without a visitor. A small white dog called Gracie was running in and out of the stones, pink tongue lolling, excited to be there. I knew how she felt.

I walked over and stood beneath the capstone. Old illustrations suggest that it is possible to pass under it on horseback while wearing a top hat. Having neither horse nor hat, I reached up and stroked the underside. From within the cromlech, the landscape becomes a picture in a frame – and everything you see takes on a greater significance. To the west is Carn Ingli, the Mountain of Angels, the angle of the capstone seeming to mirror the shape of its slope. On the skyline to the south-west are the rocky outcrops known as Carnedd Meibion Owen, the Cairns of the Sons of Owen, which are said to be the petrified bodies of giants who fought to the death over the right to inherit their father's land. To the south are the Preseli Hills, the source of Stonehenge's bluestones. The archaeologists Vicki

Cummings and Alasdair Whittle, in their book *Places of Special Virtue*, suggest that this spot was chosen because it offered views of these features, which may have been regarded as sacred sites associated with origin myths, and that the monument itself – a great stone raised up – embodies an idea of creation: 'the first rising of the earth'.

Ancient monuments are good places for reflection upon one's own origins and past. We change, they do not, so we can measure our lives against them. How many people reading this book, I wonder, have pictures of themselves as children on days out to circles and standing stones? The grown-ups who took us, who lifted us to sit on the stones, may well be gone, and we will be quite different from our childhood selves, but the monuments stay much the same. They are the constant, we are the variables, and thus they become places of memory and personal association. In her essay on Pentre Ifan, the poet Gillian Clarke recalls a family picnic in the 1940s:

> It was like a church, its stone roof balanced like a feather on its pillars, each window the wind's eye. The oldest roof in Wales, the oldest building, yet not so holy you had to whisper, not too sacred for cheese sandwiches and *bara brith* spread with Ga's salty home-churned butter and a bag of windfall apples and a flask of sweet tea.

Before leaving for Pembrokeshire, I had spoken with Pamela Petro. She was in Cambridge, Massachusetts, where she teaches creative writing, but was happy to turn her thoughts to Wales and in particular to Pentre Ifan, her favourite place in the world.

She was raised in New Jersey – amid malls and housing developments and cloverleaf highways – where she had a feeling of being cut off from history and from the physical reality of the planet. 'I was a kid who wanted some sense of anchorage. And I didn't find it.' So Wales, when she first went there to study in 1983, became emblematic of all she had lacked growing up. 'It was a place where I felt I could go back in time. It almost demanded that I *imagine*, in the way that New Jersey seemed to shut down my imagination. It felt like a portal. Not in any mystical way, but just to touch – concretely and imaginatively – the past.'

Pam visited Pentre Ifan during her first days in Wales. 'I felt I'd come home to a place that was larger than my experience and my self and my family,' she told me. 'This was a homecoming to humanity. To everything that represents us: our longing for stone to express our wishes well past our mortal years; our sense of design and place and imagination; our sense of mystery, because we can't ever know exactly what they meant by it. And you know what? It's just *beautiful.* Beyond all of this thought, there's a visceral strength and beauty and endurance that grabs me each time.'

She has made around thirty trips to Wales in the years since that first encounter. She was in her early twenties when she first came to Pentre Ifan; she is now in her early sixties and hopes to continue to make the pilgrimage for the rest of her life. To this place of meaning, she has taken the people who mean the most; parents, partner, friends. If the monument was built as a way of looking out at the landscape, for Pam it functions as a way of looking in at her lifescape – stories, feelings, identity, losses. She has written a memoir, *The Long Field*, but in a way the monument is her book, embodying and expressing personal history. Pentre Ifan, she writes, is 'an equation created by place and stone and time that needs only my witnessing presence to be solved'.

What a great line. It made me consider, when I first read it, whether it's true of all the megalithic sites. Do they require us now, whenever our now is, to be complete? Perhaps human presence around the old stones functions like an enzyme; our attention is the catalyst that creates a reaction, producing emotion and memory. Some of us need them, that is clear, but they need us too. The human imagination, Pam said, is 'the invisible fourth stone' holding up Pentre Ifan's capstone. We raised the monuments, we forgot why we did so, and now keep them alive through our wondering and our wonder.

*

I left Pentre Ifan and drove north out of Pembrokeshire into Ceredigion. A little beyond the village of Llanrhystud, at a bend in the road overlooking a valley, I pulled off the A487. I had come to see a monument with a far more recent history.

The lay-by was separated from fields by scrubby growth and the stubby remains of a low wall. Behind the wall was the gable end of a ruined cottage. Just over half of its surface was covered in red paint – on which was written two words in white block capitals, one above the other.

COFIWCH

DRYWERYN

There was no interpretation panel to explain the meaning and history, as there would be with an ancient site, but the presence of a security camera suggested that this was not ordinary graffiti. It required and deserved protection.

'Cofiwch Dryweryn' means 'Remember Tryweryn'. The wall was painted as a protest against plans by Liverpool Corporation, backed by the UK government, to flood the Tryweryn Valley in order to create a reservoir supplying the people of Liverpool.

Despite a nine-year opposition campaign, the project went ahead in 1965. The valley – and Capel Celyn, the village within it – was flooded, with the loss of twelve farms, a school, a methodist chapel, a post office and the homes of seventy-five people who had been forced to move. A few bodies were exhumed from the cemetery at the request of families who could not abide the thought of loved ones abandoned to the deep, but the rest are still there, graves sealed beneath concrete. In periods of significant drought, the level drops enough that the walls of the burial ground and what remains of the chapel emerge from the amnesiac water.

Jacquetta Hawkes, remember, wrote about the 'submerged peoples' whose ancient presence could be inferred from place names. I had noted the truth of that in Cornwall. Here in Wales the submersion of a village and way of life were suggested by those words, Cofiwch Dryweryn. It is said to have been a place of poetry and music. 'The people of Capel Celyn are an integral part of the pattern of one of the richest folk cultures in Europe,' declared Gwynfor Evans, the Plaid Cymru leader, in a pamphlet of 1956. 'No civilised person would wish to see such a community of high artistic and intellectual attainment invaded and destroyed by an alien institution.'

The flooding of the valley was regarded as an expression of English arrogance and power: Wales treated not as a partner in a union but a resource to be exploited. The fight against the plan was more than politics; it was seen in spiritual terms, a battle for the soul. The reservoir was described in a poem of 1956 as 'the devil's dam'. A letter sent to Liverpool Corporation in the same year expressed a view that the people of Tryweryn should 'shoot the first devil that puts his foot in the valley'. The Devil's Quoits. The Devil's Den. The Devil's Dam. When the day of judgement comes, one villager wondered, how are the dead of Capel Celyn, kept down by concrete, supposed to rise from their graves?

Tryweryn was politicising; Gwynfor Evans was elected to Westminster in 1966, Plaid Cymru's first MP. And it was radicalising; sparking a bombing campaign and leading indirectly to the many arson attacks on holiday cottages and second homes that took place between 1979 and 1991. There is something elemental about the story: the earth of the valley, the water of the lake, the vengeful fire. Something fearful, too. 'There are places in Wales I don't go,' wrote the poet R. S. Thomas:

> Reservoirs that are the subconscious
> Of a people, troubled far down
> With gravestones, chapels, villages even;

Within this political and cultural context, the Cofiwch Dryweryn wall has become an almost sacred expression and symbol of Welsh consciousness and nationalist feeling. However, it has also been a contested place, the words painted out a number of times and even, in 2019, the gable end partly demolished. Remember Tryweryn? Some think it better to forget. *Anghofiwch*. Wales should be more than a history of grievance.

Yet, in response to those destructive acts, the words have been painted at dozens of locations across Wales, and the original has been restored. Vandalism of historic buildings is a blight. Even Pentre Ifan was subject to a graffiti attack a few years ago. But in the case of Cofiwch Dryweryn, the graffiti itself is the cultural heritage. 'This is no static monument,' Rhys Mwyn writes in *Cam i'r Deheubarth*, his account of the archaeology of south-west Wales. 'Part of the wall and the original paint may be long gone, but the slogan is a living thing . . .'

It was painted in 1963 or 1964 by Meic Stephens, a young man living in a commune of nationalist activists in Merthyr Tydfil. The year is uncertain because he did not record it in his diary, not wishing to incriminate himself. He was part of a group engaged in painting political graffiti at prominent locations, including on the front of Cyfarthfa Castle. Stephens, by the time of his death in 2018, was a prominent man of letters much admired for his advancement of Welsh language and

literature. He wrote and edited many books in his life, but understood that those two words, Cofiwch Dryweryn, had a significance beyond the rest of his work. They were, he said, 'my most famous statement, my most eloquent poem, my most important political act'.

His choice of verb is interesting: *Cofiwch.* The slogan was painted before the valley was flooded, and yet it doesn't say Save Tryweryn or Justice For Tryweryn. It says, *Remember* – as if the village was already underwater and the present already the past. I arranged to speak with Huw Stephens, the radio DJ, about this. Meic Stephens was his father.

'I think of it as a warning,' Huw said of the graffiti. 'You're right, it didn't say Save Tryweryn or Stop the Drowning, or anything like that. It wasn't a protest in that way. It was an understanding that this was happening because of the system, and that future generations must remember what happened – for when it happens again.'

Political graffiti is, by its nature, ephemeral. It comes and goes. 'Cofiwch Dryweryn' has lasted, perhaps, because it was painted on to a ruin that, for a long time, nobody much cared about – a location chosen simply because the words would be seen and read by anyone passing on the road. The cottage, which was called Troedyrhiw, has been uninhabited, as best I can tell, since around the time of the First World War. Its roof, when it had a roof, was thatched. Looking at the place now, a shell thick with nettles, it is hard to credit anyone ever having lived there. But they did. It was divided into two properties. In one lived Sam Mitchell, a Boer War veteran, with his wife and children. The other half of the cottage was home to Winnie Griffiths and her brother John, a farm worker. It is worth setting those names down here, I think, to honour the graffiti's insistence on memory.

I learned about the history of Troedyrhiw from the journalist and broadcaster Betsan Powys. She learned it from her mother, Rhiannon, who grew up on a nearby farm.

Betsan had made an excellent podcast, *Drowned – The Flooding of a Village*, telling the story of Tryweryn and exploring the political and cultural repercussions. When we spoke on the phone, I asked what she sees as being the significance of the graffiti in Wales now? 'It's defiance,' she replied. 'It's: *We are still here.* That's what the wall is all about. It's saying that life can be tough, and it's really hard to keep the Welsh language going in a global world, but it's still here. We're still here.'

Her emphasis on language is important. It was always part of the anxiety around Tryweryn that it was a community of Welsh speakers; the flooding of the valley was understood as a further erosion of a cultural identity being worn away by modernity. And although it is now known that it was Meic Stephens who painted the words on the ruined cottage, for many years the graffiti was anonymous – as if no one person, but the very stuff of Wales itself was urging us to remember; old stones speaking the old tongue.

'The substance of Welsh nature', Jan Morris once wrote,

> is largely rock, for some four-fifths of the surface of Wales is hard upland, where the soil is so thin that stones seem always to be forcing their way restlessly through . . . The ancient constancy of the stones provides a permanent con-solation to the Welsh people. Whether they are suffering from political grievance or economic distress, whether they are homesick far away or lonely at their own firesides, the great old shapes provide a kind of reassurance.

There is a word, *hiraeth*, that seems to connect Cofiwch Dryweryn with Pentre Ifan. Those who speak both languages sometimes say that this noun is difficult to translate into English because it signifies an emotion that is distinctly Welsh, a kind of ache in the soul, a homing instinct that can never be satisfied because the thing for which you long – it could be a place, a person, a time – is impossible to reach.

The cromlech and the old wall, statements in the landscape, are sites of *hiraeth* because both are places of remembrance and yearning. If Pentre Ifan *was* a tomb, then it was raised as a memorial to a person or people whose absence demanded some sort of compensatory presence. But even if no one was ever buried there, and its purpose was otherwise, it stands now for a past that is beyond us, that we can barely imagine let alone visit: the childhood of our species. So, too, with Cofiwch Tryweryn. *Remember*, it insists – a command that is really a lament, a whisper, a breeze in the barley, a passing bell heard across a valley and soon falling into silence.

WALL

WHY WALK THE Antonine Wall? Because it isn't there.

It's not like Hadrian's Wall, which is beautiful and romantic, a symphony in stone rising and falling with the Northumberland countryside. The Antonine Wall, constructed during the reign of Antoninus Pius, Hadrian's adopted son and successor as emperor, has all but vanished from Scotland. The rampart was made from stacked layers of turf, far less durable than masonry. What you mostly notice now, when you can see anything at all, are the remains of the deep, wide ditch that the Romans dug in front of their wall. To walk its thirty-seven miles, as I did over four days, is a work of the mind as well as the body, and asks as much of the imagination as the legs. It is an act of recomposition: lost music played from a fragment of manuscript page.

We – I had my youngest with me, a boy of sixteen – had chosen to make the journey from east to west, the direction in which the Wall is thought to have been built. We began in Bo'ness on the south bank of the Firth of Forth.

It was the day of the annual Children's Fair. At eight on a sunny morning the place was buzzing. Bo'ness is short for Borrowstounness. Naming their town is the only thing people here do by halves. The Fair, which takes place on the last Friday in June, is spectacular; the highlight of the local calendar since 1897. The central ritual is the crowning of a schoolgirl as Fair Queen. The coronation takes place amid much hoopla and pomp, a curious and delightful mix of formal pageantry and pop-culture glitz. It is, above all, an expression of local pride. Lots of the old mining towns in Scotland's central belt have fair days and galas, but none on quite this scale. Most extraordinary

of all are the frontages, known as arches, which many Bo'nes-
sian families construct in front of their homes. Disney castles,
medieval fortresses, fairyland grottoes – anything goes. This
was the sight that greeted us as we set out to walk the Wall. Not
much to do with the Romans, but proof, I suppose, that almost
two thousand years later, people round here still build big.

The Antonine Wall was laid upon the waist of Scotland, its
most slender part, in or around AD 142. During its twenty or so
years of occupation, it marked the north-western frontier of
the Roman Empire. Tacitus, writing about an earlier military
advance, had noted the strategic advantage of the estuaries: 'The
Clyde and Forth, carried inland to a great depth on the tides
of opposite seas, are separated only by a narrow neck of land.
This isthmus was now firmly held by garrisons, and the whole
expanse of country to the south was safely in our hands. The
enemy had been pushed into what was virtually another island.'

That victory belonged to Agricola, the general and governor
of Britain, who later fought his way even further north, winning
the Battle of Mons Graupius, which may have taken place at the
foot of the Aberdeenshire hill we now call Bennachie. Ahead
of the engagement, the Caledonian leader Calgacus addressed
his gathered warriors. This famous speech, believed to have
been invented by Tacitus as a rhetorical flourish, is a stirring
evocation of liberty, courage and honour; it is also a scornful
denunciation of imperialism and doublespeak. The Romans
'are the only people on earth to covet wealth and poverty with
equal craving. They plunder, they butcher, they ravish, and call
it by the lying name of "empire". They make a desert and call it
"peace".'

Despite inferior numbers, the Romans won the day. Ten
thousand Caledonians, almost a third of their force, lay dead.
Yet their losses, and the far smaller numbers of Roman casual-
ties, were for nothing. The Emperor Domitian, said to have

been jealous and fearful of Agricola's success, recalled him to Rome and gave up the advances he had secured. Tacitus writes that *perdomita Britannia statim omissa* – Britain was conquered and was immediately lost.

Around sixty years later, however, the lands of the north were once again coveted by Rome. A new emperor, Antoninus Pius, came to the throne in AD 138 and ordered his legions to push beyond Hadrian's Wall. Why he did so is uncertain. Scholars have suggested that he needed to shore up his power and reputation with military success.

Whatever his reasons, the tribal people of northern Britannia would suffer the consequences. According to a fourth-century biography of the emperor, his army built a *murus caespiticius* – a wall of turf – 'when the barbarians had been driven back'. That little word, turf, tempts one to regard the Antonine Wall as flimsy and bodged, a bit 'will-this-do?' But that would be a mistake.

It had a stone base at least fourteen feet wide; this still exists for much of its length, hidden underground. The rampart, built from stacked blocks of turf, sloped inwards as it rose and is estimated to have reached a height of at least ten feet. This may have been topped by a wooden palisade and walkway, adding further height. Twenty to thirty feet north of the rampart – in other words, closer to the 'barbarians' – was a V-shaped ditch about forty feet wide and twelve deep. The earth dug out was flung northwards, forming a further obstacle known as the outer mound. The berm, the area between the rampart and ditch, is thought to have contained pits of thorns and sharpened stakes. To the south of the rampart was the military way, a wide road connecting all the forts and fortlets, allowing troops and supplies to move at speed.

Information panels along the line of the Wall state that it was defended by a force of around five thousand men. Some experts estimate that it was more than that, others less, but five thousand would make it far more densely policed than Hadrian's Wall – from which we can infer that a great force, or at least a show of force, was needed. It may be a challenge to picture now, when it has all but vanished, but this structure must have been intimidating. 'Even a distant view of the great frontier would impress the native beholder with a sense of his own helplessness against the power and majesty of Rome,' the archaeologist Anne S. Robertson has written.

The Wall was built by soldiers from the Second, Sixth and Twentieth Legions. We know this because of objects, usually referred to as 'distance slabs', discovered in the vicinity over centuries. These are inscribed stones, rather like road signs, carved with scenes of Roman victory and information about the Wall's construction that are no less boastful for being in abbreviated Latin. To give an example: the central panel of the biggest and best of the slabs, which was found in Bridgeness (now part of Bo'ness) in 1868, bears the words, IMP CAES TITO AELIO HADRI ANTONINO AVG PIO P P LEG II AVG PER M P IIIIDCLII FEC. It means – more or less – 'For the Emperor Caesar Titus Aelius Hadrianus Antoninus Pius, Father of his Country, the Second Augustan Legion completed a distance of 4,652 paces.' A Roman pace was around five feet.

If this sounds like dry stuff, the slab is enlivened by action scenes. A Roman on horseback gallops over four naked warriors, cloak flying like a flag; the spear in his right hand is about to be plunged into enemy flesh. The warriors are in a bad way. One has a shaft sticking out from his back. Another, arms bound, has been executed. His severed head looks out at the viewer, a gaze that conveys an unmistakable message: do not resist; give up your land and your freedom or else give up your lives. The scene to the right of the slab shows the sacrifice of a pig, a sheep

and a bull – a ritual carried out to purify the legion and perhaps seek the blessing of Mars, the god of war. Blood spilled in battle, blood spilled in the temple, the Antonine Wall was born of its flow.

Of course, how we see the Wall depends on where, in history, we are standing. When Britain was an imperial power out to devour the world, the territorial hunger of Rome was regarded as a benevolent and civilising force; for so we saw ourselves. The artist and writer Jesse Mothersole walked the length of Hadrian's Wall in 1920 (supposedly the first woman to do so) and the Antonine Wall in 1927. She admired the former for its 'plain straightforward purpose', which she understood as being to bring peace and stability to Britain under the 'righteous' rule of the Romans. 'In all ages the building of walls has marked a stage of advance in the evolution of human character,' she wrote, 'in so far as it has meant a progress from the offensive to the defensive position.' It is hard to imagine such a sentence being set down now. When she writes about the Bridgeness slab, she describes the purification ritual but does not mention the decapitation.

That the distance slabs have survived in reasonable condition is thought to result from them having been taken down and concealed by the Roman army during withdrawal from the frontier in the years following the death of Antoninus Pius in AD 161. Buried face down, they escaped the blade of the plough. Nineteen have been found, although only eighteen now exist, one having been purchased soon after discovery by the United States consul in Newcastle-upon-Tyne. He paid £2 to acquire the slab and had it shipped to America, intending it for a museum, but it was lost in the Chicago Fire of 1871.

Almost half of the total number of slabs were discovered in the eighteenth and nineteenth centuries as central Scotland experienced industrialisation and the intensification of agriculture. The most recent find was in 1969. There are almost certainly more out there, under the ground, awaiting their moment to astonish. The Bridgeness slab can be seen at the National Museum of Scotland. The East Millichen slab is in storage. The rest are on permanent display at the Hunterian Museum in Glasgow.

Research by Dr Louisa Noble of Glasgow University indicates that the slabs were painted in a range of colours, making the depicted violence more obvious and lurid than it is now. 'These are unique,' she had said when we met at the Hunterian. 'There's nothing else like these across the empire.'

They are 'propagandist' objects, she told me, intended to quell the oppressed and put heart in the oppressors. She believes that they were set up at the side of the military way where they would have been seen by troops and by indigenous people granted passage into the empire. The academic consensus says otherwise – that the slabs were set up on the south side of the Wall, for Roman eyes only, as a statement of imperial pride: we came, we saw, we constructed.

To encounter these carved stones now is a strange feeling. They are certainly troubling expressions of tyranny, but they are also vivid, dramatic and exciting. They have a Leni Riefenstahl air. Their aesthetic appeal is such that Dr Noble feels that the terminology used to refer to them is inappropriate.

'If these were found in any other part of the empire they would be valued for their artistic aspects,' she said. 'To call them "slabs" is derogatory. It minimises their impact, and their artistic and cultural value. I call them sculpted reliefs or distance sculptures. To me, a slab is something you use to build your garden path. Not a beautiful, articulate thing like this.'

We were looking at the Summerston stone, which was found near Balmuildy fort, north of Glasgow, and has been part of the university collection since the late seventeenth century.

Analysis shows that the eagle carved on the right-hand panel of the stone has a high concentration of lead on its beak and so had probably been painted red.

'That,' Dr Noble said, 'is a representation of Rome feasting on the blood of its enemies.'

*

My son and I began our walk on Harbour Road, across the street from the Miners' Welfare. A full-size replica of the Bridgeness distance slab had been set up close to the spot where it was found. The little garden area around the stone was bright with bunting, which flapped in the breeze off the Forth. The seabirds perched on street-lights seemed to know, with scavengers' wisdom, that this was Fair Day and that meant takeaways. If the Romans invaded Scotland now, they wouldn't carve eagles on stones. A gull with a chip in its beak would be a more appropriate emblem.

Up the hill and on to Grahamsdyke Road, we followed the line of the Wall. There was nothing visible. Any surviving traces were below the streets and gardens. But the name was a clue. 'Dyke' is Scots for wall and 'Graham' has evolved from 'Grim'. The Wall was, for centuries, known as Grim's Dyke or Grime's Dyke – surely because of a folkloric association between strange old structures and the supernatural, as we have seen with similar names in England.

Other than the fortlet behind Kinneil House and the small museum in its grounds, there was little to see in Bo'ness, but as we left the town for the countryside we came upon one of Scotland's most striking prospects. The wind blew shadows through a green field as we looked down over the Grangemouth oil refinery. Clouds rose from cooling towers and the orange flame of flaring gas blurred the outline of Dumyat, a peak in the Ochil range. Beyond the refinery was the blue estuary and beyond that the dark hills of Fife. Here was Burke's Sublime. Here was Tolkien's Mordor. It was so hideous that it was almost beautiful, a view of exhilarating disquiet.

The Wall did not become clearly apparent until we reached the town of Falkirk. In the grounds of Callendar Park and then again in a wooded area called Watling Lodge, it was possible to walk along the top of the ditch and gain a sense of its impressive depth. We called upon my friend Teddy, whose home is in Falkirk, and he offered to show us the way to the next fort: Rough Castle. The route of the Wall is not well signposted. It is easy to lose the way. Belt and braces, I was carrying in my backpack two guidebooks along with an old map that had belonged to my grandparents. You have to rely on your own sense of direction as there are no other hikers to follow. This is a walk of only niche or cult interest. 'It's your hipster wall, isn't it?' Teddy said. 'It's amazing how many people have never heard of it. When I say I live opposite the Antonine Wall, no one has a clue.'

We passed the Falkirk Wheel, a huge mechanism of gleaming steel, engineered to allow boats to pass more quickly between the Union and Forth & Clyde canals. Like the oil refinery, it seemed a spaceship come to earth, hinting at how alien the Wall must have appeared when first built here. What the Romans created was the first great infrastructure project in a landscape that would become much altered, first by the canal, then the railway, and finally the motorway system.

The Wall has suffered much from these developments. Sir James Young Simpson, an esteemed physician with deep archaeological interests, gave a lecture, in 1860, to the Society of Antiquaries of Scotland in which he decried the construction of the railway between Glasgow and Edinburgh. The 'line was driven, with annihilating effect', he said, through Castlecary, one of the forts of the Wall, and he himself, while a passenger, had witnessed a painful sight as the train sped through the fort: 'I saw the farmer in the immediate neighbourhood . . . busily removing a harmless wall, – among the last, if not the very last remnants of Roman masonry in Scotland.'

Stand in the field at Castlecary and you can still see the trains hurtling through. But it is from this point, heading west, that you begin to follow the best-preserved, most rural and by far the quietest part of the frontier.

We spent the night in the Castlecary Hotel and set off again after breakfast. We were in the central belt of Scotland, the most populous part of the country, but it was like we had dropped into no-man's-land. We would not see another person for more than two hours. Deer bounded away from us, alarmed to find humans on their patch, and a little white propellor plane came in to land at Cumbernauld Airport.

We passed a farmhouse, Westerwood, which sits on top of the site of a fort. It was to this house, one summer evening in 1963, that a fifteen-year-old called Jim Walker cycled the four miles from his home and interrupted the farmer, Mr Duncan, at his tea. Would he mind, Jim asked, if he had a look at his land? Not at all, said Mr Duncan, and the boy went off to walk a newly ploughed field. 'In the furrows I could see part of a stone lying lengthwise away from me,' Jim later recalled. 'I knew right away it was an altar.' It was a substantial piece of sandstone, still half-buried. With some difficulty, he turned it over and scraped away the worst of the muck. 'Then I could see the inscription. That was magic. My Latin wasn't fully up to it, and there was soil embedded in some of the letters, so I couldn't make out all of it, but I could read certain bits. My heart was thumping away.'

He had found an object that has come to be known as the Westerwood Altar. It is on display in Kinneil Museum. I had gone there with Jim, a few weeks before setting out on my walk, to look at his discovery. Now in his seventies, Jim is a great defender and champion of the Wall. The relationship goes back to his early life when, as a boy growing up on Seabegs Place Farm, near Bonnybridge, he realised that the frontier ran through his garden and the wood beside the house. The great ditch was his playground. He acquired a couple of books on the subject, which is how, when he spotted the altar in the furrows, he knew it for what it was and not just another stone brought up by the plough.

The altar was upstairs in the museum, dimly lit, a stuffed thrush perched on top as an atmospheric touch. I shone a torch through the glass and Jim deciphered the inscription. It was dedicated to the goddesses of the woodland and crossroads, which gives a sense of the environment in which it sat. The altar had been set up by Vibia Pacata, the wife of Flavius Verecundus. Scholars of Roman names, Jim explained, say that hers suggests an African origin. 'Now, Flavius Verecundus was a centurion of the Sixth Legion. The legion had served in Africa before they came to England, and then from England they came up here for the building of the Antonine Wall. So here was a centurion who had taken a wife in Africa. She would have been a black woman, and the children they had would have been able to accompany him north.'

If – and it is *if* – the speculation about Vibia Pacata's geographical and racial origins is correct, then she could be considered the first Briton of colour whose name is known. But that is perhaps too great a claim. Whether she, part of an occupying force, would have thought of herself as a Briton is questionable. And without her bones there is no physical evidence for her race, though we do have that in other cases of Africans living in Roman Britain. But her name carved in stone adds to our picture of the complexity brought by Roman occupation. As David Olusoga has written, 'The people of the British

Isles and the people of Africa met for the first time when Britain was a cold province on the northern fringe of Rome's inter-continental, multi-ethnic and multi-racial empire. We were colonized long before we became colonizers.'

Under Scotland's treasure trove law, Jim Walker was awarded four pounds ten shillings for the altar. He spent it on records by The Beatles and Stones. But the greater personal legacy was that his discovery spurred him to look for more. He has spent his life excavating and studying the Wall. Though never a professional archaeologist, what he has done as an amateur is remarkable. He discovered two lost fortlets – at Kinneil and Seabegs – and is the co-discoverer of a third, Cleddans.

'The Antonine Wall was every bit as important as Hadrian's Wall,' he told me. 'It was the frontier of Roman Britain for a generation and had a vital role to play in the empire. Today, we need to look after the Wall, otherwise we'll find that developers will keep trying to encroach upon it. My love for the monu-ment comes from knowing it is there and has to be kept.'

That's a strong word: love. My impression is that the Wall means nothing to most Scots. They either don't know it's there, or aren't much bothered. Does Jim truly *love* it?

'Yes,' he said. 'I do.'

*

At the foot of Croy Hill there is a giant head the colour of dried blood.

The steel sculpture of a centurion has been given the name Silvanus. Standing beside him, I only came up to his eyes. The feathers in the plume of his helmet looked machined; machete-sharp. The sculpture was installed in 2021 to raise awareness of the area's past. In that endeavour, it is a great success, but I'm not sure I like it much. It feels like a counterpoint to the severed head on the Bridgeness distance slab. At least that was an admission of the Roman method: victory through terror and violence. Silvanus, by contrast, is hard, stern and noble; an idealised soldier.

Still, if we must have public art celebrating the Roman presence in Scotland then there could be no better spot, for it was here that the legionaries faced their greatest challenge – building the Wall, for the next few miles, over steep and rocky terrain. It can be tough enough to walk; goodness knows what it must have been like to labour here. On Croy Hill the troops had to dig their ditch through stone, not earth, and of course there were no explosives to ease the job. The ditch is shallower and narrower than elsewhere on the Wall, but still almost thirty feet wide and five deep; the work must have been torture. The Scottish antiquary Alexander Gordon, walking the Wall in the 1720s, felt that this stretch, more than any other, demonstrated the Roman will: 'For it is scarcely conceivable what Pains and Expence must have been used, in cutting thro' such an amazing and rough Scene of Nature.'

The modern visitor will, perhaps, be more impressed when they arrive, sore-legged from the climb, at the top of Bar Hill. Their reward is the highest and best fort of the Wall. Finally there is plenty to see: the stone foundations of a number of structures, including the fort headquarters or *principia*. A few hundred soldiers were stationed in this exposed and blustery spot, a long way from home. The army drew its troops from across the empire. Bar Hill was garrisoned by Baetasian infantry from what is now the Netherlands, and Hamian archers from Syria. How did they feel about this posting? W. H. Auden, in 'Roman Wall Blues', imagined how it must have been for a soldier on Hadrian's Wall, and the sense of shivering futility was surely just as true of this further frontier:

> Over the heather the wet wind blows,
> I've lice in my tunic and a cold in my nose.
> The rain comes pattering out of the sky,
> I'm a Wall soldier, I don't know why.

Despite the wonderful views it offers of the Kilsyth Hills and Campsie Fells, the most atmospheric spot in Bar Hill – for me, at least – is a circular hole in the ground, a few feet in diameter, defined by a ring of stones, and covered by a modern safety grille. This was the fort well. It was identified in November 1902, during a dig by George Macdonald, who wrote that its 'discovery and clearance supplied the most exciting episode of the excavations'. The well was found to be forty-three feet deep and had been deliberately blocked when the garrison withdrew. This was done by dropping debris into the shaft. Rubbish to them, treasure to us: a sandstone altar, wooden beams; an iron hammer with a name, Ebutius, scratched into it; an oak barrel inscribed with another name, Januarius, whose ration of wine it may have held; and, best of all, parts of at least fourteen stone columns. Some of these columns are now set up in the Hunterian Museum, where they offer an evocative introduction to the Roman collection.

Much of the rest of our journey, from Twechar to Kirkintilloch and on to Lambhill on Glasgow's northern fringe, took us along the towpath of the canal. Mile after mile. Lots of roaming, nothing Roman. It was easy to relate to Auden's scunnered soldier: we were walkers of the Wall and not sure why. Still, at least it was fine weather. Bright and not a breath of wind. A pair of vapour trails, reflected in the water, made the canal resemble an airport runway – on which ducks, landing gear extended, touched down with a jaunty splash.

The Reverend John Skinner, who walked the Wall in September 1825, was much impressed by the canal. He considered it an engineering marvel in comparison with which 'the mere digging of a Dyke by the Romans will appear vastly inferior'. Skinner had travelled to Scotland from his parish in Somerset and has left us a charmingly grumpy account – in a journal and series of sketches – of his progress along the Wall. He suffered much for his antiquarian pursuits. At an inn in Bo'ness the sheets were so damp that he had to sleep in his clothes; in Kirkintilloch and again in Old Kilpatrick he could not rest for noise from the bar. 'The Scots,' he noted, 'certainly do not merit the character bestowed on them as a sober people . . .' Worst of all was Falkirk, 'dirty and ill paved', where the townsfolk went about barefoot, and observed 'another custom a hundred times worse, which shall be nameless . . .' He surely meant public urination, but was too decorous to say so. Virginia Woolf wrote about Skinner with insight and empathy in *The Second Common Reader*, laying out his losses and torment: the death of his wife and daughter, the difficult relationship with his sons. Little wonder that he took such interest in the past, the present being hard to bear. 'At last, one morning in December 1839,' Woolf tells us, 'the Rector took his gun, walked into the beech wood near his home, and shot himself dead.'

Bearsden, when we reached it, felt reassuringly visible. Most of the Roman fort is lost beneath this handsome town, its name a byword for solid and respectable affluence, but the bathhouse is the closest thing the Antonine Wall has to a tourist attraction. The entrance sign, in imperial purple, nods to the stern public notices that I remember from going swimming as a kid: *Nolite currere, urinari, desilire.* No running, no diving, no bombing. What, I wonder, is the Latin for 'no petting'? The site is overlooked by a 1970s housing development; if you are into Roman Britain then there could be no better place to live than one of these flats. Go out on the balcony to water your window boxes and you would see the whole bathhouse laid out below, its series of rooms and pools – the sudatorium, caldarium, tep-idarium – where the men of the fort could relax and sweat out their troubles.

The bathhouse was discovered in 1973 and excavation took place over the next ten summers. More than two hundred people worked on the dig, my grandparents among them. I have a photograph of Eric, taken in 1980, leaning on a spade as work goes on around him. The site is wet and muddy and he appears to be standing in the Roman latrines. Not the most glamorous or illuminating spot, one might think, but in fact that part of the bathhouse complex added enormously to the picture we have of life on the frontier. 'Forget gold and silver,' an archaeologist who excavated at Bearsden told me. 'Sewage is what you want!' The latrines were flushed by water draining from the bathhouse and the contents ended up in a nearby defensive ditch. This material was analysed post-excavation and revealed that the troops had a mainly vegetarian diet. Some of what they were eating – dried figs, lentils, dill, coriander and opium poppy seeds – was almost certainly imported from Europe, or in some cases transported north from the south of Britain. They also ate emmer and spelt, probably as porridge and bread; blackberries, raspberries, celery and hazelnuts; pearl barley in soup. They had parasite eggs in their guts – whipworm and roundworm – and seem to have wiped themselves clean with moss. It sounds like a healthy diet and, intestinal infections aside, a rather pleasant lifestyle. They had olive oil and wine, steam rooms and cold plunge pools; the bodily comforts of Rome.

From Bearsden, the line of the Wall passes through edge-lands: country roads, fly-tipped rubbish, roadkill bones; behind the crematorium, past abandoned farm buildings, under the roaring A82, and through the shadow of the Erskine Bridge with its signs advertising the Samaritans. These last few miles are not what you would call an enjoyable stroll, but they are in keeping with the Wall. Its might-is-right spirit persists in this unlovely zone of concrete and exhaust fumes. The philosopher and historian R. G. Collingwood captured something of this in 1936 when he wrote that 'on any Romano-British site the impression that constantly haunts the archaeologist, like a bad smell or a stickiness on the fingers, is that of an ugliness which pervades the place like a London fog: not merely the common vulgar ugliness of the Roman Empire, but a blundering, stupid ugliness that cannot even rise to the level of that vulgarity'.

We came at last to Old Kilpatrick. The village at the end of the Wall is one of the places that claims to have been the birthplace of Saint Patrick. That cannot be proved or disproved. What is certain is that this was once – as the official handbook has it – 'the north-western corner of the Roman Empire'.

How do empires end? In this case with a row of post-war houses, a string of tumbledown garages, a small eighteenth-century bridge over the canal, and finally a bridge-keeper's cottage with the roof falling in. Beyond that is the River Clyde, widening as it nears to sea.

A replica distance slab marks the terminus of the Antonine Wall. I had seen the original in the Hunterian. It records that the 'valiant and victorious' Twentieth Legion built this last stretch. The slab is in the form of a temple in which there sits a reclining woman, bare-breasted and winged, holding a palm frond and laurel wreath. She is a goddess risen from the river. The Romans knew this water as *Clota* so perhaps that is her name.

How does a wall look to a riverine spirit? Weak, I should think, and absurdly straight; an exercise in vainglory and delusion. People can be held back for a while, but not forever, and the tide turns, it turns as it was turning now, here on the Clyde, here at the end of the Wall that is no longer a wall, that is little more than a story seldom told, a line on a map that few consult.

It is suspected that there was a Roman harbour here. Perhaps this was one of the places from which the army left as it withdrew from Scotland. They had burned down their bathhouse, thrown columns down the well, buried the distance slabs so they would not fall into tribal hands. Clota would not see the sun for fifteen hundred years.

We crossed the little bridge and walked down to the river. It was dark and empty. There was a navigation beacon but no ships to heed its light.

*

February 1969. Snow was general over England: Manchester paralysed, Blackpool blanketed, trains and buses cancelled, football matches abandoned, snow feathering the wings of Eros in Piccadilly Circus and thickening the manes of the lions in Trafalgar Square. In the deep countryside of Northumberland, a mile south of Hadrian's Wall, a man and woman walked to the top of a hill and looked down at the nineteenth-century house that had been his childhood home. Robin Birley and Patricia Burnham had been together for only a month, but it was serious – and he had brought her to see where he had lived as a boy. Chesterholm, with its steep roofs and great chimneys, looked like something from a Russian fairy tale. And just where they were standing, its contours obscured by snow, was a large field that concealed beneath its surface a true marvel: the Roman fort of Vindolanda, its existence well known, but its extent and remarkable nature as yet unrevealed. 'Vindolanda' means 'white fields', and that – as the thick flakes fell – must have seemed entirely apt.

'Robin was explaining the site to me and how wonderful it was,' Patricia recalled when we met for morning coffee. 'You couldn't see a thing for snow, but he was so passionate that I remember thinking, "Crikey, if I take this man on, I'm probably

going to have to take this place on as well." Because it was in his heart. Of course, we had no idea about all that would be in the future. But Vindolanda, I have thought from that moment on, is a sort of female persona. She was the other person in our relationship and I came to love her as much as he did.'

We were talking in the café at Vindolanda. The site has grown over half a century from a few speculative trenches to one of the major visitor attractions of Hadrian's Wall. An excellent museum displays the best of the huge number of objects discovered here, among them the items for which the site has become famous: Roman shoes and documents. Such organic material does not usually survive, but here it has been preserved deep in a waterlogged, clay-sealed layer which, lacking the oxygen that hastens decomposition, functions as nature's own time capsule.

Among the correspondence recovered from the site is one of Britain's great treasures. On 11 September, most likely in AD 104, a woman called Claudia Severa wrote to her friend Sulpicia Lepidina, the wife of the commanding officer at Vindolanda, asking her to a birthday party. 'I give you a warm invitation to make sure you come to us, to make the day more enjoyable for me by your arrival . . .' That part was penned by a scribe, but the closing lines were written by Claudia Severa herself: *sperabo te soror vale soror anima mea ita valeam karissima et have.* This has been translated as 'I shall expect you, sister. Farewell, sister, my dearest soul, as I hope to prosper, and hail.' The small, frail tablet of ink on wood looks like nothing much; you might take it for a piece of bark from a tree. But this affectionate little greeting, dashed off no doubt by a busy military wife with a million other things to organise, is the earliest known example of writing in Latin by a woman. It has that historical importance, which is why it is in the British Museum, but it also has a human significance not so easily summed up. While it would be reductive to say, 'Oh, the Romans were just like us,' there is much about the birthday letter that feels familiar: its tone of easy friendship, its suggestion of community and social life, and most of all its use of language, those gentle pleasantries with which we bind and smooth our relationships. It is touching to see this other side of Roman life. It wasn't all SPQR; sometimes it was RSVP.

Vindolanda was founded almost forty years before work began on Hadrian's Wall – around AD 85, in the aftermath of the Battle of Mons Graupius when the troops were withdrawn into what is now England. Auxiliaries from Vindolanda were probably involved in construction of the Wall and then formed part of its garrison. The life of the fort, as a military base, spans the first to fifth centuries – much of the Roman occupation of Britain. I say 'fort', but in fact there were nine, built and rebuilt, one on top of the other, first in timber and eventually in stone. Archaeologists must go as deep as twenty or so feet to get to the earliest levels, 'the anaerobic' as everyone who digs there calls it, where the airless wonders lurk.

The fort remained in use even when the boundary line of the Roman Empire was pushed north to the Antonine Wall. The combined population of the fort and *vicus* – the neighbouring civilian settlement – would have been getting on for five thousand at its height. This busy, noisy place was part of a frontier landscape that had not been entirely pacified. In the early third century, the Emperor Septimius Severus came north to put down a native rebellion using tactics that have been described as genocidal. He quoted *The Iliad* when urging his troops to be merciless: 'Let none escape death at our hands, not even the child in the womb.' Archaeological evidence suggests Vindolanda's fortifications were strengthened at this time of strife. In 2002, a skull was found in a defensive ditch: a young man from between the Lake District and south-west Scotland. Was he a tribal leader? Was his face known to other rebels who looked upon it? The severed head was mounted on the ramparts until, we can suppose, it decomposed and fell. 'That didn't half stink,' one of the excavators recalled of the find. 'It was sitting in a pool of black goo where the flesh had rotted away. We had to light citronella candles just to be able to go down and work.'

In the two summers before he took Patricia to see Vindolanda, Robin Birley had begun to excavate the site in a minimal way, with the agreement of the farmer who owned the land. Tentative digging had convinced him that there would be much to find if ever opportunity rose for exploration on a larger scale. In 1970 the farm was bought by Daphne Archibald, a local landowner and Roman enthusiast, and given to a newly formed charity, the Vindolanda Trust, with Robin as director. The following year, Robin and Patricia resigned their teaching posts and embarked upon their life's work. Their devotion, especially in the hand-to-mouth early years, seems to have been total. On the day of their wedding, in 1971, they spent the morning excavating, went off to Hexham to get married, and then came back on site and had champagne in the trenches.

'It has been my life,' Patricia, who is now in her seventies, told me. 'I feel so privileged to have been part of the Vindolanda story. But it doesn't feel like fifty years. When you study history you realise that time means nothing. It's what you do with it that matters.'

*

What the visitor to Vindolanda sees now are the consolidated ruins of the fort and *vicus* covering a large area. Some walls survive to an impressive height and the footprints of the structures are everywhere clear; evocative of life inside. The visible stone dates from the third and fourth centuries, when Vindolanda was the base of the Fourth Cohort of Gauls. Information panels explain what each building was: tavern, bathhouse, barracks, temple, and so on.

Excavation is ongoing. The season lasts from April to September, with a break in July and most of August when temperatures are hot enough to endanger the anaerobic deposits. Exposed, they would dry out too fast. Since 1970, Vindolanda has accepted volunteer diggers. Members of the public pay to participate for a fortnight at a time. Places are in high demand. 'It's addictive,' one digger told me. 'It gets into your blood. You find after a while that this is something you can't not do.'

I spent a few days there in June, trowel in hand, keen to understand what it is about this place that gets under people's skin. 'A real community,' Sonya Galloway, who arranged my stay, told me, 'is created on the back of spending two weeks on your knees in the Northumberland mud.'

There were around thirty of us, including a field school of archaeology students from the Netherlands. People had come from all over. The chat as we trowelled was mostly a mix of Dutch and English; some American accents, too. The frontier, with its troops drawn from the empire, must have been a bit like this: the babble of tongues and the sounds of work. I was the only Scot. 'Always nice to have a barbarian here,' said Andrew Birley, director of excavations. 'We're glad to welcome you – to make up for the Wall.'

We had been put to work in the north-eastern quadrant of the fort. Roman forts, wherever in the world they are found, are shaped like playing cards. They have those rounded corners. We were about halfway up the top-right corner of the card, excavating an area of infantry barracks. We would gather early each day on the steps of the Archaeology Centre and then walk to the site. Marta Alberti-Dunn, the deputy director, is an Italian archaeologist with Jedi master energy. 'The soil is calling our name,' she announced one morning, 'and we must answer.'

Whenever anyone found a significant object – a coin, say, or part of a bronze bracelet – its precise location was recorded using a fancy surveying instrument called a total station. It looked a bit like an old Victorian camera except that it was Simpsons yellow. I didn't find anything worth recording in that way, although I was delighted to trowel up a big iron nail and, even better, a tiny fragment of Roman glass, probably from a drinking vessel, the pale blue of a spring sky. We were only a few feet below the surface, still in the fourth century, not deep enough for the really good finds, but that feeling of 'well, you never know' was motivating. One day, when I was away from the site on other business, a lovely little bead emerged just where I would have been trowelling, and I tried without success to feel happy for the young Romanian student who found it. The fear of missing out is real. They should call it Fomolanda.

Many of the more experienced diggers had my-best-find stories to share during tea break. Someone brought out his phone and showed a picture of one of last year's discoveries: a silver medal decorated with a head of Medusa, snakes writhing around her face. It put my rusty nail in the shade.

'I'm a frustrated antiquarian,' another volunteer said. 'I was born two hundred years too late.'

'Do you have a cabinet of curiosities?' I asked.

'Yes! With a human skull . . .'

I got talking with Graham Ryan, a 'Vindolanda veteran' from Cumbria. He was seventy-nine and had been coming to dig here for almost twenty years. He was twelve feet down in a trench one day, he told me, when he found a perfect leather shoe. Going by the size, it had been worn by a child of around five – it pleases him to think it was a girl – and dated from the first century. Graham had found plenty of adult shoes before, but none carried the sweet sadness of this object. It seemed to awaken some tender feeling he had for his own early life. 'I come from a big family. A very poor family,' he explained. He was one of eight children: two older brothers, two younger brothers, three younger sisters. Hand-me-down shoes were a part of life. It would be wrong to say that those personal memories, the feeling of owning nothing new, came flashing back in the moment he found the object; it was subconscious, not thought-through, but he felt it. That shoe took him back to being a boy, and it made him wonder about its wearer's life in relation to his own – 'What was her childhood like, compared to mine? What happened to her later on?' The psychology of excavation is complex. The cliché is that you touch the past, but sometimes it's more like the past touches you.

'One of the saddest things in life is that we've only got one, and we can only live one set of options,' Marta told me later that same day. 'Archaeology is fascinating because it gives you the chance to put yourself in the shoes of somebody else and live their life for a bit.'

As we all focused on our assigned bit of trench, trying to define the boundaries of the barrack rooms, Andrew Birley stopped by on his rounds to see how we were getting along. My work was slow. I had been a teenager the last time I did this, had lost whatever technique I once had, and was nervous of removing stones in case they were important. He saw this right away. 'Your worst enemy is fear,' he said. 'Fear of making a mistake. Fear of breaking something. But when you're trying to find a wall, as we are here, you can afford to be quite robust with your trowelling.' He could *see* the line of the building, as I could not, and demonstrated how to reveal it from the surrounding rubble. A few quick movements of his trowel and there it was – a wall. He had a mantra for this: 'Work from the known to the unknown.'

It would be a considerable understatement to say that he knew this ground well. He had started digging at Vindolanda when he was fifteen, was now forty-nine, and had been on and around the site since he was a baby. 'My history with this place has been all-encompassing,' he told me. 'My family have served for longer than any Roman soldier served here.'

The Birleys are an archaeological dynasty. Back in the 1970s they were already being described as 'the first family of Roman Britain'. Professor Eric Birley – Andrew's grandfather – began his excavations at Vindolanda in the 1930s, having bought the site at auction in 1929. 'Then,' Sonya Galloway had told me, 'he went off and did various things in the war.' Sonya is Eric's granddaughter, Andrew's younger sister, and her 'various things' is a splendid euphemism. Birley worked for British military intelligence. He had taught himself German in order to access foreign research into the Roman army. He was now able to take a system he had devised for estimating Roman troop numbers and apply it to analysis of intercepted German documents and information from prisoner interrogations. This allowed him to judge, among other things, the likely strength of enemy forces.

'His archaeological training, exercised on the Roman Wall, gave him encyclopaedic insight into German procedures, and he carried in his head a pattern of related facts that I have never seen equalled,' an intelligence colleague remembered in a memoir. 'Should he learn that a captured Feldwebel had started his army career in Paderborn in April 1941 with the third Ersatz battalion of the sixtieth Pioneer Regiment, that man's subsequent career was at once clear to him.'

During the planning for D-Day, his input was crucial. He was able to demonstrate that German divisions which might have overcome the Allied forces were not at full strength. Had they been so, the invasion might have had to be reconsidered and the course of the war changed. Of course, he didn't talk about this much. 'I knew Eric as a very quiet old man who smoked a pipe, walked with his hands behind his back, and said "jolly good!" a lot,' Sonya recalled. 'He was private and kind, and it was only at his memorial service that I realised what a significant person in history he was.' It's all very Powell and Pressburger. Eric Birley, had there been a film of his life, would surely have been played by Roger Livesey.

Having been appointed master of a college at Durham University, Eric sold Vindolanda in 1950 and he and his wife and children moved away. That is why when his son Robin arrived at the site with Patricia on that snowy day in 1969, it was no longer owned by the family. However, a discovery made on the morning of 23 March 1973 hugely expanded the profile and cultural importance of Vindolanda, and has caused it to become closely identified with the Birley name.

Robin had been working in a trench about thirteen feet below the surface, so deep that water had to be constantly pumped out, when he trowelled up two very small, thin fragments that he took at first to be wood shavings from some Roman workshop. He then noticed, but could not quite believe, that one of them appeared to have marks upon it. Could it be . . . though surely not . . . could this really be *writing*? 'If I have to spend the rest of my life working in dirty, wet trenches,' he later recalled, 'I doubt I shall ever again experience the shock and excitement I felt at my first glimpse of ink hieroglyphics on tiny scraps of wood.'

This was the first of the Vindolanda tablets. Since that discovery, almost two thousand ink-on-wood tablets have been recovered from the anaerobic layer, as well as four hundred or so stylus tablets that were used by incising words into wax. Nothing like these documents had ever been found in Britain before. They allow us to eavesdrop on the Roman world and their discovery was a sensation. They changed Vindolanda from a place to a story. Until they were found, the fort was a setting; now there were characters and a script; names, relationships, voices.

Vindolanda had been receiving five thousand visitors a year; by the end of 1973 it was eighty-eight thousand. This public interest didn't always sit well with locals. 'Tourists are spreading all over the countryside,' a farmer complained around that time. 'They're taking over!' Hadrian's Wall meant nothing to him, he said, it was just a nuisance. 'I don't care about delving into the past. The present is too important.'

That first tablet, though; Robin couldn't be sure about it. He *thought* he had seen writing, but then, as it was exposed to oxygen for the first time in almost two thousand years, the wood quickly darkened and nothing could be made out. Had he been dreaming? He showed it to Patricia and asked her opinion.

'He wasn't a fanciful man,' she told me, 'so I said, "Well, if you think you've seen some writing then you did." We put it in water from the excavation in a plastic margarine box and brought it to the house.'

Robin phoned his father: 'What do you think we should do?' Eric's advice was to take the piece of wood as soon as possible to Richard Wright, a specialist in Roman inscriptions.

'So,' Patricia continued, 'we got in our ramshackle car, a Ford Zephyr, and scooted across to Durham to see Richard. Robin drove like a bat out of hell. We were feeling quite urgent about things by this point. Can you imagine, sitting in a rickety old car, going vroom-vroom-vroom along the country roads, me holding this margarine box, and Robin beside me saying, "Don't let it slop about!" We were worried it was going to break into fragments.'

They sat in Richard Wright's drawing room and showed him this internationally important discovery: a black blob floating in a tub of Stork. He suggested that they take it to Alison Rutherford, a specialist in infrared photography at Newcastle University's School of Medicine. 'We went to see her on Saturday morning,' Patricia recalled. 'She photographed the tablet and developed the prints straight away. And there it was: writing. An amazing moment for all of us. You're just overwhelmed, really. Then, of course, your next thought is, "What does it say?"'

This was not so easily answered. Robin had thought, in that first glance, that the tiny writing looked like hieroglyphics. In fact, the tablets are written in cursive Latin, utterly different in appearance from the capitalised inscriptions on public monuments. It is hard to distinguish individual words, or even the letters, clearly. The Romans did not put spaces between their words, and the untrained eye slides helplessly over the text. But before any attempt can be made to decipher their meaning, they must first be conserved and then photographed. Patricia conserved most of the tablets found between 1973 and her retirement in 2015. Her daughter-in-law Barbara Birley, curator of the Vindolanda Museum, is now in charge of conservation.

They are brought to a laboratory on site as soon as possible after discovery. The days of margarine tubs are in the past, but they are still kept in water from the trench in order to prevent them drying out and falling apart.

I had imagined the tablet being rushed from the dig to the lab like a patient to casualty, but the process isn't quite as hasty. They are extremely fragile, and to break one could mean losing a piece of evidence that changes our understanding of history. Robin Birley, describing what they are like to extract from the wet ground, once explained that 'the smallest pressure – such as occurred when a bracken frond was accidentally moved – was liable to cause fractures, and most of them were effectively glued to the surrounding organic rubbish'. In order to excavate the tablets safely, a technique was introduced that is still in use today. Trowelling is no use in the anaerobic because scraping risks destroying vulnerable finds. Instead, blocks of the wet earth are sliced out with a spade and then a gentle pressure applied by hand to open them up. Any artefacts are thus revealed, like a book falling open at just the right page.

Andrew Birley, Robin's son, excavated a large cache of tablets in 2017. He recalled for me what such high-pressure excavation feels like: 'We had a large crowd gathering at the side of the fence, but there was no sound at all. You could have heard a sparrow fart. There was such an atmosphere, a buzz, an intensity. We were absolutely on our knees by the end of the day, just exhausted by the tension of making sure we didn't miss any of these things.'

Once in the lab the tablets are cleaned with dental tools, gently washed in pure water and placed in a succession of chemical baths. It takes about six weeks from a tablet being found to being clean and dry and ready for photography. Only when it has been photographed can work begin on trying to read it. This is challenging; very few people have the skills and experience. These texts were often written quickly – notes penned in haste – and without much effort at clarity. Why bother? They would be understood by the people for whom they were intended, who all wrote and talked in the same way, and obviously no one had it in mind that their shopping lists and party invitations and requests for leave would become matters for posterity. Certain letters can be difficult to distinguish from one another, there are very few capitals, no punctuation, lots of abbreviations, the spelling is often phonetic, and the actual words used are sometimes 'vulgar' – meaning Latin as it seems to have been spoken rather than the formal language familiar from classical texts.

Then there are further difficulties caused by the physical condition of the tablets. These were never intended to be kept. They were trash. A large number of tablets, found in the early 1990s, had been thrown on a bonfire to be burned – and only survived because, the theory goes, it started to rain. Understandably, therefore, the tablets are often fragmentary and in poor condition. The ink can be faded, stained, scorched or made hard to read by the grain of the wood. In the case of the stylus tablets there is no ink at all and the wax layer has gone, so all the expert has to work from are unintentional marks where the writer has pressed too hard with their stylus and scratched the wood behind the wax.

'It's the magic of code-breaking,' Dr Roger Tomlin told me when I visited him at home in Oxford to talk about his work on the Vindolanda tablets. 'You've got this message that has come out of the ether and you have to try to see how it starts to make sense if you push it this way and that.' Had he lived earlier, he said, he might have been recruited to work on decryption at Bletchley Park. The Vindolanda texts even include an incomplete tablet that has been interpreted as an intelligence report. Found in 1985, it notes that, though the native warriors do not wear armour, they have a great deal of cavalry. It refers to them using a contemptuous diminutive, *Brittunculi*, which has been translated as 'wretched Britons' or even 'horrid little Brits'.

Dr Tomlin had answered the door in bare feet, so comfortable upon Persian rugs, and led the way upstairs to a study decorated with his own landscape paintings, including one of Crag Lough, a lake not far from Vindolanda. There was a large microscope on his desk and the room was bright with daylight. This work needs sharp eyes, a sharp mind and clean windows. It requires perfect Latin, but also a deep knowledge of classical history, culture and custom, so that – for example – he can recognise a reference to the work of a particular poet or philosopher when he reads it. He has a strong visual memory and it helps that he is artistic. He takes what he calls a 'kinaesthetic' approach to deciphering the texts, meaning that he tries to identify illegible letters and words by considering the movements the writer made as they set down the strokes, bearing in mind that writing is an act of the body as well as the brain. He does this by copying out the text as best he can, thinking himself into those Roman hands, working not only by eye, but with the help of multiple photographs taken in different angles of light.

To better explain his method he showed me a strange little object. It was a strip of lead that looked like tattered old leather. Going by the handwriting scratched into its surface, which I could barely even see, he reckoned it was written in the late second or third century. This wasn't from Vindolanda; it had been found by a metal detectorist at an unexcavated temple site in Gloucestershire. Someone had written upon it, rolled it up and buried it in the ground for consideration by the divine.

Dr Tomlin had been examining the tablet, and others like it, for its American owner – and had worked out what it says. 'He's writing to Mercury: "I complain to you about my lost property, a cloak and hood." I had to reconstruct that word. I've got "pallium" which means "cloak", and then I've got a word ending in "rtium" which is probably "mafortium" – a kind of hood.'

The rest of the tablet takes an interesting turn: 'Whoever stole this, whether slave or free, whoever stole this, the god is not to let them stand or sit, to drink or eat, unless they pay with their own blood.'

Here we have a glimpse of life in Roman Britain. A man loses his cloak and hood. He assumes they've been nicked, which is very annoying, but he has no clue who took them, so accepts that he is not getting them back. What, then, does he do? Well, of course, he asks the god Mercury to afflict the thief. Over a hundred such curse tablets, or *defixiones*, have been found in Bath, thrown into the hot spring of the goddess Sulis Minerva, and a further eighty-seven from the temple to Mercury near the Cotswold village of Uley. They sometimes offer significant historical information – in the margins, so to speak. One of the Bath tablets, seeking the return of six silver coins, contains a very early reference to Christianity in Britain, while an Uley tablet, complaining of a stolen hive, is the first British reference to beekeeping.

These, though, are incidentals. The point of curse tablets is the curse. They make me shudder a bit, with their calls for offending parties to be struck dumb, to bleed, to die. I don't think I should like to touch one. They are bubbles of human malice, grievances floating up from the depths of time and popping on the surface.

I asked Dr Tomlin if he would talk about the pleasure of his work.

'It's a lovely feeling when you realise what the thing is about,' he replied. 'We had a stylus tablet from Vindolanda and I could read the word "erronem" down the bottom right hand corner. That sort of means "wandering fugitive" and is a typical phrase in the deeds of sales of slaves. And so I had some idea of what the text was going to be. It's nice when it suddenly dawns on you like that. It must have been marvellous for Alan and David when they read the famous birthday invitation.'

Alan and David are Professors Alan Bowman and David Thomas, who have been involved in deciphering the Vindolanda tablets since the earliest years. Roger Tomlin joined them later. When the work of trying to read the tablets began, no one had any idea of what sort of material they contained. When Patricia Birley looked at that infrared photograph of the first tablet, she thought that, having been written down, it was surely a matter of some importance. Which it was, in a way.

It was a private letter to a soldier, written in the early second century, informing him that the writer has sent him socks, sandals and two pairs of pants.

This, I think, must be the greatest example of bathos that has ever occurred, glorious in its mundanity; dream big, get smalls. 'To date the excavations at Vindolanda have produced over 5,000 shoes, one small sock but as of yet no sign of any underpants,' the official guidebook notes. 'We keep looking.'

A number of the best-known Vindolanda tablets have this enchantingly humdrum quality. A tablet found in 1988 was written by Octavius, a merchant supplying goods to the military. There is a feeling of stress and rush about his letter; it was folded up so soon after writing that the ink hadn't dried. Octavius needs to go to Catterick, which he calls *Cataractonium*, to pick up animal hides; indeed would have gone already, except he doesn't want to risk injury to the animals pulling the wagons *dum uiae male sunt* – while the roads are bad. Anyone who has ever whinged about potholes will feel for poor old Octavius having a bad day in Yorkshire sometime in the early second century.

It was pleasant to think of such things as I worked in the trench. In fact, the experience was altogether lovely. 'Meditative' would be the buzzword. Eyes on the ground, mind elsewhere, you are only half aware of the Vindolanda soundscape: the squeak of wheelbarrows, the car-won't-start screech of pheasants, the scrape-scrape-scrape of trowels.

The stories of exciting finds at Vindolanda make the place sound dramatic, but it doesn't feel like that. It feels *slow*. Archaeology of a sort has taken place here, on and off, since the 1830s and yet it is estimated that only a quarter or so of the total site has been excavated. There are huge areas, including the cemeteries (which are beyond the land owned by the Trust) that have not yet been touched. At the present rate of digging, it could be another a hundred and fifty years before Vindolanda is entirely revealed and understood.

A new factor, however, has introduced a note of urgency: climate change. It is believed that cycles of drought and torrential rain are allowing oxygen to penetrate the anaerobic layers, causing whatever is down there to begin decomposing before the archaeologists get to it. The most fragile material rots first, which is why the Trust believes so few textiles are found now. Wood and leather – the writing tablets and shoes – are also being affected. The situation is monitored using ground probes and the prognosis is not good. Andrew Birley told me he thought they had fifteen years until much of the anaerobic was lost.

We were talking one morning before the other diggers had arrived. Andrew, like his late father, is an early riser. He sometimes likes to sit out on the steps of the Archaeology Centre and watch deer running across the site. I was interested, I said, in the word he had used to describe the Birleys' relationship with Vindolanda. Does it really feel like 'service'?

'Yeah, it does. Service and responsibility.'

'Why?'

'Because I feel that I owe them something. The people who were here almost two thousand years ago. To find out about them and tell their stories. My mission, if you will, is to do that.

'Also, I'm the last of my family, probably, to do this. My kids have no passion or interest in following the family line, which is healthy, actually. I'd prefer them to be happy. So I understand that I'm the last one. And there is a weight of responsibility that goes with that.'

The Romans believed that places had protective spirits, the *genius loci*, hence Vibia Pacata setting up that altar on the Antonine Wall to the goddesses of woodland and crossroads. This idea seems to have found resonance with the Birley family, who have built their lives among ruins. When I spoke with Patricia she said that 'for us Vindolanda's more or less a living being. This wonderful lady called Vindolanda, in my fanciful mind, keeps saying, "I'll give you this, I'll give you that." And we never know what's going to come next.'

For Andrew Birley, no matter what his family's involvement in the longer term, he knows what he must do for the moment: keep digging.

'Most of the best stuff is yet to come,' he said. 'Out there somewhere is a municipal dump where over four and a half thousand people for ten to fifteen years tipped their rubbish. That is the huge discovery of the future. It could be fifty to sixty metres deep. That would be the motherlode. But we haven't found it . . . yet.'

NORTH

IN THE RAVEN DARKNESS of the island night, the only light came from the full moon, which silvered the sea, and from a pair of flaming torches hammered to posts on either side of a gate leading off a single-track road. These beacons carried a message that every islander would understand: the men of the Jarl Squad are about their work.

Going a little closer, passing between the torches, I could make out a large agricultural building, known as 'Da Shed', but looking more like a warehouse. Was that music I could hear? A fiddle starting up? I went around the corner, pushed open the door, and there they were: a group of twenty Vikings, beers in hand, singing lustily – how else? – a Johnny Cash tune. One of them, his shaved head covered in black runes, held up a can of Tennent's and hollered the words: *I shot a man in Reno* . . .

Well, we were a long way from Reno. We were on Unst, or *in* Unst as people here say, that preposition better expressing a feeling of nurturing embrace. Unst is the most northerly inhabited island of Britain. Sail east and you're in Norway; north-west and you're in Faroe, then Iceland. It is ten miles long by five wide and has a population of six hundred or so. To get here I had driven the length of the Shetland Mainland, taken a little ferry to the island of Yell and then another to Unst. Shetland can be a windy place and Unst the windiest of all. A sticker in my hire car warned that care should be taken when opening the doors as the insurance doesn't cover them being blown off their hinges. But I was fortunate to have arrived during a spell of calm sunshine, one of the few times in decades, I was told, that it was going to be good weather for Norwick Up Helly Aa.

Up Helly Aa? The annual fire festival. Hence those Vikings. Up Helly Aa began in Lerwick, Shetland's capital, in the late nineteenth century, and has since spread to a further nine communities across the archipelago. Unst has two Up Helly Aas, both of which take place in February. Uyeasound, in the south of the island, has been going since 1911; Norwick, in the north, began in 1985. It was Norwick's Jarl Squad – the name given to the group dressed as Norse warriors who lead and provide a focus for the festival – that had been singing Johnny Cash's 'Folsom Prison Blues' as I arrived. The country song has an outlaw swagger that somehow suits Vikings despite the obvious anachronism.

It was 'hand ower night' – the evening when last year's Guizer Jarl, the leader of the squad, hands over to his successor ahead of the following day's festivities. This was why they had gathered in their headquarters, Da Shed. That word 'da' is how people here say 'the'; 'du' is how they say 'you'. The dialect, known as Shetlaen, contains many wonderful words and sounds and is surely a linguistic echo of the settlers – perhaps too gentle a noun – who arrived in Shetland around AD 800. 'Shetlaen,' writes the poet Roseanne Watt, 'is a form of Scots shaped by sea roads. It forms something of a fraught coalition between English, Lowland Scots and old Norn: the extinct Scandinavian language of the Northern Isles. This Norse element is retained mainly in the speech patterns and grammar of the dialect, as well as in place-names, and words which describe the natural world.'

The Vikings were being kept warm by nips of Whyte & Mackay and the red glow of a portable heater. Grey cloaks hung from a clothes rail. A table was covered with black helmets, the initials of each squad member written inside. The helmets didn't have horns, they had goose wings, Unst having geese to spare. An accordion player, fiddler and guitarist kept the mood up. It was a family occasion. Lots of women and children around.

'What are we doing tomorrow?' a little girl with blonde plaits was asked.

'Viking stuff!' she replied.

*

The relationship between present-day Shetland and its Viking past is close. It's an identity thing. Ask Shetlanders whether they feel Scandinavian or Scottish and you often get a simple answer: 'Baith.' You can't go anywhere in Unst without encountering Norse names. Norwick means 'north bay'. Uyeasound is 'island strait'. Haroldswick is named for Harald Fairhair, the Norwegian king.

When Vikings first came to Unst is uncertain; proximity to Norway made it a natural landfall. The Viking Age is often seen as beginning with the attack on Lindisfarne in 793, but it seems at least possible that they were in Shetland, so much further north, earlier than that. A settlement in Norwick, discovered in 2003, has been suggested as Shetland's earliest Viking colony. The sites of sixty-two longhouses have been identified in Unst. Given the small size of the island, this would have been the most densely settled territory in the Viking world, including Scandinavia itself.

The nature of the Norse domination of Shetland – and Orkney, to the south – has been much argued. Assimilation or genocide? Whoever wrote the visitor information panels at the Shetland Museum in Lerwick was in no doubt: 'Raiders came first. They cleared out the local people, and took their land. Settlers followed, setting up house and becoming farmers and fishermen. Viking beliefs, language and architecture replaced the Pictish culture and way of life.' Whichever way it went, Up Helly Aa is a celebration of history's winners.

On my first morning in Unst I had met Christopher Ritch, a former Guizer Jarl, and we went to give breakfast to his sheep. They ran to meet him as he climbed over a gate and poured feed into a trough; a starling perched on a woolly back, iridescent in the sun. Christopher, who is in his fifties, was born and raised here. He used to be a salmon farmer and is now a crofter. He is forever finding evidence, as he walks and works his land, of fishing and farming done by Norse settlers – picking up their line sinkers, spindle whorls and sharpening stones. He feels no personal connection to the Vikings other than this sense of shared labour, being concerned, as they were, with the daily business of fish and fleece. He takes a great interest in the history of the island and its old stories. He doesn't waste words. I asked how he would characterise Unst.

'Well,' he said. 'You see it.'

The hills and moorland, he meant; the farmland and the sea. Each of the Shetland islands has its own individual character, he added, but he wouldn't know how to describe this one.

I had asked my friend Jen, a journalist from Shetland, to have a go. Unst, she thought, was '*fey* – which I suppose I use to mean "slightly in the other realm", in the faerie realm, not of us entirely, somewhere otherworldly. You could say "enchanted" in English but it sounds silly. It has this dark element, as all otherworldly things do.'

I knew what she meant. Whenever I have visited Shetland's North Isles – Unst, Fetlar and Yell – I have been told strange stories. The creepiest concerns the White Wife of Watlee, a ghost in a pale cowl who appears to men driving a particular stretch of Unst road at night, materialising in the passenger seat, like a tatter of moonlight, and smiling at the driver.

Mainly, though, what you hear are trow stories. Orkney and Shetland are rich in those. Trows are a bit like the Cornish piskie, but the emphasis is more on menace than mischief. They are little people who live in the hills and moors, places said to be 'trowie', and are much given to abduction. They are especially keen on taking fiddlers as they love the sound of that instrument. 'Time and again in the folk tales,' the late Orcadian poet George Mackay Brown has written, 'the fiddler is dragged down under the furrows, among roots and skulls.'

You needn't go back very far to find widespread belief in trows. Christopher told me that his own grandparents might have been wary of them. And I have met Shetlanders, even now, who seem agnostic on the matter. They don't quite believe, no. This after all is the twenty-first century. But why risk it by taking that shortcut home from the dance at night? The folklore of trows must, I am sure, have developed from Viking beliefs. Neil Price, in *The Children of Ash & Elm*, suggests that to the Norse the world was alive with what we would now consider supernatural beings, but which to them seemed entirely natural. These included the *álfar*, the elves, and the *dvergar*, the dwarves, and of course the trolls, creatures which 'lived in stones and underground but in more remote places, and . . . were uniformly threatening'.

Sheep fed, and the hens too, Christopher took me to see some longhouses. Unlike, say, York, which was an important Norse centre but has a city on top of it, Unst's Viking past is still clear in the landscape. The longhouse sites tend to be near the coast and it is likely that more have been lost to erosion. Some survive as low stone walls, with evidence of having been divided into two parts, living quarters for the people and a byre for cattle. The heat of the animals would have helped keep the houses warm.

We went to Underhoull in the south-west of the island. The sea was pale blue in the bay. V-shaped trenches dug into banks just above the beach are 'noosts' – where the settlers who lived here pulled up their boats to keep them safe and secure. There are two longhouses at Underhoull. Built into the walls of one, Christopher showed me, was a big broken stone that looked like it might once have been used to hold water. 'It's said that the Vikings smashed stone baths because the Christians used them to baptise infants,' he explained. 'Being heathens, they disapproved of that.'

The Vikings in time became Christian too. Just on the other side of the bay from the Underhoull longhouses is the shell of St Olaf's Kirk, which dates from the twelfth century. The most celebrated of the Norse saints is Magnus Erlendsson, whose martyrdom is told in the *Orkneyinga Saga*, an Icelandic text written around the year 1200.

Magnus was Earl of Orkney in the early twelfth century, a man of great faith and even temper, 'gentle and agreeable when talking to men of wisdom and goodwill, but severe and uncompromising towards thieves and vikings, putting to death most of the men who plundered the farms and other parts of the earldom'. He married a young woman from a noble family, but in ten years of marriage they did not sleep together. 'Whenever the urge of temptation came upon him,' the anonymous writer of the *Saga* tells us, 'he would plunge into cold water and pray to God for aid.'

This is far removed from warrior machismo. Indeed, Magnus's defining characteristic is pacifism. While accompanying the King of Norway on a raid in the Menai Strait, he refused to fight, instead chanting psalms while arrows flew. Later, on the island of Egilsay, he was killed on the orders of his cousin Hakon. 'Stand in front of me and strike me hard on the head,' Magnus encouraged the executioner. 'Take heart, poor fellow, I've prayed that God grant his mercy.'

In 1919, during restoration work in Kirkwall's St Magnus Cathedral, a pine box was discovered behind a stone high in a pillar of the choir. Inside the box were the bones of a man; skull cracked, as if from a fierce blow. These, it was decided, must be relics of the martyr, hidden during the Reformation to save them from destruction. In 1925 they were returned to their hiding place, where they have remained since. Almost a century later, I stood by the pillar with the cathedral curator Fran Flett Hollinrake. She is not a Christian, but finds Saint Magnus meaningful and approachable. 'He's my friend,' she told me. 'In times of difficulty I've come and asked for wisdom, advice and peace.' Although his bones are not on display, as they might be in a Catholic country, there is a certain power in invisibility. 'He is nice and safe up there,' she said, 'still casting his net of protection over all of us.'

*

It was the day of Up Helly Aa and I was looking for the Vikings. They weren't hard to find.

They were in full gear now, helmets on, and were being driven around Unst in a bus, axes and shields in the boot. Out front, towed by a 4x4, was a beautiful replica longship, red flag flapping in the breeze. I followed behind. We passed ruined cottages, fields of sheep, ponies with indie-boy fringes, the most northerly post office in Britain, the most northerly everything in Britain, and the construction site of the SaxaVord spaceport. We stopped at a care home so the Jarl Squad could visit the old folk, the wings of their helmets snagging Union Jack bunting strung across the lounge, and then it was on to the Final Checkout, the local shop, where they sang 'Amarillo' while marching up and down the aisles.

Such visits are an important part of Up Helly Aa, which is, above all, an expression of community. It is as much about Unst now as it is Unst a thousand years ago.

'We dinna get too hung up on tradition,' one of the squad told me. 'It's aboot Up Helly Aa noo, rather than trying to be pure Viking.'

We were talking at another of the stops. There was a speaker strapped to the longship's mast and one of the squad was playing tunes from his phone: 'A Little Respect', 'Sympathy For The Devil', 'I Walk The Line'.

What you find, when speaking with the Jarl Squad, whether in Unst or elsewhere in Shetland, is that they are reluctant or unable to articulate what the festival means on a deeper level. 'Up Helly Aa's just Up Helly Aa,' a Guizer Jarl of Lerwick once told me. 'You don't ask any questions. You just get on with it.'

It is a thing passed down that must be passed down in turn. 'Up Helly Aa was a way of preserving heritage and culture that might have been lost to twentieth-century life,' one of the Unst squad said. 'Although it was a Victorian invention, it was a good way of preserving that.'

Up Helly Aa has its roots in an earlier winter festival, nothing to do with Vikings, in which young carousers would set off home-made explosives and drag burning tar barrels through the Lerwick streets. On one occasion, in 1855, a cannon-load of dead cats were fired from the walls of the fort. An 1875 article in the *Shetland Times* gives a strong whiff of these revels, the newspaper editor denouncing the 'time-honoured institution of the tar-barrel, with its hurdle and chains, its noxious smoke and scorching flame, its yelling imps and barbarous dances, its masquerade and saturnalia, inspiring fear, and threatening destruction of property and life'.

A more genteel version of Up Helly Aa began with Prince Alfred's visit to Shetland in January 1882, and as the century moved towards its end the festival became increasingly Norse in character. There was a feeling that something was in danger of being lost, or perhaps that something almost forgotten ought, with urgency, to be rediscovered. 'This is a transition time such as never was before,' Laurence Williamson, a folklorist from Yell, wrote in a letter of 1892. 'The old Northern civilisation is now in full strife with the new and Southern one, and traditions, customs which have come down from hoary antiquity are now dying forever. The young don't care for their fathers' ways.'

It feels almost absurd and rather priggish now to talk of Up Helly Aa's ideological background. 'This is far more than just an excuse for a drink,' I was once told. 'But it is a *brilliant* excuse.' Ironic, then, that the festival has its roots in a cultural movement that was sombre and sober. Up Helly Aa, as it developed in the late nineteenth and early twentieth centuries, was shaped by socialists, teetotallers and intellectuals. Perhaps the most significant figure was the blind writer J. J. Haldane Burgess, who, in 1897, wrote 'The Up-Helly-Aa Song', an anthem still sung more than a century later. It is surely no coincidence that the lines of its closing verse – 'Our galley is the People's Right, the dragon of the free' – seem to evoke 'The Red Flag'.

An element of racial theory can also be detected in Shetland's Norse revival. When Arthur Laurenson, a Lerwick businessman and politician, wrote a paper on the superstitions and speech of island fishermen, he began by stating that, 'The native population of the Shetland Islands is Norse in blood and origin. There is not, nor has there been, any appreciable Celtic element in it. To this day the Norse physiognomy of the people is distinctly marked; nowhere do you find the Celtic type.' Laurenson was writing in 1874.

Talk of pure bloodlines may strike the modern reader as troubling. George Mackay Brown, in the late 1960s, noted that 'Such myths, in Germany only a few years ago, produced the greatest nightmare in history.' This is certainly not to claim that there is any such aspect to Up Helly Aa now. Indeed, one of the reasons that Shetland people still feel a warm connection to

Norway is because, during the Second World War, the islands were a base for Norwegian resistance to Nazi occupation. Still, Viking warrior culture continues to be vulnerable to exploitation by extremists. I once had a conversation with a young man who had covered his Norse tattoos with imagery from Pictish symbol stones, in part because he did not want to be taken for a white supremacist.

The first appearance of a Viking galley at Up Helly Aa was 1889. The Guizer Jarl, wearing Norse costume, was introduced in 1906. It is a huge honour to be Guizer Jarl, a thing that stays with you for the rest of your life. I have heard of one former Jarl who was buried in full Viking armour, which may confuse some future archaeologist. Since 1921 the Jarl Squad have all dressed as Vikings. A great deal of care has always gone into the outfits, as atmospheric old photographs show, and varying levels of poverty and affluence have influenced materials and design. The years in which the Lerwick squad wore bearskins and wolfskins coincided with the Shetland oil boom. The capital's Up Helly Aa is still far and away the biggest and most spectacular of the festivals, with thousands on the streets for the torchlit procession, but there is a view among those in outlying areas that the Lerwick men spend far too much money and take it all too seriously. It is rumoured, I was told with amused horror, that they employ a dance coach. '*This*', one of the Unst squad insisted of their local ritual, 'is the *real* Up Helly Aa.'

Authenticity is relative, of course. The Vikings of Up Helly Aa could never be like the real Vikings, nor would anyone want them to be. 'They were warlike people in conflicted times, and their ideologies were also to a marked degree underpinned by the supernatural empowerment of violence,' Neil Price writes in *The Children of Ash & Elm*. 'We should not read the Vikings backwards from our own time, but anyone who regards them in a "heroic" light needs to think again.'

In 922 the missionary and diplomat Ahmad ibn Fadlān travelled from Baghdad to what is now Russia, where he encountered Viking traders on the Volga River. He called them al-Rusiyyāh, or Rus', and wrote up his observations and interactions. His eyewitness account of the funeral of a Rus' leader, ten days of ritualised rape and slaughter leading to cremation and burial in a ship, is a document of reeking horror. I wish I had not read it.

In many ways, therefore, Viking culture is an odd thing to celebrate. But as George Mackay Brown wrote of Orkney's relationship with the Norse, what is felt for them is 'a romantic reverence . . . a kind of sentimental make-believe history, very different from the terrible and fruitful things that actually happened to our ancestors'.

*

Night had fallen. The moon had risen. We were on a headland above the beach at Norwick, waiting for the galley to be burned.

The people gathered in expectant darkness could be sensed rather than seen.

At half past seven a firework went up. This was the signal for torches to be lit and soon the water of the bay was aglow with reflected fire. The guizers, a hundred and fifty of them, marched down a steep hill to the burning place, a bright line of flame. The Jarl Squad were out front, of course, but in procession behind them were the other local squads – men and women dressed as astronauts, Santa Claus, Sherlock Holmes and goodness knows what else. Costume themes are often hyper-local in-jokes. Once, in Lerwick, I praised the outfits of what I took to be a squad of Elvis impersonators, but was soon put right. They had in fact come as members of Showaddywaddy who, many years before, played the inaugural gig at the Clickimin leisure centre.

The longship they burn at Norwick is not the same as the longship I had seen being towed around the island in front of

the bus. That one's too nice to waste. Instead they get an old fishing boat, Unst having about as many of those as geese, rig it up with a dragon head and tail, decorate it with colourful shields painted by kids at the local school, and surround it with wooden pallets and other junk in classic bonfire style. It is given a name, Norðrljós, meaning 'Northern Lights', and finished with a red sail bearing a raven emblem, wings outstretched.

It was quite a thing to see this boat enclosed in a ring of fire as the squads crowded round. This was an important occasion and demanded appropriate music. Johnny Cash would not do. They sang 'The Galley Song':

> Floats the raven banner o'er us,
> Round our Dragon Ship we stand;
> Voices joined in gladsome chorus,
> Raised aloft the flaming brand.

Every guizer has a duty
When he joins the festive throng;
Honour freedom, love and beauty
In the feast, the dance, the song.

There were three cheers for Up Helly Aa, three cheers for the Guizer Jarl, then one of the Jarl Squad yelled, 'Throw in your torches!' – and everyone did.

Within a minute the raven sail had burned away and soon the whole thing was ablaze. The dragon prow was black against the flames, forked tongue darting, snake-like, as if to taste the smoke. What had been, in daylight, a knackered old boat now looked fearsome and strange. In the morning it would be nothing more than a pile of ash and charred wood, a mess at the side of the road, but for now there was no difficulty in picturing some Viking chief laid out on deck, already halfway to Valhalla.

*

ONE ORDINARY DAY in the spring of 2003, Carole Hoey was washing dishes at the kitchen sink when a sound, or rather a sudden absence of sound, caused her to glance out the window. She had lived here, on the land between the lochs, for six years and had become used to the view, Orkney's everyday miracle: the hills of Hoy, the waters of Stenness and Harray, and, just up the road, the Ring of Brodgar – Scotland's biggest stone circle.

What snagged her attention was the realisation that she could no longer hear the tractor. It had been passing up and down, ploughing a field belonging to her neighbours, preparing for the sowing of wild flowers in ground that, for years, had been given over to barley. But the planned meadow would not now happen. A very different crop was about to emerge.

As the plough worked the southern part of the field, it had caught on something heavy and dragged it from where it lay. That was why the tractor had stopped.

Hoey watched as the plough rose from the earth. There was a slab lodged between its blades. 'It wasn't any old stone,' she recalled. 'It looked like it had been deliberately made.'

The rectangular object was a little over five feet long. Four semicircular notches along one side appeared very like hand-holds. The islands of Orkney are rich in prehistoric sites, and it was thought, at first, that the slab could be the capstone of a Bronze Age cist. The possibility of human remains prompted investigation, and when, a week or so later, two archaeologists arrived from the Scottish mainland, Hoey was given a trowel and invited to help. What was revealed, as she scraped the earth, was the top of a wall. 'It was so exciting and enthralling. I was the first person to see that in thousands of years.'

This was not a grave but a building, and not Bronze Age but older – Neolithic. And it was thought likely that there was more to be discovered. 'I didn't realise,' Hoey told me, 'how big it was going to be.'

No one did. How could they? The subsequent Ness of Brodgar excavation – 'the Ness' to its familiars – would become one of the largest and longest-running archaeological digs in Britain. And what it has revealed is remarkable: a complex of monumental structures built, rebuilt and eventually destroyed with ceremony and purpose over a period of around one thousand two hundred years. They offer, in their stately ruins, glimpses of the Stone Age people who made them, people at once familiar and deeply strange, whose voices are lost but whose sharp minds and skilled hands can be inferred and admired. The Ness is a window into the ancient past. The view is breathtaking.

*

Orkney is an archipelago of seventy or so islands lying off the north-east tip of Scotland. The largest is referred to as the

Mainland, though the Vikings knew it as Hrossey. Orkney, like Shetland, is full of Norse names and every map is a poem: Bay of Skaill, Water of the Wicks, Candle of the Sneuk. The Vikings, when they got there, found the islands covered in pre-historic sites. The *Orkneyinga Saga* tells the story of a raiding party, caught out by a snowstorm, that took shelter in what they called Orkahaugr, a Neolithic burial mound; and there, in the dark of the dead-house, two warriors lost their minds. Orkahaugr is famous these days as Maeshowe, a popular visitor attraction. You can go inside the stone chamber and see Viking graffiti carved on the ancient walls – a dragon, a serpent, a forest of runes.

I first travelled to Orkney towards the end of July, the ferry ploughing the Pentland Firth. Arriving at the terminal by the village of St Margaret's Hope, I drove north through a chain of islands linked by causeways – South Ronaldsay, Burray, Glimps Holm, Lamb Holm, the Mainland – until I came to the Ness of Brodgar. Ness, another Norse-derived word, means 'headland'. Brodgar is 'bridge farm'.

The approach to the site, especially on foot, is like entering another world. There is a strong sense of a threshold crossed. A nearly twenty-foot monolith, The Watchstone, stands at one end of a narrow little bridge leading to the Ness; you half expect it to pose a riddle in return for passage. To one side of the bridge is the freshwater Loch of Harray, on the other the saltwater Loch of Stenness; yin-yang lakes in a liminal zone.

I passed through an open farm gate and made for Carole Hoey's old house, repurposed as 'Dig HQ' – the headquarters of the excavation team.

Being on site felt like walking through a major construction project. The Ness isthmus covers an area of seven acres and large parts had been exposed – the ruins of a great settlement with origins in the mid-fourth millennium BC. Forty buildings have been identified within the excavated area. Geophysical surveying – a non-invasive imaging technology used to detect man-made structures underground – suggests a total of around a hundred and twenty, but it is thought that this is an underestimate and the true figure could be two hundred. Seen from above, a drone's-eye view, the shape and pattern of the buildings was clear, yet from the ground it appeared a chaos of stone.

'Welcome to the Ness of Brodgar,' I heard a tour guide tell his party. 'Most of the monuments you can see in this landscape date from the Neolithic, the New Stone Age. The earliest evidence of Neolithic activity in Britain is around 4100 BC. The Neolithic is defined by the adoption of agriculture. We shift from being hunter-gatherers to settling down and farming. The earliest evidence of agriculture in Orkney is 3700 BC, so it takes a couple of centuries to get here – like most things.' There was laughter at that. 'But when it does arrive, it flourishes.'

A few dozen visitors stood at the lip of a trench, trying to make sense of the structures within. Diggers, bent to their labours, paid the onlookers no mind. They were five feet down and five thousand years away. What's more, they had a deadline. This was to be the last season. The Ness was in the final weeks of its strange second life.

Unlike the celebrated prehistoric village of Skara Brae, six miles or so to the north-west, which was built from resilient stone gathered from the nearby coast, the buildings of the Ness were made from a softer, quarried stone that cannot be left exposed to the elements. 'It's going to turn to dust,' the guide explained, scooping a handful of fragments from the top of a wall and letting it fall through his fingers. 'Five, six years, I think a huge proportion of this would be gone. So it must return to the conditions that preserved it for thousands of years.'

Since its discovery, the Ness has been excavated for up to nine weeks during the summer, at the end of which time the trenches are covered by tarpaulins held down by thousands of old tyres. This year, however, would be different. All the trenches were to be backfilled with the material that had been taken out over years of excavation, and which had been piled in a huge spoil heap at the edge of the site. This season was one long farewell. Some diggers had been crying. Others were philosophical. 'It is going back into the dark,' one told me. 'But hopefully we have illuminated some things.'

Visitors to Skara Brae are often struck by its Hobbit-y appearance, but at the Ness one is very far from the Shire. These buildings, whatever their purpose, had been large and magnificent. Walls still stood to three feet or so in some places, but what impressed most was their finish. The best of them, Structure 27, was approximately fifty-six feet long by thirty-six wide, and its masonry, even now, was clearly masterful, the stone courses so elegant and smooth that it gave the misleading

impression of being newly made. Tourists had been known to ask bemused diggers, 'Why are you building this and when will it be finished?'

As I looked down into the interior, an archaeologist was at work in an exposed hearth, a scatter of charcoal across its surface. People must have warmed themselves here in the glow of a fire that, thousands of years ago, burned out for the last time.

*

In Dig HQ, Nick Card was seated at his desk, his dog Tam, a Border collie, chewing a bone by his feet. A Scot in his mid-sixties with silver hair and beard, Nick is director of the excavation and has been with it since the start. The Ness is not only a place of work and endless fascination; it's also his home. For the last few years he has lived in a farmhouse overlooking the site. He opens his curtains in the morning and looks out at the big skies and big stones of a prehistoric landscape. Every day, when he steps down into Structure 27, he can't keep from smiling.

His intellectual excitement was evident during our discussions, as was his admiration for the people who had built these structures. The quality of the work suggested specialist trades: masons, quarrymen, even some sort of architect, perhaps sketching out the design with charcoal on animal skin. He insisted upon their sophistication: 'We must never, ever underestimate what our ancestors were capable of.'

Yet while he praised the builders, Nick seemed reluctant to speculate about the use and purpose of what they had built. He had once described Structure 10, the largest building, as a 'Neolithic cathedral' – but now regretted that likening. He was coming to the view that it had been built as a residence for an individual or family of very high status.

'So, closer to a palace?' I asked.

He frowned. 'I wouldn't call it a palace. A house of renown.'

It is tempting for an outsider to look at the Ness, its grandeur, and conclude that it must have been a site of spiritual or political authority, or some mixture of the two. But those closest to the excavation are the most wary of conjecture. The furthest Nick would go was to describe it as 'a place of gathering for masses of people'.

There is evidence for this: not only the size of the buildings, but also deposits that suggest preparation and consumption of food on a huge scale. Around 2400 BC, at least four hundred cows were killed and then eaten during one feast, or so radiocarbon dating and other analysis suggests. The bones of their shins, cracked for marrow, were then arranged around the perimeter of Structure 10 — as if in celebration of wealth, abundance and consumption.

For Mark Edmonds, co-director of the Ness, this feast was a 'spectacle terrifying in scale'. The butchery must surely have meant a great deal of blood and pain?

'A huge amount. Four hundred-plus animals being slaughtered is difficult to get your head round. But the other thing it does is burst the assumption people often make: that life in prehistory was small-scale, close-grained, relatively tightly knit communities. The Ness tells you that life was sometimes massive in extent, and messy and complex.'

I'd noticed Mark around the dig. He stood out. Sunglasses and striped T-shirts gave him a Velvet Underground look. He is a serious and accomplished archaeologist, but allows himself freedom to imagine what life must have been like in the islands. His remarkable book *Orcadia* reads, at times, as if written by an eyewitness to the Neolithic.

I kept coming back to one sentence in particular: 'The past is not a world to retreat to; it is where we argue about the future.' Sitting in a hut, out of the wind, we talked about that.

'Prehistory is easily recruited for a romantic view of the past where everything's great, and everybody gets on, and everybody is in tune with the rhythms of the natural world,' he said. 'I think the story of this site is quite the opposite. We see the appetites for construction, the appetites for the marshalling of people, and for food on a grand scale. More and more stone, more and more timber, more and more people, more and more cattle – until, towards the end of the Neolithic or the beginning of the Bronze Age, it crashes. The pattern of consumption was unsustainable. And of course it's understandable why that is a theme I've been thinking a lot about recently – in terms of our contemporary situation.'

'You see our present selves in this gobbling of resources?' I asked.

'Definitely. We're facing a period of intense and dramatic risk to many aspects of the world now, but it's not the first time that's happened – and it's not the first time that we've been responsible for it. There was a very complex social and political world here, and it fell apart. So rather than seeing prehistory as a place where you can go for sentimental escape from the character of our relationship with the world now, archaeology can give insights into the human capacity to do that kind of thing over and over again.'

Who were the feasters of the Ness? Ancient populations are tricky to estimate. Mark thought that the numbers would have varied significantly with poor harvests and disease, but when times were good then there could have been as many people across Orkney during the Neolithic as there are now: around 20,000.

It is almost certain, though, that those congregating here were not only people from the islands. Material found at the site, such as glossy volcanic glass from Arran, hint at social and trade links with Scotland's west coast. But the connections go much further. Orkney seems to have been a cultural and technological innovator during the Neolithic. It has been argued that the nearby Stones of Stenness is the earliest stone circle in Britain, a few hundred years older than Stonehenge. Similarly, so-called Grooved Ware, a distinctive style of flat-bottomed pottery, perfect for serving food, appears to have originated in the archipelago and spread across Britain and Ireland.

Ideas – and the people who carried them – were on the move.

*

That the Ness was a gathering place, something akin to a pilgrimage site, is an attractive thought. Indeed there is a certain poetry in the way that, for the last two decades, it has exerted a similar pull on those who have come, summer after summer, to dig there. The wind howling across the lochs is a call to prayer.

During excavation season, there have been up to a hundred or so people working at the Ness at any one time. Volunteers mostly; a mix of students, locals and archaeologists from elsewhere in Britain. Artists, too. Jeanne, a painter at work in Structure 10, explained how she copes with gusts that can easily blow over an easel. She works on canvases small enough to grip in one hand, and dresses in seven layers of clothes – 'One day it was eight!'

For some novice diggers, the Ness has offered a first taste of a real excavation, and the chance of an electrifying find. Jessica Heupel was a twenty-year-old archaeology major at Willamette University in Salem, Oregon, when in 2012 she discovered an object that has come to be known as the 'Sky Axe'. This is a polished-stone axe-head, patterned blue-black and white, which, when she lifted it from the earth, appeared to reflect the clouds passing above. The look on her face as she held it, Nick Card had said, would stay with him forever.

When I called Jessica in St Louis, Missouri, she was still excited as she remembered that moment: 'You really do feel connected to the past. You're like, "Holy cow! This was something someone held, like, five thousand years ago." To find an axe that beautiful and intact, and to feel the weight of it, I was kind of in awe.'

This is the elegant serendipity of archaeology. A person is born towards the end of the twentieth century, on the other side of the Atlantic, and, through a series of choices and coincidences, happens to be in precisely the right spot at the right time – not a foot to the left or right, not five minutes later coming back from tea break – to uncover an axe-head that someone, around 2800 BC, had put into the earth for reasons of their own.

The Sky Axe was not lost or discarded; it was a meaningful object made from a type of stone not native to Orkney and seems to have been placed in Structure 14 as part of a ritual deposit marking the end of that building's life before the interior was filled with rubble. Neolithic axe-heads were not always made for use, but rather for aesthetic power; they may have been given as gifts, expressions of alliance and esteem, and it is possible that some had a symbolic importance – carrying associations with particular people and places. The Sky Axe may have spoken, to those who knew its origins, of distant horizons; and now, thanks to the young woman who found it, the skies of the American Midwest are part of its story too.

Jessica Heupel is not the only digger moved by a discovery at the Ness. Jo Bourne, an archaeologist and writer from Kent, was a week or so into the first of ten summers at the site when she found the 'Butterfly Stone' – a heavy slab incised with two examples of the motif that has become emblematic of the Ness. The main 'butterfly' is, from wing-tip to wing-tip, about the length of a human hand, and has been deeply carved, probably with a piece of flint.

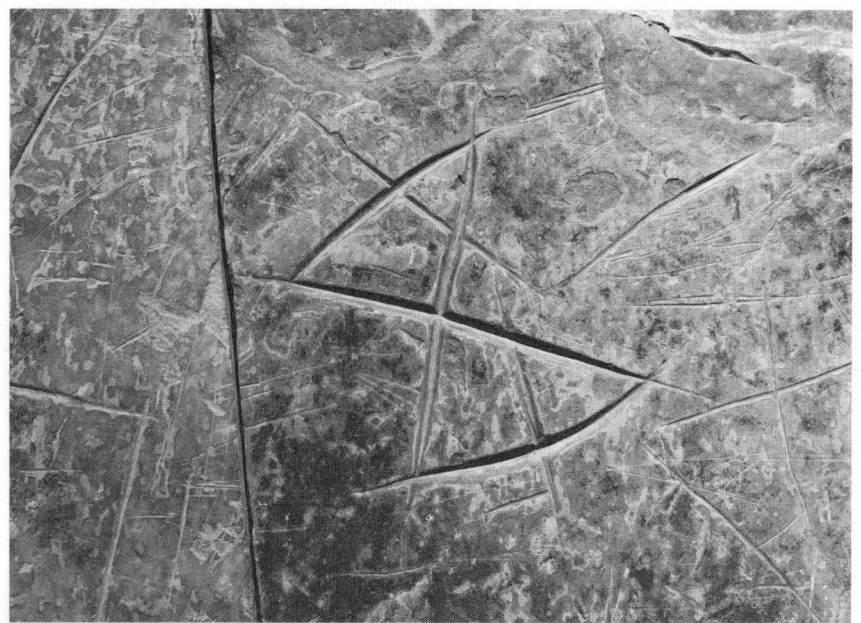

It was a cold, wet day when Jo found the stone. She had been tasked with removing a small pile of rubble blocking the northern entrance to the annex of Structure 12. She had taken away the first couple of stones when she saw the butterfly. There was a woozy unreality about that first glimpse. 'It was,' she recalled, 'like going underwater in a swimming pool when everything is kind of loud and noisy and real around you, and you just dip into some more silent place.'

There is an intimate moment when a digger finds something, when it is just them and the object and the hovering ghost of whoever touched it last. Then they finish trowelling it from the ground and it belongs to the world, destined for the museum storage box, or, in the case of special finds, the exhibition case and admiring gaze of visitors.

The Butterfly Stone, being special, falls into the second category. I had seen it in London, in the British Museum, cocooned within glass; as had Jo Bourne. 'I found that, on a dig in Orkney,' she had told a little girl who was looking at it. Having come into its presence once again, she didn't want to walk away. Numbered and recorded, the stone was now part of the material culture of human civilisation – and always will be.

But does Jo feel that, on some level, it is hers?

'Secretly, I do. There's a feeling of ownership even though, intellectually, I know that's not the case. Yeah, I kind of love it.'

*

More Neolithic 'rock art' has been discovered at the Ness than in the rest of the UK put together. In excess of one thousand two hundred examples have been recovered from the site, some of it similar to what I had seen on Anglesey. In addition to the butterflies, there are scratches and incisions of various kinds – crosses, diamonds, triangles, zigzags – as well as the pecked and ground depressions known as cup-marks. These shapes don't seem to be representational, nor are they a language, and even the word 'art' is probably the wrong way to think about them.

'Art is a very post-Renaissance term that we're putting on to the ancient past, and it may not apply,' explained Antonia Thomas, an archaeologist at the Ness and expert on Orkney's decorated stones. 'But there's something fundamentally human about our need to make a mark, to decorate, to leave our imprint for the future. That's why these carvings speak to us now, I think, and transcend the millennia.'

Looking for meaning in the carvings is a frustrating business, but they certainly have a *tone*. There is something anxious about them, something nerve-jangling and twitchy. Some, Antonia suggested, may have been apotropaic – that is, intended to ward off evil. A number of diggers, I noticed, had commemorated their time at the Ness with tattoos of designs discovered at the site. One, though, explained that she wouldn't be comfortable having a butterfly inked on her body, because she simply did not know what it had meant. What if it was a spell? A warning?

The Ness is well named. Strange*ness*, uncanni*ness*, mysterious*ness* – it conveys all these. The Neolithic mind is unknowable. We are so like and yet so unlike those people. We can walk within their buildings, pick up their tools, look out over the same water and hills, and yet how they saw and understood their world is beyond us. They did some really weird things.

One day, around 2500 BC, four centuries after it had been built, Structure 10 – the building Nick Card had called 'a house of renown' – was abandoned. Its walls were brought low, and its interior, where who knows what chief or priest held court, was filled with rubble and a substance known as midden – rotted refuse and ash. Buried, it became a great mound that, until twenty years ago, was thought natural, just another swell in the Orkney landscape. The archaeologists, digging into it, found the house; within the house they found a hearth; within the hearth they found an object placed there long ago as, one assumes, some sort of closing offering: the skull of a cow, inverted.

Cattle were fundamental to Neolithic Orkney. They provided leather, milk and meat, but their value, according to Mark Edmonds, was more than physical and economic. The emphasis on breeding and bloodlines, he thought, would have made herds proxies for human communities. 'So, yes,' he said, 'they are a great source of material wealth, but also a rich source of metaphor. You talk to farmers here and they get that.' The skull in the hearth could have been a known beast – an animal with a name and life history, associated with a particular person or family. It may have been a sacrifice. George Mackay Brown has imagined such a scene: 'The offered throat of a bullock, a chant, a stone knife – these instruments and elements were required before the ceremony was complete and the honey-dripping lord of summer walked in power through the sky.'

The Ness is not the only Orcadian site at which ritual deposits of animals have been found. At Links of Noltland, on the island of Westray, a ring of twenty-eight cattle skulls were set upside down within the foundation of a Neolithic house. On Cuween Hill, the skulls of two dozen dogs were placed in a burial chamber. A tomb above the cliffs of South Ronaldsay was excavated in 1976 and found to contain the bones of fourteen white-tailed sea eagles mingled with human remains. Five curved talons are on display in the Kirkwall museum; tiny drinking horns laid out for a fairy feast. One bright day, during my time in Orkney, I took the ferry to Rousay, an island of many tombs, and followed a steep path to Knowe of Yarso, a chambered cairn built around five thousand three hundred years ago. It was a grassy mound above a heathery hillside looking over Eynhallow Sound. A little wooden door allowed access, and three skylights gave enough light to see that the stones of the chamber were green with algae. Here archaeologists had found the skulls of seventeen people placed around the walls, facing into the room, and the bones of at least thirty-six red deer.

It is tempting to regard all these as marks of identity: the deer people, the dog people, the cattle clan, the eagle folk. But whether they were placed in tombs and dwellings as acts of assertion, propitiation, remembrance or thanksgiving is uncertain. At the time, such gestures would have been well understood, their meaning and resonance clear, but the skulls and claws have come down to us, the forgetful inheritors, as objects that perplex and disturb.

*

I returned to the Ness of Brodgar at the end of summer. Cattle lay in cold fields; black ribbons of geese streamed through the pale sky. The farm gate was closed and locked, the excavation over.

Nick Card was in Dig HQ. On the desk was his favourite trowel, his name carved into the handle. He intended to bury it on site as a memento of his involvement. 'In hundreds of years, perhaps someone will dig it up and go, *Nick who?* We walked through the house to the kitchen and stood by the window. 'So,' he said, 'this is where it all started.'

He pointed to where Carole Hoey saw the tractor stop and where the first stone must have come up. We were looking out at what was, once again, farmland. The spoil heap was gone. Most of the trenches had already been filled, and over the next week or so, if the weather held, the rest would be put back underground. A goose flying overhead would not, now, make much of the Ness. Just another field on the way to the wintering grounds.

But for Orcadians, hardly that. This place makes you proud to be an islander, is how one local digger, Sigurd Towrie, summed it up. Why proud? Something to do with the enabled connection to Orkney folk of the past. 'They undoubtedly went through the same things as we do,' he said. 'The darkness of midwinter, the joy of equinox when the days are equal and you know that the daylight's coming back; midsummer and knowing that darkness is coming. Cold, wind. They *knew* this place. It's the continuation of a long, long human story.'

Nick and I went outside. Mud squelched underfoot. Trench J was gone, and Trenches X and Y, and Trench P – where the Sky Axe and Butterfly Stone had been found – was almost completely covered. Almost all that remained of Structure 10 was the hearth where the cow skull had been placed upside down.

The director led the way past Dig HQ, past two lichen-shaggy standing stones and down a slope to Structure 27, Tam running ahead and stopping at the edge of the trench. Work had not yet begun on backfilling this building. It was the last to be excavated and would be the last to be buried.

For Nick, the Ness is his legacy. Even though there were many structures that hadn't yet been excavated, even though it was frustrating that he would never explore them, he knew that covering the site was for the best. It had to be returned to the earth's protective embrace. Besides, there were years of post-excavation analysis ahead. There were books to be written, stories to be told. And yet he was finding it difficult to witness the buildings disappear. He had often been close to tears during our conversations.

'The Ness has been such a big part of my life for the last twenty years,' he said. 'It's filled many of my waking hours and sometimes sleeping hours as well. It has fulfilled many boyhood dreams when I thought about being an archaeologist, all those years ago, and making a discovery like this. It's the discovery of not just one lifetime, but several.'

We walked down some steps cut into the earth bank and stood by a large upright slab that had formed one side of the building's narrow entrance. Nick invited me to notice the inner edge, how rounded it was. It had been worn by thousands of people brushing against it as they passed in and out. This is what we leave of ourselves: a smooth edge on an old stone.

Very early the next morning, as I drove through the dark to catch the ferry home, I passed the road leading to the Ness. There was a single light on, out there on the isthmus, and I wondered if it was Nick. It would surely be strange for him to live there now, overlooking the buried site, no longer able to see the buildings he loves. Yet it feels right that he will have their keeping, like The Watchstone on the other side of the bridge. I had told him, the last time we spoke, that I imagined him, in years to come, as a watcher or guardian of the Ness.

He is a highly practical person, and I had expected him to dismiss this as whimsy. But he nodded.

'You don't own the land. You don't own the house. You are just here for a moment in the history of this landscape. So, a guardian? Yeah, I'd go with that.'

SCION

THE ICE. THE WALL. THE TREE. US.

That is the story, in seven words, of Sycamore Gap.

Now let me try to tell it better.

Two men walked along Hadrian's Wall, in conversation about deep time. 'We humans like to talk about ourselves,' the older man said, 'and yet we are less than the shaving off the end of a fingernail in the great scheme of things.'

Ian Jackson is a geologist. He is retired after a long career with the British Geological Survey and now expresses his passion for rock in books for a general readership. Jacquetta Hawkes saw geologists and archaeologists as kindred thinkers. They were, she wrote in *A Land*, 'instruments of consciousness who are engaged in reawakening the memory of the world'.

It was midsummer morning, already warm. I had met Ian at Steel Rigg car park and we climbed the steep path up Peel Crag. We were heading east, to a crime scene.

Ian had grown up at one end of the Wall, in Carlisle, gone to university at the other, in Newcastle, and lives with a Roman road, the Stanegate, running through his garden. I wanted to see Wall country through his eyes. He has an extractive gaze; can look at a landscape and strip away millions of years. I think he was intrigued by my request to meet: 'One thing nobody ever asks about Sycamore Gap is *why* it's there.'

Hadrian's Wall was built in AD 122. At seventy-three miles it is almost twice the size of the Antonine Wall. This central section is especially scenic, the Wall clinging to hills and valleys, a rollercoaster of stone. Much of its masonry has been robbed over the centuries and put to other use. William Hutton, who walked its length in 1802, observed that 'Half the churches, houses, barns, partition-walls, and roads, nay, even down to a very horse-block, were raised out of this Wall.' Nevertheless, it still stands in these parts to four feet or so. Long grass growing on top waved in the breeze as we passed along its southern face.

Time and nature have gentled the Wall. It has an accidental beauty. Wild flowers flash among the stones; foxgloves, rock rose, wild thyme. We are so used to thinking of the Wall as picturesque that we have lost sight of how violently out of place it is. Charlotte Higgins, in her book on Roman Britain, captured its unnerving surrealism: 'Visually, it makes about as much sense as René Magritte's open door suspended in a cloudscape.'

The Wall, here, was built along a rocky ridge, the Whin Sill, which is very high in places, making it an even more formidable barrier for anyone approaching from the north. The Romans had used topography to define and defend their empire. Ian and I dropped down into a dip, at the bottom of which were the remains of Milecastle 39, known as Castle Nick, and then climbed sharply again to the top of the next rise. 'Before,' he sighed, 'this would have been the big reveal.'

That 'before' said a lot. We were looking down into Sycamore Gap, or what had been Sycamore Gap.

Out of habit and stubborn defiance, locals still call it that – but the tree from which it took its name is gone. On the morning of 28 September 2023, it was discovered lying across the Wall, having been cut through close to the base of its trunk. At first it was thought, or hoped, that it had blown down in the storm of the previous night. Such a loss would have been more easily borne. But it soon became clear that this had been a deliberate act. The tree had been 'murdered' – the verb many used at the time. The felling made international headlines, but closer to home it felt tribal. As Andrew Poad, the National Trust's senior manager in the area, told me: 'This was an attack on everybody who lives here; on Northumberland, on the north-east, on Hadrian's Wall, and on all those who felt a connection with the tree.'

The Sycamore's status as icon and emblem is all the more interesting for being a recent development. Like the Wall, sycamores are a foreign intervention in the landscape; they are native to central, eastern and southern Europe, and were probably introduced to Britain in the sixteenth century. The tree in the gap is thought to have been around two hundred years old. According to the National Trust, it was planted by John Clayton, a lawyer and landowner who, beginning in the 1830s, bought up estates that included stretches of the Wall in order to preserve it from destruction. By the time of his death, Clayton owned almost twenty miles of Hadrian's Wall and five forts including Vindolanda.

We can imagine that the sycamore, as it grew to maturity, was often admired. But it was not much remarked upon, at least not in print. Jesse Mothersole, walking the Wall in 1920, noticed it in passing: 'At Steel Rigg Gap the ground falls very steeply, and the Wall-stones are laid horizontally. Here in the gap is a small walled enclosure, with a sycamore growing in it.' Hunter Davies, half a century later, makes no mention of the tree in his book on the Wall – and such a sharp-eyed journalist would certainly have done so if he thought there was decent copy in it.

As for the name, 'Sycamore Gap' is said to have been coined by Lawrence Hewer, a poet and National Trust ranger, when asked by the Ordnance Survey – in the mid-1980s – if that particular place on the Wall was called anything. That is the story you're told, anyway, if you ask around, but the name does not actually appear on OS maps, at least none I've seen, so it's a bit of a mystery. What is certain is that the sycamore's profile was boosted by its appearance in the 1991 film *Robin Hood: Prince of Thieves* and then again, in 2016, when it was named England's

Tree of the Year. The power of social media did the rest. It was impossible to take a bad photograph of the tree, cupped as it was by the rising land, and so it became an Instagram honeypot, as well as a sort of westward companion to that other lonely sentinel, the Angel of the North.

We walked down the steep path to where the tree had stood. I had been here years before with my wife and children, when the boys were small, and we had enjoyed the delightful oddness of the tree, the way it sat like a pearl in a goblet. There was a swooping pleasure in the approach that no child could resist. We began high above its crown, descended into its green shade, then over the Wall and up again on the other side.

The absence, now, was brutal. A protective fence had been built around the stump in the hope that it would show signs of new life. What a resurrection that would be. The fence was low enough to lean over and look at what was left. Tributes had been placed by the roots: a cross made from twigs bound with grass, and a number of small stones on which people had written messages of condolence and thanks; one pebble was painted with a picture of the tree under a crescent moon. This was a kind of shrine.

Eight months had passed since the felling and the cut wood had darkened. Large, sticky patches of orange and black were a mix of bleeding sap and human ashes. On and around the stump, people had scattered their dead. 'This will help it to grow,' they had been overheard to say, but in fact the opposite was true and a sign would soon go up asking the public to desist.

People wished to be part of the tree, to be drawn into its roots. You might dismiss that as sentimental; I'd say it comes from some lingering sense that trees can be sacred and that cutting them down is an assertion of power over spirit.

Tacitus tells us that woods were the holy places of the Germanic tribes, and that the Romans, on invading Anglesey, destroyed groves devoted to the 'barbarous superstitions' of the druids. The excavation in 1984 of a medieval church on the Swedish island of Frösön revealed the stump of a birch below the floor of the choir. On top of its roots was a scatter of bone: elk, deer, piglets, sheep, goats and at least seven brown bears. Radiocarbon dating indicates that the animals died in the late tenth to early eleventh centuries. The site has been interpreted as evidence of a *blót* – a rite of sacrifice and sacred feasting. Parts of the bodies, mostly lower jaws, were laid around the tree, giving the gods their share. It was cut down in the late eleventh century and the church is thought to have been constructed in the twelfth. The birch may have represented Yggdrasill, the great tree at the centre of Norse cosmology. Building a place of Christian worship upon its remains could be seen as a statement of dominance or perhaps appropriation of spiritual authority. No doubt there were people on Frösön who regretted the end of the old faith and were sad and angry to see the tree brought low.

Anger could be felt at Sycamore Gap in the immediate aftermath of the loss. But that was passing now. The word I heard most often was: 'Why?'

That's what people wanted to know. Who did it was important, of course, but what they hoped most of all was that the motivation would come out at the trial.

I spent most of the day near the tree, talking with walkers as they came by.

Mel and Andy from Devon were on their way up to Scotland to visit their daughter and had broken their journey here. It was a pilgrimage of sorts, Mel said.

Andy was shaking his head. 'I felt the need to go and say sorry to the tree. That someone could do that to it . . .'

'Why is it your place to apologise?' I asked.

'Because I'm part of the species that does this to nature.'

David from Whitley Bay was walking with one of his mates. The last time they were here, the tree was still lying across the Wall, but had not yet been sawn up to be taken away. 'We came over from Housesteads to see it and say goodbye. I was crying me eyes out. It's just all the memories that are mixed up here. It's like something being ripped out of you. Sounds daft, but it's like a family member.'

A party of schoolkids from Yorkshire stopped by the fence for a photograph.

'Mr Wilkinson and I serenaded each other under the branches of this tree last year, didn't we, Mr Wilkinson?' one of the teachers said.

'We did, yeah,' Mr Wilkinson replied. 'But I don't think it would be appropriate to sing "Everything I Do, I Do It For You" beside a stump.'

Victoria and Darren from Lincoln were on holiday in the area. They had come to pay their respects.

'It fills me with sadness,' Victoria said.

Darren nodded. 'It's just another tree but not just another tree.'

No one could stop and talk for long. There was a film being shot, a zombie movie, and walkers were being held back, out of frame, until the end of each take. A child actor with a bow and quiver of arrows walked past the fenced-off stump and climbed over the Wall, heading north. He was followed at a distance by a camera-drone, gliding through the gap with an insectoid buzz.

'You making a documentary?' a walker asked one of the crew.

'No, a feature film.'

'What, *Robin Hood 2*, without the tree?'

'Hah, not that. But the tree will be there when we're fin-ished. We're putting it back with CGI.'

If only it was that simple. But all was not lost.

SCION

Rachel Ryvar, a horticulturalist, lives a few miles from the tree, and visited the site as soon as possible after the felling, aware that the wind would be drying out the trunk. The leaves were already curling, a bad sign. 'But there was some remnant life in it,' Rachel told me. 'You have a window, ideally in the first twenty-four hours, where you can collect what we call scion material.'

Scion is the name given to the tips of branches, the most recent growth of twigs and buds. It is a word more commonly used in relation to human lineage, but in its botanical sense it refers to a cutting that can be grafted to living rootstock. The advantage of scion material is that anything that grows from it will be genetically identical: not the offspring of the Sycamore; the Sycamore reborn.

The horticulturalist and two rangers filled six compost bags with scion and seed, collecting them from the crown as it lay on the northern side of the Wall. Rachel sorted through what they had gathered, selecting the most promising specimens, and took them to Hexham Post Office to send to the National Trust. At the Trust's Plant Conservation Centre in Devon, grafts were made and the seeds tended. In time it might be possible to plant a new sycamore, grown from this material, at the spot where the tree was felled, but it would likely struggle in the wind and exposure of the gap.

The best thing would be for the tree to regrow from the stump. There was no sign of that, but it was too early to give up. Sycamores are vigorous and there was potential for a dense thicket of shoots, which could then be thinned, allowing one dominant shoot to develop into a trunk. As this would emerge from the side of the stump, the new tree would not grow straight. 'It'll be slightly off-kilter,' Rachel had said, 'which is perhaps a way of remembering what happened. Like a scar from a wound.'

That would be fitting. The land itself is a kind of wound, a broken place, or so I understood from Ian Jackson. Sycamore Gap, like every dip on this stretch of Wall, was created by melt-water flowing from the north fast enough, hard enough and for long enough to breach the barrier of the Whin Sill and drain south to lower ground. The Sill came into being 295 million years ago when molten magma deep underground cooled and hardened as dolerite. It is a very tough rock, but there must have been weaknesses at the points where the water broke through. This could have happened incrementally during the planet's four glacial periods, so between 2.6 million and twenty thousand years ago, and what you have to imagine, Ian explained, is ice pressing down on the land where we now stood, from a height of at least two thousand feet. But the world was warming, the glacier thawing, and so rushing beneath the ice was a river strong enough to drive through dolerite and leave a gap – a gap in which, one day, the Romans would build a wall, and in which, later, a sycamore would grow beautiful, beloved and mourned.

This is why Sycamore Gap mattered, I think; why deep down we found it special. It was the collision and collage of time. The great chasms of geological time. The distant lives of the Romans. The long lifetime of the tree. And we were the fourth element, knowing ourselves fleeting, coming here with people we loved, our days spinning away like sycamore keys.

Us. The tree. The wall. The ice.

We are here for a moment, a breath between glaciers, a ring in a trunk. Our history contains all other histories. We are seeded by the people of the past and seed the future in turn. Will we appear as strange to our descendants as our ancestors seem to us? Will they curse us for the troubles we are handing on?

Chopping down trees is one of the things that defines us as humans. It was how we began to change the earth. The first farmers cleared forests for timber and to open the land for fields. In the British Museum I had seen a perfect elm leaf spotlit behind glass. It fell sometime around 4000 BC. On the wall behind it was a display of stone axe-heads, slanted like rain. For six thousand years we have swung the axe. We are the cutting edge and it has brought us to a precipice.

So you look for hope where you can.

Though I did not know it then, as I turned back along the Wall, heading for home, deep within the sycamore something was happening. Dormant buds, unseen behind the bark, had been stirred by the trauma of felling, and within a few weeks the stump would put out twelve shoots. Tiny, fragile, vulnerable, but there.

It might be two hundred years before the tree fills its gap once more. No one now living will be here to see it, and who knows what sort of world it will inherit and inhabit? But it is a comfort to think of it growing there: survivor, witness, idol, friend.

The author, 1980s, Islay.

Selected Sources

RING

Anstruther, Eleanor, *A Memoir in 65 Postcards & The Recovery Diaries* (Troubador Publishing, 2024)

Braithwaite, Stuart, *Spaceships Over Glasgow: Mogwai, Mayhem and Misspent Youth* (White Rabbit, 2022)

Brophy, Kenny, 'Urban Prehistoric Enclosures: Empty Spaces/Busy Places' in *Empty Spaces: Perspectives on Emptiness in Modern History* (University of London Press, 2019)

Caesar, Julius, *The Conquest of Gaul*, trans. S. A. Handford (Penguin Books, 1951)

Chippindale, Christopher, *Stonehenge Complete: Everything Important Interesting or Odd That Has Been Written or Painted, Discovered or Imagined, About the Most Extraordinary Ancient Building in the World* (Thames & Hudson, 1983)

Cleal, Rosamund, K. E. Walker and R. Montague, *Stonehenge in its Landscape: Twentieth Century Excavations* (English Heritage, 1995)

Cleal, Rosamund and Joshua Pollard, 'The Revenge of the Native: Monuments, Material Culture, Burial and Other Practices in the Third Quarter of the 3rd Millennium BC in Wessex' in Michael J. Allen, Julie Gardiner and Alison Sheridan (eds.), *Is There A British Chalcolithic?* (Oxbow Books, 2012)

Cocker, Mark and Richard Mabey, *Birds Britannica* (Chatto & Windus, 2005)

Cocker, Mark, *Crow Country: A Meditation on Birds, Landscape and Nature* (Jonathan Cape, 2007)

Daniel, Glyn, *The Origins and Growth of Archaeology* (Penguin Books, 1967)

Darwin, Charles, *The Formation of Vegetable Mould, Through the Action of Worms, with Observations on their Habits* (John Murray, 1881)

Selected Sources

Davies, Martin J. P., *A Distant Prospect of Wessex: Archaeology and the Past in the Life and Works of Thomas Hardy* (Archaeopress, 2011)

Dickens, Charles, *A Child's History of England* (Bradbury & Evans, 1852)

Druce, Carol, *Stonedaws: The Jackdaws of Stonehenge* (CreateSpace Independent Publishing Platform, 2016)

Druce, Carol, *Rooks at the Rocks: The Rooks of Stonehenge* (CreateSpace Independent Publishing Platform, 2017)

Druce, Carol, *Hares in the Henge: The Hares of Stonehenge* (CreateSpace Independent Publishing Platform, 2021)

Fagan, Brian, *A Little History of Archaeology* (Yale University Press, 2018)

Forster, John, *The Life of Charles Dickens* (Chapman and Hall, 1872)

Garrow, Duncan and Neil Wilkin, *The World of Stonehenge* (The British Museum Press, 2022)

Gilbert, Oliver, *The Lichen Hunters* (The Book Guild, 2004)

Goldsmith, Ben, *God is an Octopus: Loss, Love and a Calling to Nature* (Bloomsbury Wildlife, 2023)

Goodwin, Derek, *Birds of Man's World* (Cornell University Press, 1978)

Hardy, Thomas, *Tess of the D'Urbervilles: A Pure Woman* (James R. Osgood, McIlvaine & Co., 1891)

Hardy, Thomas, *Personal Writings*, ed. Harold Orel (Macmillan, 1967)

Harper, Charles G., *The Exeter Road: The Story of the West of England Highway* (Chapman & Hall, 1899)

Harris, Barney, 'Landscapes of Labour: A Quantitative Study of Earth-moving and Stone-shifting in Prehistoric Northern Wessex' (thesis, Institute of Archaeology, University College London, 2019)

Hauser, Kitty, *Bloody Old Britain: O. G. S. Crawford and the Archaeology of Modern Life* (Granta Books, 2008)

Hawkes, Jacquetta, *A Land* (Cresset Press, 1951)

Hawkes, Jacquetta, *A Guide to the Prehistoric and Roman Monuments in England and Wales* (Chatto & Windus, 1951)

Hill, Rosemary, *Stonehenge* (Profile Books, 2008)

Hutton, Ronald, *Blood and Mistletoe: The History of the Druids in Britain* (Yale University Press, 2009)

Hutton, Ronald, *Pagan Britain* (Yale University Press, 2013)

King, Clive, *Stig of the Dump* (Kestrel Books, 1981)

Michell, John, *Megalithomania: Artists, Antiquarians and Archaeologists at the Old Stone Monuments* (Thames & Hudson, 1982)

Michell, John, *The New View Over Atlantis* (Thames & Hudson, 1983)

Moss, Stephen, 'Keir Starmer: "I wouldn't characterise myself as a bleeding heart liberal . . ."', *Guardian*, 21 September 2009

Orwell, George, *The Orwell Diaries* (Harvill Secker, 2009)

Parker Pearson, Mike, *Stonehenge: Exploring the Greatest Stone Age Mystery* (Simon & Schuster, 2012)

Pendragon, Arthur and C. J. Stone, *The Trials of Arthur* (Amazon, 2012)

Pepys, Samuel, *The Diary of Samuel Pepys: A Selection* (Penguin Classics, 2003)

Piggott, Stuart, *The Druids* (Thames & Hudson, 1968)

Pitts, Mike, 'Does Stonehenge's Scottish source reveal a project uniting ancient Britain?', *Observer*, 18 August 2024

Potton, Ed, 'The KLF's Jimmy Cauty: We want to be No 1 in Bavaria', *The Times*, 6 May 2023

Richards, Julian, *Stonehenge* (English Heritage, 2023)

Rifkind, Hugo, 'Sanitised solstice shows we're all hippies now', *The Times*, 19 June 2023

Roy, Rob, *Stone Circles: A Modern Builder's Guide to the Megalithic Revival* (Chelsea Green Publishing Company, 1999)

Sheldrake, Merlin, *Entangled Life: How Fungi Make Our Worlds, Change Our Minds, and Shape Our Futures* (The Bodley Head, 2020)

Stout, Adam, *Creating Prehistory: Druids, Ley Hunters and Archaeologists in Pre-war Britain* (Blackwell Publishing, 2008)

Stukeley, William, *Stonehenge A Temple Restor'd to the British Druids* (London, 1740)

Tacitus, Cornelius, *The Annals of Imperial Rome*, trans. Michael Grant (Penguin Books, 1978)

White, Gilbert, *The Natural History of Selborne* (B. White & Son, 1789)

Whitlock, Ralph, *Salisbury Plain* (Robert Hale, 1955)

Woolf, Virginia, *A Passionate Apprentice: The Early Journals 1897–1909*, ed. Mitchell A. Leaska (Chatto & Windus, 1990)

Worthington, Andy, *Stonehenge: Celebration and Subversion* (Alternative Albion, 2004)

*

Recollections of the Stonehenge Free Festival from www.ukrockfestivals.com

HENGE

Bradley, A. G., *Round About Wiltshire* (Methuen & Co., 1907)

Burl, Aubrey, *Prehistoric Avebury* (Yale University, 1979)

Causey, Andrew, *Paul Nash: Landscape and the Life of Objects* (Lund Humphries Publishers, 2013)

Cleal, Rosamund, *Avebury: A Souvenir Guide* (The National Trust, 2022)

Cope, Julian, *The Modern Antiquarian: A Pre-Millennial Odyssey Through Megalithic Britain* (Thorsons, 1998)

Cope, Julian, *How I Wrote 'The Modern Antiquarian' . . . And Why* (Head Heritage Press, 2023)

Dunn, Jane, *Antonia White: A Life* (Jonathan Cape, 1998)

Eliot, T. S., *The Waste Land* (Boni and Liverlight, 1922)

Hopkinson, Lyndall P., *Nothing To Forgive: A Daughter's Life of Antonia White* (Chatto & Windus, 1988)

Leary, Jim and David Field, *The Story of Silbury Hill* (English Heritage, 2010)

Leary, Jim, *Footmarks: A Journey Into Our Restless Past* (Icon Books, 2023)

Matless, David, *Landscape and Englishness* (expanded edition, Reaktion Books, 2016)

Milton, John, *Paradise Lost* (Samuel Simmons, 1667)

Murray, Lynda J., *A Zest for Life: The Story of Alexander Keiller* (Morven Books, 1999)

Nash, Paul, 'The Life of the Inanimate Object', *Country Life*, 1 May
   1937 in Andrew Causey (ed.), *Paul Nash: Writings on Art* (Oxford
   University Press, 2007)

Montagu, Jemima et al., *Paul Nash: Modern Artist, Ancient Landscape*
   (Tate Publishing, 2003)

Piggott, Stuart, *William Stukeley: An Eighteenth Century Antiquary*
   (revised and enlarged edition, Thames & Hudson, 1985)

Powell, Anthony, *John Aubrey and His Friends* (revised edition,
   Hogarth Press, 1988)

Rawlins, Marjorie, *Butcher, Baker, Saddlemaker: Village Life in Avebury
   from 1920 to 1974* (Antony Rowe, 1999)

Soar, Katy (ed.), *Circles of Stone: Weird Tales of Pagan Sites and Ancient
   Rites* (British Library, 2023)

Spalding, Frances, *John Piper, Myfanwy Piper: Lives in Art* (Oxford
   University Press, 2009)

Stukeley, William, *Abury, a Temple of the British Druids, with Some
   Others Described* (London, 1743)

Thorpe, Adam, *On Silbury Hill* (Little Toller Books, 2014)

White, Antonia, *Diaries 1926–1957: Volume I*, ed. Susan Chitty
   (Constable, 1991)

LOCH

Christison, Robert, 'On an Ancient Wooden Image, Found in
   November Last at Ballachulish Peat-Moss' in *Proceedings of
   the Society of Antiquaries of Scotland* (Session 1880-1, Volume 15;
   Neill and Company, 1881)

Gearey, Benjamin, 'The Discovery of the Ballachulish Goddess,
   "This Strange Relic of Paganism . . ."' in *The Pallasboy Project*
   (www.thepallasboyvessel.wordpress.com 14 August 2017)

Stevenson, Robert Louis, 'Thrawn Janet' in Louise Welsh (ed.),
   Ghost: 100 Stories to Read With the Light On (Head of Zeus, 2015)

Stewart, Alexander, Report on the Ballachulish discovery in the
   Inverness Courier, 9 December 1880

CHALK

Allen, Mike, 'A Tale of Three Giants? New Evidence for the Evolution of Cerne Abbas' Chalk Colossus', *Current Archaeology*, Issue 410, May 2024

Betjeman, John, *Letters Volume One: 1926 to 1951*, ed. Candida Lycett Green (Methuen & Co., 1994)

Betjeman, John, *Letters Volume Two: 1951 to 1984*, ed. Candida Lycett Green (Methuen & Co., 1995)

Butterworth, Jez, *Jerusalem* (Nick Hern Books, 2009)

Castledon, Rodney, *The Cerne Giant* (Dorset Publishing Co., 1996)

Darton, F. J. Harvey, *English Fabric: A Study of Village Life* (George Newnes, 1936)

Fenwick, Simon, *The Crichel Boys: Scenes from England's Last Literary Salon* (Constable, 2021)

Garner, Alan, *Treacle Walker* (4th Estate, 2021)

Gordon, Helen, *Notes From Deep Time* (Profile Books, 2021)

Hamer, Richard, *A Choice of Anglo-Saxon Verse* (Faber & Faber, 1970)

Hardy, Thomas, *The Return of the Native* (Smith, Elder & Co., 1878)

Harris, Alexandra, *Romantic Moderns: English Writers and the Imagination from Virginia Woolf to John Piper* (Thames & Hudson, 2010)

Heaney, Michael, *The Ancient English Morris Dance* (Archaeopress Publishing, 2023)

Holst, Imogen, *The Great Composers: Holst* (Faber & Faber, 1974)

Judah, Hettie, *Lapidarium: The Secret Lives of Stones* (John Murray, 2022)

Kingsnorth, Paul, 'Oak, Ash and Thorn' in *Jersualem* (John Good, 2022)

Kipling, Rudyard, *Puck of Pook's Hill* (Macmillan and Co., 1906)

Macfarlane, Robert, *The Old Ways: A Journey on Foot* (Hamish Hamilton, 2012)

Marples, Morris, *White Horses and Other Hill Figures* (Country Life, 1949)

Selected Sources

Massingham, H. J., *Downland Man* (Jonathan Cape, 1926)

Massingham, H. J., *Fee, Fi, Fo, Fum or The Giants In England* (Kegan Paul, Trench, Trubner & Co., 1926)

Massingham, H. J., *Remembrance: An Autobiography* (B. T. Batsford, 1941)

Mead, Rebecca, 'The Mysterious Origins of the Cerne Abbas Giant', *The New Yorker*, 12 May 2021

Miles, David et al., *Uffington White Horse and its Landscape: Investigations at White Horse Hill, Uffington, 1989–95, and Tower Hill, Ashbury, 1993–4* (Oxford Archaeology, 2003)

Miles, David, *The Land of the White Horse: Visions of England* (Thames & Hudson, 2019)

Morcom, Thomas and Helen Gittos, 'The Cerne Giant in its Early Medieval Context', *Speculum: A Journal of Medieval Studies*, Volume 99, Number 1, January 2024

Nielsen, Poul Otto, National Museum of Denmark – *Danish Prehistory*, trans. David Earle Robinson and Anne Block (Narayana Press, 2016)

Pollard, Joshua, 'The Uffington White Horse Geoglyph as Sun-horse', *Antiquity*, Volume 91, Issue 356, April 2017

Pratchett, Terry, *A Hatful of Sky* (Doubleday, 2004)

Ravilious, Eric and Alice Pattullo, *White Horses* (Design For Today, 2019)

Semple, Sarah, 'A Fear of the Past: The Place of the Prehistoric Burial Mound in the Ideology of Middle and Later Anglo-Saxon England', *World Archaeology*, Volume 30, Number 1, June 1998

Simmons, Gail, *Between the Chalk and the Sea* (Headline, 2023)

Sutcliff, Rosemary, *Sun Horse, Moon Horse* (The Bodley Head, 1977)

Vale, Vivian and Patricia, *The Parish Book of Cerne Abbas: Abbey and After* (Halsgrove, 2000)

Whittle, Alasdair, A. Bayliss and M. Wysocki, 'Once in a Lifetime: The Date of the Wayland's Smithy Long Barrow', *Cambridge Archaeological Journal*, Volume 17, Supplement S1, February 2007

Young, Rob, *Electric Eden: Unearthing Britain's Visionary Music* (Faber & Faber, 2011)

*

Eric Ravilious: Drawn To War (Foxtrot Films, 2022; written and directed by Margy Kinmonth)

GRAVE

Adams, Max, *The First Kingdom: Britain in the Age of Arthur* (Head of Zeus, 2021)

Bede, *Ecclesiastical History of the English People*, trans. Leo Sherley-Price (Penguin Books, 1990)

Bentley, Diana, 'The Dark Secrets of the Bog Bodies', *Minerva: The International Review of Ancient Art & Archaeology*, March/April 2015

Brown, George Mackay, *Northern Lights: A Poet's Sources*, ed. Archie Bevan and Brian Murray (John Murray, 1999)

Carver, Martin, *Sutton Hoo: Burial Ground of Kings?* (The British Museum Press, 1998)

Carver, Martin, *The Sutton Hoo Story: Encounters With Early England* (Boydell Press, 2017)

Clarke, D. V., T. G. Cowie and Andrew Foxon, *Symbols of Power at the Time of Stonehenge* (National Museum of Antiquities of Scotland, 1985)

Cole, Henri, 'Seamus Heaney: The Art of Poetry No. 75', *The Paris Review*, Issue 144, Fall 1997

Connolly, Peter, *The Roman Army* (Macdonald Educational, 1975)

Doig, Sarah, *The Real Basil Brown: From Rickenhall to Sutton Hoo and Back* (Quatrefoil, 2023)

Dronfield, Jeremy, 'Subjective Vision and the Source of Irish Megalithic Art', *Antiquity*, Volume 69, Issue 264, September 1995

Edmonds, Mark, *Orcadia: Land, Sea and Stone in Neolithic Orkney* (Head of Zeus, 2019)

Edmonds, Mark and Alan Garner, *The Beauty Things* (Group VI Press, 2016)

Selected Sources

Evans, Angela Care, *The Sutton Hoo Ship Burial* (The British Museum Press, 1986)

Gardner, John, *Grendel* (Alfred A. Knopf, 1971)

Garner, Alan, *Powsels and Thrums: A Tapestry of a Creative Life* (4th Estate, 2024)

Giles, Melanie, *Bog Bodies: Face to Face with the Past* (Manchester University Press, 2020)

Glob, P. V., *The Bog People: Iron-Age Man Preserved*, trans. Rubert Bruce-Mitford (Faber & Faber, 1969)

Grice, Elizabeth, 'A chilling tale of ritual murder', the *Daily Telegraph*, 7 January 2006

Heaney, Seamus, *Death of a Naturalist* (Faber & Faber, 1966)

Heaney, Seamus, *Wintering Out* (Faber & Faber, 1972)

Heaney, Seamus, *North* (Faber & Faber, 1975)

Heaney, Seamus, *Field Work* (Faber & Faber, 1979)

Heaney, Seamus, *Beowulf* (Faber & Faber, 1999)

Heaney, Seamus, *Beowulf: A Verse Translation*, ed. Daniel Donoghue (W. W. Norton & Company, 2002)

Heaney, Seamus, *The Letters of Seamus Heaney*, ed. Christopher Reid (Faber & Faber, 2023)

Kelly, Eamonn P., 'Kingship and Sacrifice: Irish Bog Bodies and Boundaries' in *Archaeology Ireland* (Heritage Guide No. 35, 2006)

Kennedy, Maev, 'Arrival of Beaker folk changed Britain for ever, ancient DNA study shows', *Guardian*, 22 February 2018

Mantel, Hilary, *Giving Up the Ghost: A Memoir* (Fourth Estate, 2003)

Marzinzik, Sonja, *The Sutton Hoo Helmet* (The British Museum Press, 2007)

Minter, Faye, *Rendlesham Revealed: The Heart of a Kingdom AD 400–800* (Suffolk County Council, 2023)

Morgan, Edwin, *Beowulf* (Carcanet Press, 2002)

Morris, Marc, *The Anglo-Saxons: A History of the Beginnings of England* (Hutchinson, 2021)

Morrison, Toni, 'Grendel and His Mother' in *The Source of Self-Regard: Selected Essays, Speeches and Meditations* (Alfred A. Knopf, 2019)

Selected Sources

Moss, Sarah, *Ghost Wall* (Granta Books, 2018)

Mulhall, Isabella and Elizabeth Kim Briggs, 'Presenting a Past Society to a Present Day Audience: Bog Bodies in Iron Age Ireland', *Museum Ireland*, Volume 17, 2007

Mulhall, Isabella, 'Bog Bodies from Ireland's Peatlands' in G. Plunkett, I. Stuijdts and C. McDermott (eds.), *Life and Adaptation in the Irish Wetlands During the Holocene* (INQUA Congress Field Guide, 2019)

Newton, Sam, *The Origins of Beowulf and the Pre-Viking Kingdom of East Anglia* (D. S. Brewer, 1993)

Newton, Sam, *The Reckoning of Raedwald: The Story of the King Linked to the Sutton Hoo Ship-Burial* (Red Bird Press, 2003)

Ó Floinn, Raghnall, 'Irish Bog Bodies', *Archaeology Ireland*, Volume 2, Number 3, Autumn 1988

Orwell, George, *The Lion and the Unicorn: Socialism and the English Genius* (Martin Secker & Warburg, 1941)

Phillips, Charles W., *My Life in Archaeology* (Alan Sutton, 1987)

Pryor, Francis, *Britain BC: Life in Britain and Ireland Before the Romans* (HarperCollins, 2003)

Pryor, Francis, *Home: A Time Traveller's Tales From Britain's Prehistory* (Allen Lane, 2014)

Reynolds, Ffion, 'Regenerating Substances: Quartz as an Animistic Agent', *Time and Mind: The Journal of Archaeology, Consciousness and Culture*, Volume 2, Issue 2, July 2009

Reynolds, Ffion, 'Tracing Neolithic Worldviews: Shamanism, Irish Passage Tomb Art and Altered States of Consciousness' in D. Luke, C. Adams, A. Waldstein, B. Sessa and D. King (eds.), *Breaking Convention: Essays on Psychedelic Consciousness* (Strange Attractor Press, 2013)

Shippey, Tom, *J. R. R. Tolkein: Author of the Century* (HarperCollins, 2000)

Skelcher, Mary and Chris Durrant, *Edith Pretty: From Socialite to Sutton Hoo* (Leiston Press, 2006)

Stead, I. M., J. B Bourke and Don Brothwell, *Lindow Man: The Body in the Bog* (British Museum Publications, 1986)

Sutcliff, Rosemary, *Beowulf* (The Bodley Head, 1961)

Tacitus, Cornelius, *The Agricola and The Germania*, trans. H. Mattingly and S. A. Handford (Penguin Books, 1982)

Tacitus, Cornelius, *Agricola and Germany*, trans. A. R. Birley (Oxford World's Classics, 1999)

Tolkien, J. R. R., *Beowulf: A Translation and Commentary, together with Sellic Spell*, ed. Christopher Tolkien (HarperCollins, 2016)

Videen, Hana, *The Word Hord: Daily Life in Old English* (Profile Books, 2021)

Webster, Diana Bonakis, *Hawkeseye: The Early Life of Christopher Hawkes* (Alan Sutton, 1991)

Wienraub, Bernard, 'Ulster women tar 2 girls for dating British soldiers', *New York Times*, 11 November 1971

LOUGH

Flechner, Roy, *Saint Patrick Retold: The Legend and History of Ireland's Patron Saint* (Princeton University Press, 2019)

Foley, Claire and Emily Murray, 'Excavations at Dreenan, Caldragh Graveyard, Boa Island, Co. Fermanagh' (Queen's University Belfast, 2012)

Freeman, Philip, *St Patrick of Ireland: A Biography* (Simon & Schuster, 2005)

Hickey, Helen, *Images of Stone* (Fermanagh District Council/ Regency Press, 1976)

Lowry-Corry, Dorothy, 'The Stones Carved with Human Effigies on Boa Island and on Lustymore Island, in Lower Lough Erne' in *Proceedings of the Royal Irish Academy: Archaeology, Culture History, Literature* (1932–4, Volume 41; Royal Irish Academy, 1934)

O'Brien, Edna, *A Pagan Place* (Weidenfeld & Nicolson, 1970)

O'Brien, Elizabeth, *Mapping Death: Burial in Late Iron Age and Early Medieval Ireland* (Four Courts Press, 2020)

Warner, Richard, 'Two Pagan Idols – Remarkable New Discoveries', *Archaeology Ireland*, Volume 17, Number 1, Issue 63, Spring 2003

Williams, Mark, *Ireland's Immortals: A History of the Gods of Irish Myth* (Princeton University Press, 2018)

*

The Loughsiders (BBC Northern Ireland, 1976; narrated by Seamus Heaney; produced by David Hammond)

WEST

Baker, Denys Val, *A View from Land's End: Writers Against a Cornish Background* (William Kimber, 1982)

Baring-Gould, Sabine, *A Book of Dartmoor* (Methuen & Co., 1900)

Bates, Selina and Keith Spurgin, *The Dust of Heroes: The Life of Cornish Artist, Archaeologist & Writer John Thomas Blight, 1835–1911* (Windowbox Books, 2006)

Bord, Janet and Colin, *A Guide to Ancient Sites in Britain* (Paladin Books, 1979)

Clarke, Gillian, 'The Poetry of Stone' in David Walford Davies (ed.), *Megalith: Eleven Journeys in Search of Stones* (Gomer Press, 2006)

Colquhoun, Ithell, *The Living Stones: Cornwall* (Peter Owen, 1957; Pushkin Press, 2025)

Cummings, Vicki and Alasdair Whittle, *Places of Special Virtue: Megaliths in the Neolithic Landscapes of Wales* (Oxbow Books, 2004)

Cummings, Vicki, 'Imagining Prehistoric Landscapes' in Andy Burnham (ed.), *The Old Stones: A Field Guide to the Megalithic Sites of Britain and Ireland* (Watkins, 2018)

Du Maurier, Daphne, *Vanishing Cornwall: The Spirit and History of Cornwall* (Victor Gollancz, 1967)

Evans, Gwynfor, *Save Cwm Tryweryn For Wales* (Plaid Cymru, 1956)

Garner, Alan, *The Weirdstone of Brisingamen* (William Collins Sons & Co., 1960)

Garner, Alan, *The Owl Service* (William Collins Sons & Co., 1967)

Green, Matthew, *Shadowlands: A Journey Through Lost Britain* (Faber & Faber, 2022)

Hale, Amy, *Genius of the Fern Loved Gully: The Supersensual Life of Ithell Colquhoun, Artist and Occultist* (Strange Attractor Press, 2020)

Hannigan, Tim, *The Granite Kingdom: A Cornish Journey* (Head of Zeus, 2023)

Hunt, Robert, *Popular Romances of the West of England, or The Drolls, Traditions and Superstitions of Old Cornwall* (J. C. Hotten, 1865)

King, Richard, *Brittle With Relics: A History of Wales 1962–1997* (Faber & Faber, 2022)

Lynch, Frances, Stephen Aldhouse-Green and Jeffrey L. Davies, *Prehistoric Wales* (Sutton Publishing, 2000)

MacBeth, Lally, *The Lost Folk: A Journey from the Forgotten Past to the Emerging Future of Folk* (Faber & Faber, 2025)

May, Jo, *Fogou: A Journey into the Underworld* (Gothic Image Publications, 1996)

Morris, Jan, *The Matter of Wales: Epic Views of a Small Country* (Oxford University Press, 1984)

Marsden, Philip, *Rising Ground: A Search for the Spirit of Place* (Granta Books, 2014)

Mwyn, Rhys, *Cam i'r Deheubarth: Safleoedd Archaeolegol yn Ne-orllewin Cymru* (Carreg Gwalch, 2019)

Petro, Pamela, *The Long Field: Wales, and the Presence of Absence, a Memoir* (Little Toller Books, 2021)

Pettit, Paul, *Prehistoric Dartmoor* (David & Charles, 1974)

Pitcher, Ben, *Back to the Stone Age: Race and Prehistory in Contemporary Culture* (McGill-Queen's University Press, 2022)

Shaw, Matthew, *Atmosphere of Mona* (Annwyn House, 2020)

Stephens, Meic, 'Cofiwch Tryweryn?' (BBC Cymru Fyw, 25 March 2015)

Stephens, Meic, *My Shoulder to the Wheel: An Autobiography* (Y Lolfa, 2015)

Thomas, R. S., 'Reservoirs' in *Not That He Brought Flowers* (Rupert Hart-Davis, 1968)

Thomas, Wyn, *Tryweryn: A New Dawn? The Legacy of the Drowning of Capel Celyn* (Y Lolfa, 2023)

Selected Sources

Worth, R. Handsworth, *Worth's Dartmoor*, ed. G. M. Spooner and
F. S. Russell (David & Charles, 1967)

*

A Year in a Field (Anti-Worlds Releasing, 2022; directed by
Christopher Morris; produced by Denzil Monk, Bosena)

*

Drowned – The Flooding of a Village (BBC Sounds, 2023; written and
presented by Betsan Powys; produced by Maria David and
Huw Meredydd)

WALL

'Antoninus Pius' in *Lives of the Later Caesars: The First Part of the
Augustan History, with Newly Compiled Lives of Nerva and Trajan*,
trans. Anthony Birley (Penguin Books, 1976)

Auden, W. H., 'Roman Wall Blues' in *Collected Poems* (Faber & Faber,
1994)

Birley, Eric, 'A Centurion of Leg. VI Victrix and his Wife' in
Zeitschrift für Papyrologie und Epigraphik (Dr Rudolf Habelt
GmbH, 1984)

Birley, Robin, *Vindolanda: A Roman Frontier Post on Hadrian's Wall*
(Thames & Hudson, 1977)

Birley, Robin, *Chesterholm: From a Clergyman's Cottage to Vindolanda's
Museum 1830–2000* (Roman Army Museum Publications, 2000)

Bowman, A. K., J. D. Thomas and R. S. O. Tomlin, 'The Vindolanda
Writing-Tablets (Tabulae Vindolandenses IV, Part 1)', *Britannia*,
Volume 41, 2010

Bowman, A. K., J. D. Thomas and R. S. O. Tomlin, 'The Vindolanda
Writing-Tablets (Tabulae Vindolandenses IV, Part 2)', *Britannia*,
Volume 42, 2011

Bowman, A. K., J. D. Thomas, R. S. O. Tomlin, A. Birley and
A. Meyer, 'The Vindolanda Writing-Tablets (Tabulae
Vindolandenses IV, Part 3)', *Britannia*, Volume 50, 2019

Breeze, David J., *Bearsden: A Roman Fort on the Antonine Wall* (Society
of Antiquaries of Scotland, 2016)

Selected Sources

Breeze, David J., 'The Army of the Antonine Wall: Its Strength and
Implications' in David J. Breeze and William S. Hanson (eds.),
The Antonine Wall: Papers in Honour of Professor Lawrence Keppie
(Archaeopress Roman Archaeology 64, 2020)

Campbell, L., 'Polychromy on the Antonine Wall Distance
Sculptures: Non-Destructive Identification of Pigments on
Roman Reliefs', *Britannia*, Volume 51, 2020

Collingwood, R. G. and J. N. L Myres, *Roman Britain and the English
Settlements* (Oxford at the Clarendon Press, 1936)

Coupar, Sally-Anne and Donal Bateson, *The Antonine Wall: An
Illustrated Guide* (The Hunterian, University of Glasgow, 2012)

Davies, Hunter, *A Walk Along the Wall* (Quartet Books, 1976)

Dobson, Brian, 'Eric Barff Birley 1906–1995' in *1997 Lectures
and Memoirs: Proceedings of the British Academy – 97* (Oxford
University Press, 1997)

Keppie, Lawrence, *Roman Distance Slabs from the Antonine Wall: A Brief
Guide* (Hunterian Museum, 1979)

Kepppie, L. J. F., 'Roman Inscriptions from Scotland: Some
Additions and Corrections to *RIB* I', *Proceedings of the Society of
Antiquaries of Scotland*, Volume 113, 1984

Keppie, Lawrence, *Roman Inscribed and Sculptured Stones in The
Hunterian Museum, University of Glasgow* (Britannia Monograph
Series Number 13, The Society for the Promotion of Roman
Studies, 1998)

Keppie, Lawrence, 'A Walk Along the Antonine Wall in 1825: The
Travel Journal of the Rev John Skinner', *Proceedings of the Society
of Antiquaries of Scotland*, Volume 133, 2003

Macdonald, George, *The Roman Wall in Scotland* (James MacLehose
and Sons, 1911)

Meyer, Alexander, Alex Mullen and Roger Tomlin, 'Slavery on the
Northern Frontier: A Stylus Tablet from Vindolanda', *Brittania*,
Volume 55, 2024

Montgomery, Alan, *Walking the Antonine Wall: A Journey from East to
West Scotland* (Tippermuir Books, 2022)

Mothersole, Jessie, *In Roman Scotland* (John Lane, The Bodley Head, 1927)

Olusoga, David, *Black and British: A Forgotten History* (Macmillan, 2016)

Pryce-Jones, Alan, *The Bonus of Laughter* (Hamish Hamilton, 1987)

Reid, John H., *The Eagle and the Bear: A New History of Roman Scotland* (Birlinn, 2023)

Robertson, Anne S., 'The Roman Frontier' in Gordon Menzies (ed.), *Who Are the Scots? A Search for the Origins of the Scottish Nation* (British Broadcasting Corporation, 1971)

Robertson, Anne S., *The Antonine Wall: A Handbook to Scotland's Roman Frontier*, rev. and ed. Lawrence Keppie (Glasgow Archaeological Society, 2015)

Simpson, James Young, 'Archaeology: Its Past and Its Future Work' in John Stuart (ed.), *Archaeological Essays by the Late Sir James Y. Simpson, Bart.* (Edmonston and Douglas, 1872)

Skinner, John, *Journal of a Somerset Rector 1803–1834*, ed. Howard and Peter Coombs (Oxford University Press, 1971)

Stewart, Rory, *The Marches: Border Walks With My Father* (Jonathan Cape, 2016)

Sutcliff, Rosemary, *The Eagle of the Ninth* (Oxford University Press, 1954)

Sutcliff, Rosemary, *The Mark of the Horse Lord* (Oxford University Press, 1964)

Walker, James J., 'The Importance of Fieldwalking: The Discovery of Three Fortlets on the Antonine Wall' in David J. Breeze and William S. Hanson (eds.), *The Antonine Wall: Papers in Honour of Professor Lawrence Keppie* (Archaeopress Roman Archaeology 64, 2020)

Woolf, Virginia, *The Common Reader: Second Series* (The Hogarth Press, 1932)

*

The Antonine Wall: A 37 Mile Landmark (Seannachie Films, 2022; produced and directed by Liam Anderstrem)

Selected Sources

NORTH

Bourne, Joanne, *Flint: A Lithic Love Letter* (Eye Books, 2024)

Brown, Callum G., *Up-Helly-Aa: Custom, Culture and Community in Shetland* (Mandolin, 1998)

Brown, George Mackay, *An Orkney Tapestry* (Quartet Books, 1973)

Brown, George Mackay, *For The Islands I Sing: An Autobiography* (John Murray, 1997)

Edmonds, Mark and Alan Garner, *The Beauty Things* (Group VI Press, 2016)

Edmonds, Mark, *Conversations With Magic Stones* (Group VI Press, 2017)

Edmonds, Mark, *Ness of Brodgar: Past, Present & Future* (Ness of Brodgar Trust, 2024)

Ibn Fadlān, Ahmad, *Ibn Fadlan and the Land of Darkness: Arab Travellers in the Far North*, trans. Paul Lunde and Caroline Stone (Penguin Classics, 2011)

Greig, David, *Columba's Bones* (Polygon, 2023)

Hedges, John, *Tomb of the Eagles: A Window on Stone Age Tribal Britain* (John Murray, 1984)

Irvine, James W., *Up-Helly-Aa: A Century of Festival* (Shetland Publishing Co., 1982)

Jamie, Kathleen, *Surfacing* (Sort Of Books, 2019)

Jarman, Cat, *River Kings: The Vikings from Scandinavia to the Silk Roads* (William Collins, 2021)

Laurenson, Arthur, 'On Certain Beliefs and Phrases of Shetland Fishermen', *Proceedings of the Society of Antiquaries of Scotland*, Volume 10, 1875

Moore, Hazel and Graeme Wilson, 'Sands of Time: Domestic Rituals at Links of Noltland', *Current Archaeology*, Issue 275, February 2013

Orkneyinga Saga: The History of the Earls of Orkney, trans. Hermann Pálsson and Paul Edwards (Hogarth Press, 1978)

Price, Neil, *The Children of Ash & Elm: A History of the Vikings* (Allen Lane, 2020)

Watt, Roseanne, *Moder Dy/Mother Wave* (Polygon, 2019)

Williams, Thomas, *Viking Britain: A History* (William Collins, 2021)

SCION

Crow, Jim, 'The Tale of a Tree: An Archaeological History of Sycamore Gap on Hadrian's Wall', *Current Archaeology*, Issue 405, December 2023

Fox, Kate, *On Sycamore Gap: A Celebration of the Tree We Lost and Those to Come* (HarperNorth, 2024)

Garner, Alan, *Red Shift* (William Collins Sons and Co., 1973)

Higgins, Charlotte, *Under Another Sky: Journeys in Roman Britain* (Jonathan Cape, 2013)

Hutton, William, *The History of the Roman Wall* (John Nichols and Son, 1802)

Jackson, Ian, *Northumberland Rocks: 50 Extraordinary Rocky Places That Tell the Story of the Northumberland Landscape* (Northern Heritage Services, 2021)

Jackson, Ian, *The Rocks at the Edge of the Empire: 50 Extraordinary Rocky Places That Tell the Story of the Romans and the Landscape of their Northern Frontier* (Northern Heritage Services, 2024)

Magnell, Ola and Elisabeth Iregren, 'Veitstu Hvé Blóta Skal? The Old Norse Blót in the Light of Osteological Remains from Frösö Church, Jämtland, Sweden, *Current Swedish Archaeology*, Volume 18, 2010

Mothersole, Jessie, *Hadrian's Wall* (John Lane, The Bodley Head, 1922)

Rackham, Oliver, *Trees and Woodland in the British Landscape* (Weidenfeld & Nicolson, 2020; first published in 1976 by J. M. Dent)

Acknowledgements

The poet George Mackay Brown wrote that 'the Orkney imagination is haunted by time'. I have felt similarly haunted over these last years while working on *A Tomb With A View*, *Steeple Chasing* and especially *Upon A White Horse*. Although not a formal series, my books are linked by a common subject – the marks we leave upon the earth that seem to ask a hopeful question: 'We matter, don't we?' I have come to think of them as the Fox Trilogy, after the delightful little animal slinking across each of the covers, but perhaps they are better thought of as a trilogy of stone.

I have been fortunate, while writing this book, to have benefited from the insight and comradeship of Richard Roper, my editor, and Holly Purdham, my publisher at Headline. Many thanks to both for their company along the way. Kevin Pocklington, my agent at The North Literary Agency, believed in this book from the moment I suggested it to him – and for that I thank him. Rosie Margesson, head of publicity at Headline, has been a great support in spreading word of my work and helping it to find new readers.

A word, too, about those readers. Many people have told me that *Steeple Chasing* and *A Tomb With A View* have been meaningful books for them. I'm always very happy to hear from readers and am grateful that the work has brought them pleasure and consolation. I hope that this book will find such a generous and welcoming readership.

A book is a joint effort, the work of many minds and hands. I'd like to thank the following people: Edward Bettison for the beautiful cover; Juliet Brightmore for picture research; Wilf Dickie, typesetter; Patrick Insole, art director; Linden Lawson for copyediting; Rabeeah Moeen, audio; Caitlin Raynor, publicity director; Louise Rothwell, book production manager; Alan Rutter, indexer; Rebecca Swales, sales; Nicola Thatcher, at Keystone Law, for legal advice; Alexia Thomaidis, head of marketing; Helena Towers, publicist.

Acknowledgements

I am grateful to Dr Jennifer Wexler for reading the manuscript and offering expert comment and suggestion.

My thanks to Polly Jean Harvey for allowing me to quote from 'White Chalk' as an epigraph. It's one of my favourite songs from her incredible body of work, and it means a lot to be able to include it. Thanks, too, to George Service at ATC Management.

Dani Garavelli has been a good friend throughout the writing of this book. It has been a pleasure to share my work with her. Thank you, Dani, for the encouragement and support.

There are a number of people whose interest and friendship has been important to me during this period of work. They include Kelly Apter, Brian Donaldson, Kenny Farquharson, Rob Fraser, Jane Graham, Joe Hodrien, Teddy Jamieson, Laura Kennedy, Jamie Lafferty, Barry and Fiona Leathem, Damien Love, Paul McNamee, Stephen Phelan, Helen, David and Michael Ross, Graeme Smith, Jen Stout, Alison Stroak, Graeme Virtue, Lindsey Ward, Paul and Christine Ward.

Much of *White Horse* was written in the company of our white rabbit, Jenny, for whose calm presence I am thankful.

Finally, with all my heart, to Jo, James and Jack – for the good times at Sycamore Gap and beyond. I love you.

SHRINE

My thanks to the Keeper of the Stones.

RING

Thanks to: Jessica Gray, Bloomsbury; David Jones, Ordnance Survey; Richard Oliver and Gerry Zierler, Charles Close Society; Jane Thomas and Jessica Trethowan, English Heritage; Vicki Steward, Normal For Glastonbury; David Waters, Great Bustard Group.

HENGE

Simon Fyles, National Trust; Rebecca Lambert; Jenny Lemon and Heather Sebire, English Heritage; Gordon Rimes; James Ross; Rev-

Acknowledgements

erend Maria Shepherdson; Katy Soar, University of Winchester; John Vigar.

Loch

Bruce Blacklaw, National Museums Scotland; Benjamin Gearey, The Pallasboy Project; Parris Joyce, Glencoe Museum; Rob Malpas, Ballachulish Community Council.

Chalk

Jo Atkins, Katy Dunn, Liz Flight, National Trust; Mark Fisher, XTC Limelight; Alan Garner; Maddy Irvine; Shauna McLarnon, Shameless Promotion PR; Peter Metcalf, Wessex Morris Men; David Miles.

Grave

Kevin Barry; Jacq Bernard, David Breeze; Chris Dix, Catherine Hoy, David Keeble, Tim Kirk, David Pryor, The Sutton Hoo Ship's Company; Martin Carver; Murray Cook, Pamela Forsyth, Stirling Council; Ann Daly, Eamonn Mcloughlin, Isabella Mulhall, Maeve Sikora, National Museum of Ireland; Sarah Doig; Oliver Dunne; Francesca Hillier, British Museum; Flemming Kaul, John Fhær Engedal Nissen and Samantha Scott Reiter, National Museum of Denmark; Neil Macfarlane; Neil Macnab, AECOM; Valerie A. Maxfield; Hector Muir; Claire Mullaney, Historic Environment Scotland; Sam Newton; Ian Orkney; Jeanne Robinson, The Hunterian, University of Glasgow; St John's Kirk – Walls Heritage, Hoy; Martin Timoney; Will Troughton, National Library of Wales; Hana Videen; Tristram Whyte, Irish Peatland Conservation Council.

I am especially grateful to Lorna Main, who responded to an unexpected voice from the past with great generosity. Without her willingness and perseverance I would not have been reunited with the beaker we found so long ago.

This chapter includes some material adapted from the essay 'Whaligoe Steps' in *The Passion of Harry Bingo*, published in 2017 by Sandstone Press.

Acknowledgements

Lough

Ann Allen, Fermanagh Live; Eamonn Fitzsimons and Hazel Long, Lough Erne Landscape Partnership; Joe Graham, Castle Archdale Boat Hire & Watersports; Helen Lanigan Wood; Séamas Mac Annaidh; Kizzia Mildmay; Fr Eugene O'Neill; Marilyn Quinn, Fermanagh House; Archbishop Noel Treanor; Francis Young.

West

Ríbh Brownlee, Pushkin Press; Maria David, BBC Wales; Denzil Monk, Bosena; Steve Patterson; Rob and Laura, Rosemerryn; Alasdair Whyte, University of Glasgow.

It was a great pleasure to meet Rhys Mwyn in Caernarfon and to spend time speaking about his life in music and archaeology.

Wall

Ben Archibald, Big Partnership; David J. Breeze; Mandy Eversett, Devon Archaeological Society; Emma Ferrier and Frank McGarry, Bo'ness Children's Fair Festival; Teddy Jamieson; Valerie A. Maxfield; Jack Ross.

I am especially grateful to Jim and Anne Walker for their hospitality, and to Jim in particular for his kindness in giving up so much time to share with me his deep knowledge of the Antonine Wall.

I also want to express my thanks to Sonya Galloway for her generosity in allowing me to spend a week excavating at Vindolanda and speaking with the Birley family and others.

The opening of the section on Vindolanda contains a reference to the closing paragraph of James Joyce's classic short story 'The Dead'.

North

Molly Bond; Simon Edge, Eye Books; Derek Jamieson, Fraser Paul, Ashley Spence, Michael Thomson and the rest of the Norwick Jarl Squad; Jeanne Bouza Rose; Mark Smith, Shetland Museum & Archives; Jen Stout.

Acknowledgements

I am especially grateful to Maurice Henderson for his help with my work in Unst.

This chapter includes material adapted from an article I wrote in 2011 for *Scotland On Sunday*, which subsequently appeared as the essay 'Up-Helly-Aa' in *Daunderlust*, published in 2014 by Sandstone Press.

I wrote about the Ness of Brodgar excavation for the January/February 2025 issue of *Smithsonian*. The account of the dig that appears in this book is adapted from that article. I'm grateful to Arik Gabbai at *Smithsonian* for asking me to return to the Ness and for working with me on the story. My thanks, too, to the photographer Kieran Dodds.

SCION

Chris Collett and John Walker, Historic England; Rachel Ladd and Claire Masset, National Trust; Richard Oliver.

*

Thanks also to Libby Brooks, Murdo Macleod and Andy Pietrasik, the *Guardian*; Frazer Capie, Stephen Driscoll, Bill Grieve, Tom Horne and all those who make Govan Old such a wonderful and fascinating church; David Greig; Christine Finn; Neil Hooper; Neil Johnson-Symington, Glasgow Museums; Duncan Jordan, Bella Union; Mary Ann Kennedy; Hamish Lamley; Daniel Lee, UHI Orkney; Caz Mamwell, Swandro-Orkney Coastal Archaeology Trust; Duncan McLean; Suzanne Rough, Glasgow Life; Ola and Arnie Tait; Neil Wilkin, British Museum.

Acknowledgements

PERMISSIONS ACKNOWLEDGEMENTS

Quote from *A Land* by Jacquetta Hawkes on p. vi reproduced with permission of HarperCollins Publishers Ltd © 1951 Jacquetta Hawkes

Lyrics from PJ Harvey's 'White Chalk' on p. vi reproduced with kind permission from PJ Harvey and ATC Management

Lines from 'Digging' by Seamus Heaney from *Death of a Naturalist* on p. vi reproduced with permission of Faber and Faber Ltd © Seamus Heaney 1966

All photos copyrighted to Peter Ross, except:

p. 14   Dave0/Shutterstock.com
p. 68   Heritage Images/Getty Images
p. 80   Photograph by Harold St George Gray, public domain
p. 87   © National Museums of Scotland
p. 102 John Henshall/Alamy Stock Photo
p. 119 Graham Hunt/Alamy Stock Photo
p. 157 Photograph by Barbara Wagstaff ARPS © Trustees of the British Museum, digital image © National Trust
p. 173 © National Museum of Ireland
p. 185 David Lyons/Alamy Stock Photo
p. 195 © Lorna Main
p. 247 © National Museums of Scotland
p. 261 Courtesy of the Vindolanda Trust
p. 297 Courtesy of Ness of Brodgar Trust, photograph by Scott Pike

Index

Index

Index

Index

Index

RAISING READERS
Books Build Bright Futures

Dear Reader,

We'd love your attention for one more page to tell you about the crisis in children's reading, and what we can all do.

Studies have shown that reading for fun is the **single biggest predictor of a child's future success** – more than family circumstance, parents' educational background or income. It improves academic results, mental health, wealth, communication skills and ambition.

The number of children reading for fun is in rapid decline. Young people have a lot of competition for their time, and a worryingly high number do not have a single book at home.

Our business works extensively with schools, libraries and literacy charities, but here are some ways we can all raise more readers:

- Reading to children for just 10 minutes a day makes a difference
- Don't give up if your children aren't regular readers – there will be books for them!
- Visit bookshops and libraries to get recommendations
- Encourage them to listen to audiobooks
- Support school libraries
- Give books as gifts

Thank you for reading.
www.JoinRaisingReaders.com